BREAK-
ING THE
MOULD

Celebrating 35 Years of
Penguin Random House India

ADVANCE PRAISE FOR THE BOOK

'In an era of rising global protectionism, should India follow the Chinese path of low-end manufacturing and expect it to facilitate a march to prosperity? Or should India concentrate on services, including those embedded in new-era manufacturing? Finally, can India achieve a rapid and meaningful economic transformation without enhancing citizen freedoms and making knowledge institutions freer and more vibrant? Rajan and Lamba masterfully address these vitally important questions for India's future. They display impressive knowledge of the global economic and technological trends, combine it with a clear-eyed treatment of India's needs, policy process and political economy, and chart an innovative way forward. An eye-opening read!'—Ashutosh Varshney

'Finally, a book on the Indian economy that is non-partisan (it avoids aligning itself with political talking points) while providing clear-eyed prescriptions on difficult choices Indian policymakers must make. The authors rightly celebrate the achievements of the Indian economy while pointing to the difficult road ahead—on the opportunities that shifting global supply chains present for Indian manufacturing, the need to export high-value services and the urgent necessity to generate jobs. In these polarized times, *Breaking the Mould* makes for clear and calm, if cautionary, reading'—Vinay Sitapati

'One of the world's brightest minds, Raghuram Rajan, along with Rohit Lamba, has written an extremely engaging book on India. It is a deep examination of India's place in the global economy and is rich in both anecdotal evidence and analytical rigour. Anyone interested in the country's future will find the book a compelling and essential read'—Ruchir Sharma

'A wise book! This lively, lucid and persuasive book is basically correct about the future of jobs in India. A must-read for anyone who cares about India's economic future'—Gurcharan Das

'Timely and urgent reading on India's economic future, which policymakers would do well to heed. In a departure from conventional wisdom, the authors highlight India's potential as a supplier of high-end services, including services that are an integral part of manufacturing'—Montek Singh Ahluwalia

BREAK-ING THE MOULD

REIMAGINING INDIA'S ECONOMIC FUTURE

RAGHURAM G. RAJAN
ROHIT LAMBA

PENGUIN
BUSINESS

An imprint of Penguin Random House

PENGUIN BUSINESS

USA | Canada | UK | Ireland | Australia
New Zealand | India | South Africa | China | Singapore

Penguin Business is part of the Penguin Random House group of companies
whose addresses can be found at global.penguinrandomhouse.com

Published by Penguin Random House India Pvt. Ltd
4th Floor, Capital Tower 1, MG Road,
Gurugram 122 002, Haryana, India

First published in Penguin Business by Penguin Random House India 2023

10 9 8 7 6 5 4 3 2 1

The views and opinions expressed in this book are the authors' own and the
facts are as reported by them which have been verified to the extent possible,
and the publishers are not in any way liable for the same.

ISBN 9780670099894

For sale in the Indian Subcontinent only

Typeset in Adobe Garamond Pro by Manipal Technologies Limited, Manipal
Printed at Thomson Press India Ltd, New Delhi

www.penguin.co.in

To our wives

Contents

Part III: Wrapping Up

Introduction

Where is India going today? Is it surging, having just overtaken the United Kingdom to become the fifth-largest economy in the world? Or is it flailing, having settled at a growth rate that is grossly insufficient to provide jobs for the millions joining the labour force? Are manufacturers across the world jostling to make in India? Or does the stagnant share of employment in manufacturing over decades suggest India has missed the manufacturing bus? Is India preparing for the future? Or is it too focused on battling the past? Are Indians uniformly doing well? Or is India becoming more unequal, with the upper class experiencing the best of times, while the middle class sinks slowly?

These questions reflect two sides of the debate over India's economy, one side relentlessly bullish and unwilling to see, speak or hear any concerns about India's foreordained march into the ranks of the wealthiest and most powerful countries in the world. The other side is much more critical, unpersuaded there is any good in what is happening. Is it, as Cambridge economist Joan Robinson said, 'Whatever you can rightly say about India, the opposite is also true?' Or is there more truth to one side than the other?

The answer matters because the cheerleaders feel the government should impose its will wherever needed, even at the risk of turning authoritarian. After all, is this not how China grew, from economic parity with India in the 1960s to becoming one of the world's two superpowers today, with an economy over five times the size of India's? The critics believe the current government is better at perception management and suppressing unpleasant facts than creating real well-being for the masses, but this side has been unable to offer persuasive alternatives.

There is certainly a restlessness in India today, most noticeable among our youth, who are unwilling to settle for the old bromides. They want new answers—answers that give them good jobs not handouts, which will improve their lives today, not ask them to continue to endure. Many are temporarily sustained by the optimism that it is now India's turn to soar.

No matter which side of the debate you are on, we can hopefully all agree that India needs a vision of where it wants to get to, for that will determine the choices it needs to make today. To see what that might be, we first need to understand the debate between the cheerleaders and critics on India's current trajectory.

We will explain in this book why we think the critics are largely right on the facts—the relentless cheerleaders paper over the real fault lines that are emerging in the Indian economy. Too many of our youth don't have jobs and don't have a hope of getting one. So they stop looking. The fraction of working-age women employed is an abysmal one in five, the lowest in the G20 countries, and the fraction of men employed is nothing to be proud of either. India wastes too much of its human capital and is in danger of frittering away its demographic dividend—the supposed dividend from having a growing share of working-age population—because it is not creating enough jobs.

And new storm clouds are emerging. Geopolitical tensions, as well as disruptions caused by the pandemic and catastrophes like the Fukushima earthquake, are causing firms to rethink their global supply chains. Many multinationals are contemplating near-shoring or even re-shoring their manufacturing. Jobs in manufacturing and services are also at risk of being automated, either by robots or by artificial intelligence algorithms.

India needs solutions. The cheerleaders are correct in thinking the government is getting some things right. Reforms like the switch to a Goods and Services Tax, which unifies the Indian market, had long been proposed but were executed under the current government. India is building highways, tunnels and rural roads faster than before. Direct benefit transfers, enabled by the digital stack and mass opening of bank accounts, allow the government to reach the beneficiaries directly with minimal leakage on the way. And in September 2023, India ended its turn as the G20 president with a well-organized meeting in Delhi, culminating in a statement that achieved a consensus on some very fractious issues.

This is all progress. The government's strength has been implementation, especially when the required actions, such as building roads, tunnels, toilets or even statues, are clear, or when frameworks such as the digital stack had been initiated by previous governments. For a country that all too often has faltered in implementing its plans, this is a welcome change.

However, not everything the government has initiated—especially some of its own ideas—has been successful. The move to develop smart cities that are sustainable and citizen-friendly; the production-linked incentives (PLI) to increase manufacturing in India; the reforms to agricultural markets; the dramatic demonetization of Rs 500 and Rs 1000 notes in November 2016—have ranged from the ineffectual to the truly damaging. Reflecting its lack of confidence in the future, private sector investment has stayed tepid over the last decade.

Perhaps most worrisome is that economic thinking on how we will create jobs seems stuck in the past, with a combination of protectionism and subsidies intended to spur manufacturing. Successive Indian governments, including this one, have done little to prepare India's most precious asset, its people's capabilities, for the mounting challenges ahead. To see why this is so important, we must understand how the economics of growth have changed.

How the Global Supply Chain Has Changed

Transportation costs for goods came down tremendously in the 1960s and 1970s. Multinational firms started looking for the cheapest place to produce, for finished goods could be easily transported to the developed countries, where they would be consumed. In the early years of China's liberalization in the 1980s, global firms compared its cheap albeit low-skilled workers with expensive American and European workers when deciding where to produce. It made sense to outsource low-skilled manufacturing—essentially, the task of assembling together imported parts to make final products, like radios and televisions—to China. The cost savings from such labour arbitrage were so large that firms ignored some of the early difficulties of producing in China, such as its primitive infrastructure, and set up factories there. Production grew tremendously fast as China followed this export-led manufacturing path because factories could produce at scale, catering to the enormous demand in developed countries.

Eventually, as China grew richer, it fixed its infrastructure, and as its workers became more educated and skilled, manufacturing costs in China came down even for more sophisticated manufacturing—such as making the radio and TV components that were imported earlier. So firms moved all their manufacturing to China. China went from poor to middle income in less than four decades. Since such an export-led manufacturing path, starting with low-skilled assembly, also worked for other East Asian countries, like Japan, Korea and Taiwan, it is natural, then, that India's current government should think of following this path.

This simple narrative, as we will argue later, misses some important details as to why China was successful. Nevertheless, it suffices for now to say that the China and East Asian development path starts with cheap labour attracting global (and local) manufacturers who engage in local low-skilled assembly of goods for exports. Everything else builds on the cost advantage and the profits cheap labour offers.

Unfortunately for would-be late developers like India and Indonesia who want to follow the China path, the labour cost advantage no longer exists. For one, China has a large population, and it still has not exhausted its reservoir of cheap workers in agriculture, especially in its western provinces. So, today, workers in late developers compete with still-cheap Chinese workers (and with each other), not with expensive workers in the United States or Japan. The climb towards more sophisticated manufacturing is similarly not assured, because China and other emerging markets, like Malaysia and Thailand, have developed their logistics tremendously, so they can ship more sophisticated manufactured components easily and cheaply across the globe. Put differently, every segment of the manufacturing portion of global supply chains has become extremely competitive. Furthermore, a country's presence in low-skilled assembly does not assure profits or entry into other higher-skilled manufacturing segments.

Different degrees of competition in every segment have created what is sometimes called the smile curve of value added in a product's global supply chain.[1] The value added in the early services segments of a supply chain, including the R&D and design that go into a product, is very high. The middle segments of the supply chain, that is, the actual manufacturing, adds only a modest amount of value. The end services segments of the supply chain before the product reaches the customer—branding, marketing, advertising, sales, financing and product content—once again constitute a lot of value added. When we plot valued added in the sequence of segments in a global supply chain, we get a smile.

So, for instance, Apple does not manufacture any of its iPhones; the Taiwanese company Foxconn does, largely in China. Apple's market capitalization today is over $3 trillion. Foxconn's market capitalization is just below $50 billion. Apple is sixty times as valuable, even though it manufactures nothing! That is because it provides the R&D and product design services at the beginning of the global supply chain for iPhones, as well as the branding, marketing and content (think iTunes and the App Store) at the end. There is only a modest amount of competition in all these segments of the supply chain, so they are very profitable. When an iPhone is bought in the store, only about one-third of the value-added is manufacturing, of which a small fraction is assembly, and the profit for this step of the production chain is tiny because it is so competitive.[2] That explains the difference between Apple's and Foxconn's market values. Not all global supply chains have this pattern, but many do.

India, for a variety of reasons we will come to later, missed the manufacturing bus when China took it. But having missed it, it is trying to attract firms to assemble in India by offering large subsidies. Should it? In part, we already have the answer. The China path—of starting with low-skilled assembly and moving up from there—will not work well for us because China and others are already there and have competed down the profits. This is not being pessimistic about India's capabilities; it is being realistic about how the world has changed.

More important, however, using our understanding of how value addition in the global supply chain has changed, we can embark on a more unique Indian way of development, one that is more aligned with India's strengths. India should compete for the future rather than for the past.

We should not despair if the path up from low-skilled manufacturing exports has narrowed significantly, for technology is opening up the possibility of direct services exports as well as higher-skilled manufacturing-related services exports, such as chip design. They offer a whole new set of activities that India can flourish in.

Furthermore, apart from exports, Indian employers can cater to a growing domestic market, where the pathway we propose will create many new jobs, especially in education and health care. For success in most economic activities today requires India to invest heavily in enhancing the capabilities of all its people. A focus on education, skilling and health care will enable our people to do the jobs that are available, and also attract employers looking for better-skilled workers to India.

To truly break the mould, we must simultaneously create an environment that fosters ideas and entrepreneurship so that many more firms with radically different, useful product offerings are started in India, with the intent of capturing the high value-added segments of supply chains. In other words, India must pivot from brawn to brain, even at this early stage of development. That requires efforts to be made on a countrywide scale.

Perhaps the best way to illustrate the India we have in mind is with a few examples, one hypothetical, others actual. The first showcases a business school that directly provides high-value services to the world, the others illustrate how manufacturing and services can be combined in different ways to create entirely new products that are a mix of both.

Exporting High-Value Services Directly in the Near Future

Professor Vinod Erali got out of his Ola taxicab and bid a good day to the sari-clad driver. As he walked through the well-kept grounds of the Well-Known Institute of Management in Western India (WIMWI), he could see the institute's entrepreneurship hub just across the compound wall, where many of the institute's past students had started firms that were now household names across the world. In the far distance, he could see the steel towers of the local Indian Institute of Information Technology, whose students had collaborated with WIMWI's students in their start-ups. So much had changed in India over the last few years . . .

Indeed, so much had changed even in WIMWI. He thought back to when he joined WIMWI in the early 2020s. At that time, a classroom was typically a large room with whiteboards, desks and chairs, and was full of chattering students if you were a popular instructor. This form of instruction had not changed for hundreds, if not thousands, of years. He still taught such classes in the afternoons. This morning, however, his 'classroom' was a cabin crammed with cameras, microphones and other electronic equipment. There was a small circular area in the middle, enclosed by a plexiglass fence; his playground, as he jokingly called it, where the magic happened. Samia, his technician, had just finished her checks and gave him a thumbs up.

He put on his virtual-reality headset. A large virtual classroom awaited, modelled on the executive MBA classroom of old. And steadily, avatars of the students started taking their seats, eighty in all. They were all busy executives from all over the world, doing an MBA while holding a full-time job. Each student had their virtual-reality headset on—over the years the headsets had morphed from clunky opaque helmets to transparent headpieces, so that he could make out each one's face. He knew each student was in front of a specially equipped computer in their office, transmitting their images into the virtual classroom. His equipment was even more sophisticated, because he was always a blur of movement, summoning videos, charts and data from the ether, while engaging his students in an intense discussion.

Professor Erali introduced the case, 'Dantu Corporation and Carbon Taxes', one of his favourites. It was about a start-up that wanted to open a factory in Bhiwadi, Rajasthan, but had to negotiate with the local government over the size of the carbon taxes it would have to pay. The students had already gone through the necessary calculations in small groups, aided by a chatbot as well as a human teaching assistant. In the classroom, they would now learn from each other. This was what they all looked forward to—the experience that made their simultaneous presence in this global classroom so worthwhile.

Professor Erali started the discussion asking how much they, as Dantu's CEO, would offer to pay the local government. Zuri's avatar on the right side of his headset lit up: 'I would start by refusing to pay.

I would ask the city government to first fix the potholes in the road leading to my factory,' she said.

Yang joined in to ask if one should assume the city officials had also done their calculations.

Zuri said, 'You must be joking. No official in my city has the time or the ability to do them. They are simply trying to estimate how much you will pay to get them off your back.'

Yang responded disapprovingly, 'Here it is different. Firms typically have to upload both their data and their calculations before a meeting, and the officials question every assumption we make.'

'Good to know,' responded Zuri. 'I am travelling to your neck of the woods next week to persuade your government to finance our forest preservation effort.'

And so the case went, challenge and counter-challenge, debate and argument, until everyone, even Professor Erali, emerged wiser than before.

As he was driven back home, Professor Erali reflected on why WIMWI was so successful. The technology to do this largely existed when he joined WIMWI a few years ago. Moreover, the need for such a programme was obvious—it allowed busy students across the world to stay in their jobs while getting the experience of a top-quality business school, without the overhead costs. WIMWI, like any start-up, simply needed to believe it could do it, and Erali proudly remembered his role in persuading his colleagues.

But why did the students come to WIMWI when they had so many choices? India's growing economic importance was obviously a plus, since international businesses had to engage with India. Students sought professors like Erali, who not only knew about India, but had also done consulting and research across the world. The varied backgrounds of the students in class made it even more attractive. That the programme was in English helped, though instant real-time language translation was getting better.

An important attraction to students was WIMWI's image of being open to all opinions, ethnicities, genders and nationalities, epitomizing the Sanskrit phrase *Vasudhaiva Kutumbakam* (meaning, the world is one family). India's history of diversity and open dialogue, as well as its continuing efforts at inclusion helped enormously. Zuri was scathing throughout the class about the behaviour of her country's government officials, while Yang was the opposite. Yet they both had no qualms about making their views known, since they felt the classroom was a safe space, in a safe institution, in a safe country.

Professor Erali recognized that technology was the easy part. Ideas, generated through debate and argument, and developed with the appropriate doses of creativity and hard work, were the scarce resources. WIMWI had succeeded in persuading the world that it could be the place for world-changing ideas. This was also why his afternoon class in a regular classroom had plenty of students from outside India, including from neighbouring countries in South Asia, from Africa and from the Middle East. They added enormous value, even in a country that had more people than any other on the planet.

WIMWI did much for the local economy, not just by earning foreign exchange but also by employing so many, ranging from Erali himself and Samia, who managed the technology, to the myriad teaching assistants who supplemented his lectures, the programmers who fine-tuned the chatbot assistants, the gardeners who maintained WIMWI's grounds and, indirectly, the cab driver who dropped him off, his own household staff and so on.

Direct Services Exports: The New Frontiers

In the past, services have been much harder to export than manufactured goods. But the times they are a-changin', as Bob Dylan would say. Professor Erali and his class is imaginary, but they are not far from the realm of the possible. In 2021, IIT Madras began offering an online three-year bachelor's degree in programming and data science.[3] Erali is exporting a service, education. Many such services have become exportable. For, today, video conferencing has become easy, and the pandemic has made it acceptable. A friend of Raghu's, based in London, a senior partner in a large consulting firm, is expanding their India operations manifold.

'Oh, is demand in India growing that fast?' Raghu asked.

'No, we are going to serve all of Europe,' she replied.

'Ah, a back office,' Raghu said.

'No, a semi-front office, where the Indian consultants will deal directly with our clients. No more putting together PowerPoint presentations for our London consultants to deliver. Our Indian consultants will present, and do the underlying work, of course, working with our London people,' she said.

'Why does this make sense now?' Raghu asked.

'Well, during the pandemic our London consultants interacted with clients entirely on Zoom. It became clear that consulting could be done at a distance and did not require constant physical presence. Of course, local knowledge is important, but we infuse that by bringing local consultants into the team. The youngsters we can recruit in India are so good, speak English well and cost a fraction of the salary of our London consultants,' she said.

Both Professor Erali and Raghu's friend are exporting services directly from India. India is typically known for exporting IT services. But in the last four years, professional and management consulting services exports have grown faster, at a compound growth rate of 31 per cent.[4] Beyond such direct services, services are also embedded in manufactured products. Many of the world's top manufacturers now have large R&D and design outfits in India. It is estimated that 20 per cent of chip design is done in India.[5] Such work, done out of what are now termed global capability centres (GCCs), has contributed significantly to exports since the pandemic. India has roughly 1600 of the centres, more than 40 per cent of the number worldwide.[6] The rapidity of expansion is visible in the jobs generated—Nasscom data indicates 2,80,000 GCC employees were hired in the financial year

2023 vs 3,80,000 added in the previous five years.[7] And many more GCCs are expected to start in India.

Manufacturing Embedded in Services and Vice Versa

Products can combine manufacturing and services in different ways. We will encounter Tilfi, which has one shop in Varanasi but is selling Banarasi silk saris across the world through its website, thus creating work for traditional artisans while preserving India's heritage. Outfits like Tilfi add new appealing designs to traditional work. They offer an overall brand that assures buyers quality and create many new jobs while increasing incomes for the artisans.

We will also meet firms that are disrupting traditional markets at the intersection between services and manufacturing in innovative ways. Lenskart is an eyewear firm whose branches are ubiquitous in cities, and whose advertisements appear frequently on TV and online. It has developed a clever business model of custom manufacturing attached to direct service delivery—browse frames online, get your eyes tested in a local Lenskart store and order your glasses. Everything from the frame, lens and fitting is done at their Gurgaon factory, and the product is delivered within two days at your doorstep.

Another such disruptor is Moglix, a business-to-business supply platform. Need a nut or a lathe for your factory? Moglix has constructed a massive database of where to source it from, and once you order it they will deliver it at your factory. Both Lenskart and Moglix are home-grown innovators, one merging services and manufacturing, and the other creating a service for manufacturers—both adding substantial value and jobs through the judicious use of new technology.

ID Fresh Food and the Power of Education

Services can even be combined with the manufacturing of a traditional product like idli batter, which the firm iD Fresh Food makes and distributes. P.C. Musthafa, its co-founder, has had an extraordinary life, epitomizing the new India we would like to see more of. His father was a labourer in Wayanad, Kerala, digging up ginger root, cleaning it and loading it on to trucks. For young Musthafa, three meals a day was a distant dream. There was a single school near the village they lived in, and when Musthafa failed in class six, he dropped out of school to work with his father.

One day soon after, a kind mathematics teacher at the school, 'Mathew Sir', came by the field and took Musthafa aside. He asked him, 'Do you really want to be a labourer all your life, or do you want to learn and be like your teachers? If so, come back.' Musthafa went back to school, enduring the humiliation of starting sixth standard again with students who had been a class below him and being the butt of their jokes. His teacher, Mr Mathew, advised him, 'When you are low on confidence, focus on small steps.' So Musthafa focused on mathematics and topped the class in the subject. The students started accepting him as one of their own. Having gained confidence, Musthafa eventually topped the class overall, and got admission to a bachelor's course in computer science at the prestigious National Institute of Technology Calicut.

On graduation, Musthafa got a job paying Rs 14,000 monthly. When he gave his first monthly pay cheque to his father, the latter was astonished at the amount. 'Why, your first month's pay is more than what I earn all year,' he exclaimed.

After stints in the Middle East and the UK, Musthafa came back to India and enrolled for a business degree at IIM Bangalore with the intent of eventually starting a firm. At that time, his cousins, who owned a small grocery shop, were selling idli batter. The batter was in a plastic packet, with an elastic band holding its mouth closed. The shop constantly received complaints about the freshness or the quality of the batter, but the supplier did little to change. Musthafa and his cousins, like generations of entrepreneurs before them, felt they could do better.

Together with his cousins and with Rs 50,000 in savings, Musthafa spent a year in a shed with one grinder, one weighing scale and one sealing machine, mixing and grinding rice, urad dal and fenugreek in different ratios to get the idli batter right. Eventually, they launched their batter in 2006, with the brand name iD Fresh Food (iD stands for 'idli dosa'), producing hundred 1-kg packets a day. Of these, ninety went unsold. Even as sales picked up within a couple of years to 2000 packets a day and 300 stores, 500 packets went unsold.

Musthafa realized he needed a more sophisticated way of predicting what each store would sell. He put his MBA learning to work. Soon enough, he improved iD's data capture and analytics so that iD could predict how much a store would use, thus reducing wastage. Today, overall batter wastage is 4 per cent, and in the well-understood Bangalore market it is 1 per cent. What is left is sold to hotels and restaurants. What is left after that is donated to charities to help feed people. And finally, the residue is turned into animal feed. The just-in-time processing helps maintain the signature freshness of products, leads to low wastage (since near-term demand is more predictable) and allows the whole operation to be run on low inventories.

Musthafa has been through tough times when he could not pay a salary to his employees or his son's tuition fees. Perhaps because he knows what deprivation is, he has tried to run the whole operation with little debt, ploughing profits back into the business. Today, with five factories, 650 vans and 2500 workers, many from little known places in India (Musthafa empathizes with workers from remote rural areas), iD has solidified its market for idli and dosa batter, and expanded to new products, such as parathas, chapatis, paneer, yoghurt, coffee and bread.

As the name suggests, all of iD Fresh Food products emphasize freshness, natural ingredients (that your grandmother would use!) and simple, hygienic production processes. Indeed, the firm has placed cameras inside its factory linked to a website, so that customers can inspect the factory at any time. The firm has also moved to selling abroad, with one of its factories in Ajman and one-third of its sales now coming from the Middle East.

As Musthafa reflects on his life thus far, he notes the importance of education in transforming him and the tremendous role people like Mathew Sir can play by giving hope to even one child. Musthafa also remembers the sacrifices his father made, skipping a meal every day, to put him through school. He counsels would-be entrepreneurs not to walk past simple problems that can be fixed, thinking someone else will do that. No one will, and an opportunity will be wasted. At the same time, he cautions entrepreneurs against me-too products—innovative solutions are so much more fulfilling and likely to succeed.

Jobs, Jobs, Jobs

Musthafa's inspiring story suggests the power of education. But it also suggests how products today are so much more a composite of services and manufacturing—the year the founders spent in a shed trying batch after batch to design the right-tasting idli mix that would remain fresh for a few days; the branding, packaging and communication via factory-embedded cameras that assure buyers of hygiene and quality; the fleet of vans, the demand forecasting and the logistical operations that ensure on-time manufacture and delivery are all critical components of the product Musthafa sells, over and above the making of the batter.

The broader point is that while low-skilled manufacturing jobs are certainly welcome in India, putting all our hopes, resources and efforts into attracting such jobs betrays both a lack of ambition and imagination. Success in low-skilled manufacturing will not bring more sophisticated manufacturing with higher value added to India. If, instead, we can enhance our ability to export services directly or export the services that are intertwined with manufacturing, we will create good jobs. Indeed, the skills our workers acquire could allow Indian firms to break into high-skilled manufacturing. Later, we will describe Chennai-based Agnikul, which designs and makes 20-foot-long 3D-printed liquid fuel rockets. These will send payloads of up to 100 kg 400 miles into space. For Agnikul, manufacturing is largely printing. Indeed, just as most Indians acquired cell phones without first acquiring landlines, India could substantially leapfrog over low-skilled manufacturing.

As our discussion of the smile curve in the supply chain suggests, growing rich is not just about services or manufacturing but about acquiring the core aspect of a valuable business around which everything else is built. Ownership of intellectual property, including R&D, design and software that goes into the product, is the high ground in today's business battles, from which everything else is controlled. That is what gives Apple ownership of the iPhone. It is why Tejas Networks, an Indian company we will encounter later, hopes to be able to sell 5G networks to emerging markets and developing countries, something no company outside the superpower blocs can do today.

India creates a lot of intellectual property today, as suggested by the amount of chip design done in India, but mainly for global firms. There is no Indian chip firm like Qualcomm or Nvidia, designing chips that it then gets manufactured by TSMC in Taiwan and sells worldwide. India needs to increase its creation of intellectual property and own it in India.

Apart from increasing the capabilities of its people, this requires India to move from incremental research and development that is the basis of much of our current success in manufacturing, including in two-wheelers and generic pharmaceuticals, to fundamental research and product development. The critical need, then, is to construct more 'temples of modern India', first-rate universities doing the research that leads to breakthrough products, such as innovative therapeutic drugs. The universities should collaborate with businesses to commercialize these ideas; Indian pharmaceutical manufacturers should be selling patented drugs around the world and be worth orders of magnitude more than their worth today, which, with notable exceptions, largely reflects their sales of generic off-patent drugs. Universities also must train the PhD students who will populate research laboratories and will become instructors in the many universities and colleges across the country. And colleges should teach many more students like Musthafa, who can make the leap from poverty to well-being in one generation by becoming entrepreneurs.

The examples throughout this book will suggest that a lot of good is happening in India because of the undoubted energies and capabilities of our people. Even as we write, the Indian Space Research Organisation (ISRO), the superb public-sector undertaking, has landed a rover on the moon's south pole, making India the first country to do so and the fourth country to land on the moon.

Aren't we then doing enough already? Such achievements reflect what India is capable of, its potential. India can do far more, and it will have to if we are to break the development mould. A country that accounts for one-sixth of humanity should aspire for one-sixth of all Nobel laureates, patents, multinational CEOs and Olympic gold medallists. We certainly have some way to go. As another measure of the distance we have to make up, not one Indian university ranks in the top 200 in the world in the Times Higher Education World Universities Ranking for 2024.

But any Indian development path cannot focus only on improving the lot of people at the top. We also need to do far more to employ the tens of millions who are looking for work and the many who have become discouraged. We need to create better work for those who are struggling on the fringes of poverty. In the last full year before the pandemic, agricultural employment increased by 3.4 crore while industry and services employment only grew by 93 lakh, so the share of workers in agriculture actually increased, a rarity for a fast-developing country. By such metrics, India is going backwards! There is a lot to be done, and we must start by getting our priorities right. As of now, they are not.

Take, for instance, the Micron semiconductor plant agreed upon in June 2023, intended for a site in Gujarat. Assuming it goes through, it is a $2.75-billion investment, out of which 70 per cent is a direct subsidy coming from the Central and Gujarat governments. This is expected to create 5000 jobs. So, we are spending nearly $2 billion for 5000 jobs, which is $400,000, or Rs 3.2 crore, per job. Note that this is envisaged to be assembly and some testing, not R&D.[8] Even if this leads eventually to some chip manufacture—and that will require significantly more subsidies—it will not be the kind of sophisticated logic chips that power your mobile phone, and India will still be dependent on wafer imports and on imported machinery for chip making.

That $2 billion, or Rs 16,500 crore, is effectively a grant to a foreign company for crumbs. It is over a third of the Central government's entire annual budget of Rs 44,000 crore for university education! How many first-class universities, how much research, how many thousands of engineers and scientists could be created instead of those 5000 low-level jobs? To choose the grant to Micron over better schools and universities—and we are still a country with limited resources—reflects misplaced priorities, which translate into poor outcomes.

How Do We Get There?

While ideas generated by universities and embedded into products by daring entrepreneurs will give India more of the high ground that leads to many good jobs, too many of our youth have inadequate skills and training. We need to create jobs for those looking for them, but also equip people to do the jobs that they aspire for.

We have to start with a realistic assessment of our current state. Year after year, the meticulous Annual Status of Education Report (ASER) highlights learning gaps in our education system. For example, in 2018, less than 30 per cent of students in grade three were able to achieve grade-two levels of reading and writing, and less than 30 per cent of students in grade five were able to do maths problems associated with grade two.[9] The pandemic has set us back even further. In addition, India continues to have inordinately high levels of child malnutrition. So, it is harder for our children to absorb skills in school and many drop out with rudimentary skills. Most jobs in manufacturing, even 'low-skilled' ones, require workers with stronger skills, resulting in the common refrain from manufacturers that they cannot find workers.

Of those who finish school, many go to college. While we have a creamy layer of elite graduates from the best universities that multinationals are salivating over and that will initially staff the creative economy we aim for, we don't produce enough of them. Many more go through college programmes that give them precious little in the way of useful skills. Indeed, a 2023 report by Wheebox says that around 50 per cent of college graduates in India are unemployable.[10]

While traditional economic conflicts, such as worker strikes, have been on the wane, the vicious circle of low employability, leading to few jobs, mass unemployment and frustration, is now showing up in new forms of social conflict. The bloody clashes in the summer of 2023 between the Meiteis and Kukis in the border state of Manipur have their roots in the lack of economic opportunities for the youth, which then spills over into anger over the perceived unfairness of reservations or restrictions on land purchases. There is much to do.

In Part I of this book, we will explain how ideas, creativity and human capital are becoming much more important in growth and development, whether in manufacturing or services, or even in the agri-processing industry. We will argue that direct services exports (of the kind Professor Erali does) or services embedded in manufacturing exports (of the kind Tilfi, Tejas Networks or the captive multinational GCCs do) are increasingly possible, and can create many more high-quality jobs in India. They are already adding significantly to our exports and can contribute far more. We will also argue that services oriented to the Indian market, including education, health care and finance, will generate more jobs across the skills spectrum.

In pointing to the opportunities in high-skilled services, we do not, of course, imply India should neglect other areas of productive activity. Manufacturing, centred on innovative new products and our strength in engineering, should flourish. Of course, in a growing India, construction, transport, tourism and retail sectors will also expand, providing jobs for those with moderate skills.

A common factor in all these possible jobs, however, is the need to enhance the capabilities of our people and their opportunities to flourish. Part II of this book is about how we do so. Reforms, we will argue, need to be in three areas: governance reforms, reforms to human capital formation and reforms that will create an environment for innovation.

We start with governance reforms because we believe that underinvestment in our people's education and health care cannot be laid at one government's door. It has a lot to do with the way the Indian state is structured, a structure that worked at the time of Independence but is now showing its age. Without governance reforms, including strengthening democratic institutions and greater decentralization, which will make the government more responsive to the bottom-up demand of our people for better public services, other reforms will have little effect. But when accompanied by governance reforms, we believe that the reforms we suggest to education and health care can make an enormous difference. Throughout, we will highlight success stories and what we can learn from them on how best to increase investment in our people.

In Part II we will also discuss how we get an environment where our people can flourish, develop innovative new products and firms, thus becoming job creators rather than continuing as jobseekers. In part, that will require stronger connections with the world outside India. How can we persuade the world to be more open to India's exports, including the new range of services that technology permits us to offer, such as telemedicine and legal consulting? For instance, can we get more countries to recognize our professional degrees, or to offer our students exams that allow them to show their qualifications are equivalent to other countries' professional degrees? Innovation will also require enhancing fundamental research, starting in our first-rate universities, as we noted earlier, but spreading to business and government laboratories.

We conclude our argument in Part III of the book. For the creative, high-value-added breakthrough growth that we are proposing, India's most important advantage over more authoritarian countries, like China and Vietnam, is our inclusive liberal democracy. Pluralism, free speech, independent institutions, a vibrant civil society, and checks and balances on government are not just a concern for the liberal elite in Lutyens's Delhi, they are essential for the creativity-based growth path we propose.

The villager who wants to protest teacher absenteeism in the local government school should not fear being locked up by the teacher's police inspector brother-in-law; business people offering critical assessments of the government's performance should not find investigative agencies at their door the next day; data that reflect unfavourably on government performance should not be suppressed, leaving society navigating in the dark; foreign buyers of services from a domestic company like Tejas Networks should not fear that our government, unbound by privacy laws, will insist on the company embedding backdoors into the network through which government agencies can spy on their data; an Opposition leader who wants to protest cronyism at the highest level should not see trivial cases accelerated by a lower judiciary, seemingly intent on ejecting him from Parliament.

The possibility of abuse of power is embedded in our state structure; we have experienced centralized authoritarianism before, during the Emergency in 1975. Today we are confronted with the additional spectre of divisive majoritarianism, pitting our citizenry against each other along religious lines. None of this is good for the creativity-based growth path we advocate.

Study after study shows that authoritarianism suppresses innovative thinking—whether in the political arena, where it could challenge the existing power structure, or within research laboratories, where it could subvert the dominant scientific paradigm. If India chooses creativity and innovation, it will have to foster arguments and debates. Radical youths should be encouraged to challenge orthodoxy (non-violently, of course), and hopefully more within the university than on the street, but not locked up because they dare to speak.

Similarly, entrepreneurship flourishes in a peaceful, inclusive environment, less so in one where some community or other is targeted by hate groups. Rather than endlessly battling over our past on WhatsApp groups, we must prepare ourselves to capture the future. We cannot afford to be prisoners of history.

To address the huge challenges India faces, it must embark on a new path that involves a whole-of-country effort. Thus far, no developing country has grown rich by focusing on enhancing its human capital—certainly not within the generation or so we would aim for. No government can get it right on its own, because the path is one for which there are no blueprints. That means we need data, analysis, debate and, yes, criticism. This is not a path that an authoritarian government—which distrusts experts, suppresses inconvenient data, and isolates and harasses critics—can deliver on, even if it accepts the need for change. Before we conclude, we argue our case with an imaginary figure who is convinced of India's current trajectory. And, well, then we conclude.

Why This Book?

Both of us are professors, Rohit early in his career, while Raghu is much older and hopefully wiser than he used to be. We both have worked in government positions in India and care passionately about the country. We believe that India is capable of so much good, both in terms of its own development and the message it offers to the world.

What about you? If you are an upper-class Indian, you have probably had a good decade, with India's economic position and stature growing in the world. The news media is overwhelmingly supportive of government policies, so it is easy to feel that all is well. The reality, however, is that growth is too slow for the many jobs our people need.

If you are in a less-advantaged segment of society, you are likely experiencing an economic environment that has become more precarious, with enormous competition to get children into decent schools and public universities, and few good jobs afterwards. Your social supports are few, especially in the anonymous big city; so one medical emergency can push you or your neighbours into poverty. Most Indians are like you, enduring the present while hoping for something better.

With limited ideas on how to assuage the broader public's economic anxieties, the reaction of many of our leaders is to deflect the public's attention so that they forget the grim reality of today. For instance, the sparse data on poor job growth can be buried by an avalanche of inaugurations and announcements, so that an illusion of robust job growth is maintained. Instead of the jobseeker blaming government policies for her plight, she blames herself. We can still remedy matters, but for that we must snap out of the collective sense that our current path is fine.

If we break the mould to follow a truly Indian way, our future could be one of extraordinary well-being within a couple of decades. If, instead, we allow our thinking to be moulded by the past experiences of other countries, without accounting for how India is different and how the world has changed, it will be left to our children to lament as they think of the India that might have been.

We don't want India to be faux China; there are plenty of those already around. We need, instead, an irreverent, diverse and argumentative society, at harmony with its energetic chaos, one from which creative ideas emerge that will change the world. Instead of seeing our journey so far as an aberration and our democracy as a weakness, we should find our strengths in them and chart a path going forward that draws on the capabilities of all Indians, and builds on India's historic culture of tolerance and respect for all. The path will not be easy, but it can be the basis for change. As we write, more than three quarters of a century after Independence, we believe India's best days are still ahead. We have work to do. Let us get to it!

PART I

DEVELOPMENT: AN INDIAN WAY

Prelude

'Between the 60s and the 70s, Indonesia's GDP growth increased from 3.9 to 7.5 . . . I do not see how one can look at figures like these without seeing them as representing possibilities. Is there some action a government of India could take that would lead the Indian economy to grow like Indonesia's . . .? If so, what, exactly? If not, what is it about the "nature of India" that makes it so? The consequences for human welfare involved in questions like these are simply staggering: Once one starts to think about them, it is hard to think about anything else.'

—Robert Lucas, Nobel laureate in economics, 'On the Mechanics of Economic Development', 1988

How might India grow faster to produce the jobs its people need? In Chapter 1, we will explain how a country develops and grows richer. We will focus on how Asian economies like China and Korea grew quickly over the last few decades following a manufacturing-exports-led strategy. In Chapter 2, we will examine why India did not follow the China strategy, even after India's liberalizing reforms in the early 1990s. This will highlight some of the weaknesses that make it difficult for India to excel in low-skill manufacturing. Historically, services have been hard to export, for reasons we will point out in Chapter 3. But across the world, even as the manufacturing-exports-led growth strategy is becoming harder to follow, both direct services exports as well as the export of services embedded in manufacturing are becoming easier, especially after the pandemic. India has strong advantages in such exports, demonstrated by a significant existing share of such exports worldwide. In Chapter 4, we will argue that it is a mistake to elevate manufacturing over all else as the means for India to grow. It can also grow by expanding service exports as well as services oriented at the domestic market. More important, the government has to build the basis for growth in any sector by strengthening the human capital of our people. The government also has to create an environment where people can be creative and entrepreneurial, where new firms can flourish and create the jobs the country desperately needs. All of this requires a reimagining and reorienting of the trajectory we are on. The proposed path, which we will draw out in Part II, will utilize India's strengths better and depend less on capabilities where India is weak.

1

How Do Countries Grow Rich?

What does it mean for a country to be rich? Broadly speaking, richer countries produce more economic output per person—more food, such as grains and milk; more goods, such as cars, clothes, electronics and oil and natural gas; and more services, such as haircuts, doctor consultations, restaurant meals, hotel stays, films and software code. The more everyone in the country produces, the higher the incomes will be. So, the key to greater incomes is greater production per person, also called productivity.

Clearly, someone has to buy all those goods and services and pay for them—there has to be demand for all that is supplied. (As a side note, 'supply' and 'demand' are two of the most important words in economics, and if you speak fast and sprinkle what you say with these words, people will think you are a real economist.) A French economist, Jean-Baptiste Say, pointed out that the income from selling all that production becomes the means to buy that production. So, the farmer sells vegetables and uses the proceeds to pay for his laundry, while the laundry operator charges for laundering the farmer's clothes and uses that to buy vegetables. Well, matters are a little more complicated, but to a first approximation, production is what matters.

Where Do Higher Incomes Come From?

What allows a worker to produce more? First of all, tools or machines. In preparing the ground for a building's foundations, a labourer with a spade digs more slowly than the operator of an earth mover. The latter's work is both easier and more productive, because it is aided by an immensely powerful machine. In the economist's parlance, the earth mover operator's labour is augmented by capital, the earth mover itself. Of course, an operator who does not know how to drive the earth mover or operate its shovel can damage production. So the worker's skills, or human capital, also affect how much they produce or how valuable their output is.

What else goes into increasing productivity? The organization of production matters. If the labourer shovels the earth into a wheelbarrow, which he then carts to a landfill, where he compacts the earth with a heavy roller and then starts laying the foundation of a building—each part of the production process may require specialized skills, yet one person does it all. What if, instead, the operator uses the earth mover to dump earth into a truck, which a truck driver takes to the landfill site, where the dumped earth is compacted by other operators driving steamrollers, and finally, bricklayers take over to build the foundation? Productivity is much higher in the latter operation, not just because workers use machines but also because workers specialize, and specialists are typically better at their specific tasks than generalists. The great Scottish economist Adam Smith noted the benefits of division of labour in enhancing production. Of course, such division of labour is possible only if the operation is sufficiently large, that is, if the scale of production is high. The chain of workers would make little sense if we were moving earth within a small kitchen garden—everyone would get in each other's way.

Also critical to capital and the organization of production is the technology that underpins both. A more fuel-efficient or powerful earth mover will allow the operator to generate more value with her labour. Here, technology refers to the quality of the capital that augments labour.

Finally, it's also important to consider how workers are incentivized and how their output makes its way through the economy. Economists club these aspects into a catch-all word: 'institutions'. These could include incentive contracts for workers, the nature of ownership, logistics, the existence of markets, contract enforcement, regulations and the independence of courts. In a rich country, the operator might own the earth mover and so has an incentive to dig up as much and as quickly as possible. Furthermore, the truck that collects the dug-up earth would then travel over fast highways to the coast where a property developer, who purchased the earth in an online auction, would dump it into the sea to reclaim land, on which he would build a luxury hotel, earning a lot of money. In effect, there is a supply chain, linked through enforceable contracts, that utilizes what is produced well.

In a poor country, there would be very few immediate uses for the earth. Left on the side of the hole, the dug-up earth would blow away steadily in the wind, causing costly dust pollution elsewhere, with some even settling back into the same hole. Something as mundane as digging a hole can be done far more productively in a rich country than in a poor country.

So how does a poor country—where almost everyone is a farmer, herder or fisherman, or is part of a household dependent on someone who practises these occupations—develop? That is to say, how does it get rich? From the above example the answer is clear. Labour needs to be educated or trained so that human capital improves; it should be supported with more equipment or capital; the equipment has to get better through technological improvements; and institutions have to be created and strengthened, all with the aim of enhancing production and productivity (the value of production per worker).

Unfortunately, there is only so much that can be done to improve productivity in sectors like agriculture. The use of fertilizers, irrigation, tractors and even giant combines can increase yields, but ultimately there is only so much land. In India, each agricultural worker had, on an average, only 0.67 hectares of arable land in 2020, while in the United States, the comparable figure was 46.6 hectares.[1] The Indian worker cannot produce much from a small plot of land, even if they use the best agricultural techniques. They could add value to their produce—for instance, by making pickles out of vegetables, or keeping chickens and goats—and many do, but it cannot get them anywhere near the wealth of the Americans.

Historically, workers had to move out of agriculture into manufacturing to increase productivity significantly. For much of the now-developed world, this was a slow process. One estimate suggests the share of labour in agriculture in England shrank steadily from around 63 per cent in the 1550s to 35 per cent in the 1750s.[2] Most workers who left agriculture spun, wove, stitched, sawed or hammered to make goods in their homes. The Industrial Revolution accelerated the pace of transformation. With the advent of the factory system, the increasing use of steam-powered machines, coupled with better organization of manufacturing, increased the efficiency of production.

Growth took off because a virtuous circle developed. As people left agriculture, those who stayed behind could consolidate land into larger farms. Mechanization in tilling, better-quality seeds, irrigation and new techniques of crop rotation helped the output produced per worker go up significantly. It turned out that many of the farm workers who had been employed earlier were not really needed, especially as farmers found more productive methods of working the fields when labour became harder to find.

Wealthier farmers had incomes to spend, and they spent it on finer clothes, stylish hats and shoes, better furniture and larger dwellings, thus consuming the products being churned out by the urban factories. As factory owners became richer, they invested their profits in better machines that would allow their workers to produce more. As workers became more productive, they were paid more, and they too started contributing to demand.

New needs emerged. The local tavern allowed the factory labourer to relax, even make merry, after a hard day's work in the factory. So, an industry developed around fermenting grain, distilling it and delivering beer to every part of the city. The employment of bartenders and barmaids also increased.

Initially, workers leaving agriculture for the factories did not have much education, nor did they need much. But as machines became more sophisticated and complicated, workers needed more training, even some knowledge of mathematics, physics and chemistry, to operate, maintain and repair those machines. Clever workers innovated on the shop floor, jury-rigging machines together to make them more efficient.

Furthermore, as factories became bigger, new positions, such as those of manager, engineer and accountant, had to be filled. As clothing came to be mass-produced, consumers demanded some diversity in styles, so factory owners started looking for clothing designers. Many existing jobs as well as these new jobs needed more skills and education. Given the scarcity of educated workers, wages went up for these positions.

Seeing that education paid off with higher wages and productivity, urban dwellers, supported by factory owners, demanded more and better schools for their children. From simply being seen as vehicles for imparting a civilizing and religious discipline to children, schools became an economic imperative, a way to forge the worker of the future.[3] In other words, along with an expansion in physical capital, the human capital of populations also improved, once again increasing productivity.

Perhaps most important for longer-run growth was technological progress. Scientists, engineers and workers improved on existing machines or invented new products (think of James Watt or Thomas

Edison), while managers streamlined production processes to make them more efficient (think of Henry Ford).

So countries grew richer. Between 1820 and 1870, income per person in Western Europe and the United States grew at a rate of 1–1.3 per cent a year. This was painfully slow compared to the growth of per capita incomes in China and India in recent years, but spectacularly fast compared to the previous 5000 years of human history.

Why Has Developing-Country Growth in Recent Years Been So Much Faster?

Why could the early industrializing countries not grow faster? Even though large-scale production was more efficient in the past, a factory owner could not simply set up a gigantic factory and produce at scale. For one, he might not have had the funds or financing to make the investment. Also, he could not produce much more than the existing demand for his product, in the hope that it would be bought. Instead, he had to plan for gradual demand growth, driven by steadily increasing incomes and higher spending by the country's people. This, in turn, was made possible by the steady increase in physical and human capital employed. Of course, some industrializing countries, such as Great Britain, had colonies like India, which could be used to absorb manufactured goods. But the ability of the poor colonial population to buy the colonizer's goods was small to begin with and fell further as machine-made imports crowded out local handicrafts, further impoverishing the colonial population. In the long run, imperialism was not a sustainable source of demand growth.

Technological progress could improve production and income growth significantly—with better sewing machines, garment workers could produce more per hour, earn more, and spend more on food and entertainment. But since these countries were already using the best technologies available at that time, better technologies had to be invented. Innovation at the knowledge frontier is slow.

Yet, in recent years, we have seen some countries grow spectacularly. Most impressive has been the growth of the Asian economies, starting with Japan, proceeding to Korea, Malaysia, Singapore and Taiwan, and then, most recently, China (we will come to India shortly).

In his illuminating book *How Asia Works*, journalist and author Joe Studwell explains how Asian economies undertook the traditional transformation from agriculture to manufacturing somewhat differently—with a very active role played by the government.[4]

The starting point was land reform, which distributed land ownership (or rights to its produce in China) to the tiller. This allowed the small farmer to thrive, generating surpluses that could be deployed in manufacturing. The government recognized, however, that if manufacturing had to wait for the domestic demand for goods to build up, manufacturing scale would remain small and productivity low for a long time.

Think, for example, of a poor country that is good at making top hats. If it wants scale through its own demand, it needs income to grow enormously so that there are a huge number of high-society events, such as balls and horse races, where top hats are de rigueur. That could take a long time. But if it targets demand in rich countries, there is a ready need for top hats that it can cater to.

Therefore, economies of scale in manufacturing could be achieved by targeting world markets where the developing country's initial comparative advantage was the cheap labour that richer industrialized countries no longer had. So the government cajoled producers to focus on export sectors, especially those where low or moderately skilled labour was needed in large quantities—such as textiles, leather goods, toys and the assembly of electronic goods. In these sectors, demand from the rich world would supplement local demand, ensuring that growth and production scale would not be held back by low demand.

Nor was it held back by technology. Since these developing Asian countries were not yet at the technological frontier, they could buy, imitate, rent or even steal technologies, and didn't have to innovate—initially, they bought rudimentary sewing machines for their garment workers, then more sophisticated ones. All these technologies were available since industrial countries had already done the necessary innovation. Catch-up growth was therefore easier and faster than growth at the frontier.

Manufacturing productivity also did not remain static. Workers learnt by doing and became more skilled, with more pieces produced per hour, and error rates and spoilage coming down. Furthermore, with increasing scale, automation increased—buttons were stitched by machines rather than by hand, reducing costs and improving productivity. Managers also learnt by doing, figuring out new and better ways to incentivize workers, configure assembly lines, and manage the logistics of supplies and dispatches. Foreign producers set up base domestically, bringing their productive practices to the country, allowing domestic producers to learn by imitation.

As workers became more skilled and better educated, manufacturers moved to more sophisticated goods, such as cameras, motorcycles, cars and machinery, leaving low-skilled manufacturing to newcomer countries on the development ladder.[5] Countries nearing the technological frontier started doing their own research and development. The technological gap with the industrial countries closed, and Japanese cameras, Korean TVs and Chinese electric vehicles became global leaders.

Finally, better practices from the competitive export-oriented sector spread throughout the manufacturing sector, as well as to other sectors in the economy. The exporter who needed just-in-time inventory and reliable delivery demanded better service from transporters, who improved their truck maintenance to reduce breakdowns and unexpected delays. As logistics and transportation improved, the local property developer could source raw materials efficiently to build apartments more quickly. In the jargon, productivity improvements did not stay in the export-oriented sector; they spread to other parts of the economy, such as construction. Manufacturing was indeed the ladder to riches.

Asian export-led growth accelerated the typical shift in labour between sectors, but the transformation was similar to the one that rich countries had already gone through. First manufacturing expands, drawing workers from agriculture, accounting for a greater share of the total economic output of the country. Strong productivity growth in manufacturing increases worker incomes. As the population gets richer, people start demanding more services. When a country is poor, most services are done in-house—people cook their own food and someone in the household cuts their hair. As some people get richer, they employ a cook and go to a barber. As the country gets richer still, household help becomes expensive, and people go to a restaurant when they don't want to cook. In short, productivity growth in manufacturing increases the demand for services and eventually reduces the need for workers in manufacturing.

The growth of services consequently picks up, and draws workers from both agriculture and manufacturing, reducing their share of workers. The services sector eventually dominates employment in the economy. Thus, the manufacturing share of employment in an economy as a function of its income per person first increases as workers move from agriculture to manufacturing, then decreases as they move from manufacturing to services. Typically, manufacturing's share of workers decreases only when a country becomes quite rich, and indeed even then, given the high productivity of manufacturing jobs, its share of the economy's output does not decrease as fast.

How Has India Fared?

Add up all the incomes paid for goods and services in the country and we get the country's gross domestic product or GDP. Divide GDP by a country's total population to get income per person (in the jargon, GDP per capita).

In 1961, India's income per person was $86, South Korea's was $94 and China's was $76. India was right in the middle of a very poor pack of countries. India's income per person today is around $2300, China's is around $12,500 and Korea's is around $35,000.[6] India is no longer in the middle of the pack; it is at the bottom by a long way. Indians can have three immediate reactions to these statistics. First, of course: the comparison is unfair. We have selected two of the most successful growth stories in the history of humanity and have set India up against them. The second response is despondency: How did we get it so wrong? The third is to get defensive: India chose a different path, prioritizing stability and democracy in a diverse country rather than economic growth at any costs. There is some merit to all three reactions.

For instance, we have indeed selected two of the fastest-growing large countries for comparison. Compared to the rest, India does not fare so badly. Between 1980 and 2018, India's GDP per capita grew at an average of 4.6 per cent per annum, and the decadal average never fell below 3 per cent. If we filter countries by those that have grown at 4.5 per cent or more for at least thirty-eight years in this period, and during which any consecutive ten-year average has not fallen below 2.9 per cent, only nine countries make the cut, and only Botswana, other than India of course, comes close to being a persistent democracy.[7]

There is another aspect of growth worth noting. We mentioned earlier that the share of workers in manufacturing typically peaks at some point in a country's development, and then falls. As Dani Rodrik of Harvard University has documented, since 1990 the share of manufacturing, in terms of both total workers and total output, has started decreasing in a number of countries in Africa and Latin America. This has happened long before these countries reached the levels of per capita income at which a country's share of manufacturing typically started declining in the past. He argues this is also true for India, with the manufacturing employment share starting to decline from 2002.[8] While there is some controversy about whether India is deindustrializing, it is undoubtedly true that services employment has picked up a bigger share of those leaving agriculture than is typical for developing countries, while the share of workers in manufacturing has stayed relatively flat. Whether this is a bug or a feature of late industrializers like India is something we will examine in the next few chapters.

Whichever way you cut the data, it is clear that India came late to the manufacturing exports game, only beginning with its reforms in the early 1990s. Its growth since the early '90s has certainly benefited from its increasing exports, both of manufacturing and services. But why has it not built a greater manufacturing presence? What kinds of manufacturing is it adept at? That is what we now turn to.

2

Why Has India Not Built a Global Manufacturing Presence?

As we noted in the last chapter, India did not do as well in improving the standard of living of its people as the East Asian growth leaders, probably because we did not build a strong global manufacturing presence. Perhaps the most appropriate comparison is with China, which started off at similar levels of per capita income in the 1960s and has a similar population size.

Why Has India Not Industrialized to China's Extent?

Roughly speaking, China started modernizing its economy a decade before India did in the late 1970s. Not only did China start earlier, it also grew at a brisker pace. Compounding, as students of mathematics know, does the rest—India's total economic output today is where China's was in 2007, so India is about sixteen years behind, even if, going forward, it grows at the same pace that China grew at. Of course, such high growth rates may now be elusive, and catching up will require yet more time even if all goes well for India, since China will not remain stagnant.

There are plenty of differences between the two countries, including their history, their peoples' diversity, their political systems, even their demographics. So any focus on a few key differences runs the risk of missing many others, as with the six blind men in the Buddhist Tittha Sutta text.[1] Nevertheless, here goes.

Basic Education

Communist regimes in the twentieth century typically invested heavily in basic education, partly because of their emphasis on equality, and perhaps also because widespread literacy allowed common people to get acquainted with the Communist scriptures. China was no exception. The average years of education in India in 1950 was one; in that year in China, a year after the Communists took over, it was 1.8.[2] By 1980, when China started its reforms, this number was 5.7 for China and 2.5 for India. When India started reforms in the early 1990s, it had only crept up to 3.6.

Why does this matter? Yasheng Huang, of the Massachusetts Institute of Technology (MIT), suggests that China's growth story was bottom-up, with myriad small businesses starting up in rural areas in the 1980s, aided by cheap credit and a liberalized business environment. These small township and village enterprises (TVEs), many of them found in clusters that specialized in specific products—door handles here and machine screws there—became essential elements of China's very competitive production chains. Huang argues that the reason India did not take off in a similar way was because average levels of Indian education, especially in rural areas, were much lower. It takes a certain amount of literacy, numeracy and basic accounting to run a small business, and more Chinese had that when their economy was liberalized. India invested more in education only when liberalization gradually highlighted the need for more educated workers.[3]

Why did India fare poorly on mass early education? In his classic book *The Child and the State*, MIT professor Myron Weiner argues that India's inability to put a vast majority of its children through compulsory primary schooling in the first four decades after Independence was rooted in caste and economic hierarchies. The elite simply did not have an interest in educating the underprivileged castes and the poor. How would education benefit an agricultural worker other than raising her above her station, and increasing her dissatisfaction with her lot?

Strangely, democracy also did not push politics towards greater public spending on primary public education and health. Perhaps caste-based village hierarchies rendered the poor powerless, as B.R. Ambedkar argued; perhaps it took some minimal education for the citizenry to become aware and able to push for their rights to these public services, or perhaps the public deemed these public services unimportant until liberalization created the jobs that highlighted the education gap. The truth is, once again, probably a composite of all these.

As India liberalized its economy in the 1990s, average years of education moved up rapidly in the population, so that India was only 1.5 years behind China in 2015. This is no mean achievement, but our educational attainments are still of variable quality. For many children, the gap between what they are meant to know in their grade and what they do know is large. Now that India has got the vast majority of its children into schools, it has to improve the quality of their learning.

Government Decentralization and Support

A second key ingredient in China's industrialization was its system of competition among local governments. As with much of the developing world, China does not score particularly high on indicators of ease of doing business, such as the days it takes to complete all the formalities for opening a business. According to a World Bank database measuring the regulations governing business and their enforcement, China ranked number 91 in 2006, with Yemen slightly ahead, and Serbia and Montenegro behind it.[4] It had the same rank in 2013, with Jamaica in front and the Solomon Islands just behind. India was at number 116 and 132 in those years. In short, both countries fared poorly on measures of ease of doing business.

So does ease of doing business not matter? It does, but the Chinese got around it in a uniquely Chinese way. Despite the outward perception of centralization of power at the top of the Communist Party, growth-facilitating policies were decentralized to municipalities and city governments. Once Deng Xiaoping pivoted the economy away from communist ideals in the late 1970s, the Beijing leadership did formulate broad policies, but the local governments were at the forefront of the growth juggernaut.

As Chang-Tai Hsieh from the University of Chicago has argued, city mayors had many ways of benefiting a favoured company. They had the power to override or turn a blind eye to regulations that they administered, and to lobby higher-ups to waive the regulations that were outside their control. They could offer land at below-market prices and loans at subsidized rates, sometimes in return for an equity stake for the city in the company. They could even block competition from outside firms in areas under their jurisdiction. A city official's success in promoting local growth led to promotions up the party hierarchy. So mayors were empowered to promote growth and incentivized to do so.

Hsieh describes a 2013 visit to a Chinese city, where seven vice-mayors were primarily tasked with attracting new firms to the city as well as managing the problems of existing favoured ones. Around thirty firms were allocated to each vice-mayor. In the case of General Motor's Shanghai joint venture, assistance included ensuring that all the taxis operating in the city were GM cars.

Invariably, some of the corporate profits generated from local government support also enriched the helpful party officials. But corruption was a lubricant, not necessarily the prime motivator. Indeed, competition among localities helped limit the implicit demands from local officials for bribes. Richard McGregor, former bureau chief of the

Financial Times, describes the phenomenon thus: 'What is obvious for anyone who travels around the country is how much of the economy is driven by another factor altogether, a kind of Darwinian internal competition that pits localities against each other . . . each Chinese province, city, county, and village furiously compete to gulp down any economic advantage they can lure their way.'[5]

We use the past tense in these descriptions since the centralization during President Xi Jinping's administration, as well as the sometimes-selective drives against corruption, have curbed some of this Darwinian rule-bending. Local government officials do not want to bend the rules and make themselves vulnerable to allegations of corruption any more. China's growth has, perhaps not entirely coincidentally, also slowed, suggesting that the favourable business environment was important to Chinese growth.

India, by contrast, always had a more centralized system of governance. The Constitution decentralized governance only to the state level, and even state governments were easily dismissed by the Centre in the early decades. Local government at the city, municipality or village level was initially neither empowered nor funded nor adequately staffed, for reasons we will go into later. Even after constitutional amendments created a third tier of government, too little power has been decentralized thus far.

So while India's state governments compete with each other for business today, they govern over enormous numbers of people. The industry secretary in an Indian state capital does not have the narrow jurisdiction or the broad power that the deputy mayor in a Chinese city had, while the Central government-appointed district collector in India has little incentive to push for growth. The occasional exceptional Indian officer who breaks the mould with development work only verifies the rule. The kind of competitive cronyism we saw in China's years of fast development, which facilitates growth while checking excessive cronyism and corruption, has not taken hold in India.

Suppressing Market and Democratic Forces

China also needed to give its firms, especially those in the export sector, an edge. There were many ways it did this. Starting in the 1990s, China worked to keep its exchange rate from appreciating even as its exports and trade surpluses increased. What does this mean?

China's goods are priced in the Chinese currency, the renminbi. There is a market exchange rate that determines how many dollars a renminbi can buy. China's strategy was to keep this exchange rate low, typically through the central bank buying up dollars in the market, so that fewer dollars were being offered to the broader public against renminbis. Consequently, a dollar bought more renminbis. This ensured China's exports would be cheap in dollar terms, and it would be able to outsell other nations. Many foreign firms set up production facilities in China to take advantage of the beneficial exchange rate, while Chinese exporters got a boost. Of course, this also meant Chinese households would find it very costly to buy imported goods, which limited their imports and made them buy mainly Chinese goods.

In addition, China offered firms cheap credit, kept worker wages low and built out infrastructure. The government told banks to set a low bank deposit interest rate for households, which allowed the largely state-owned banks in turn to offer firms cheap loans without losing money on them. The Communist Party controlled the labour unions, and ensured that wages did not keep pace with labour productivity. This gave firms an extra margin of profitability. The government also built out excellent infrastructure by acquiring land as needed from citizens, which gave firms factory sites with uninterrupted access to power and fast transport connections, to where workers resided and to markets.

Ultimately, Chinese households paid the price, because their wages and the returns on their deposited savings were artificially low. Household consumption was a much lower share of China's GDP than it was in other countries with similar income levels. For example, in 2010, China's household consumption as a share of GDP was 34 per cent. The same number for a poorer India was 54 per cent, a richer America was 68 per cent, and somewhat more comparable Korea and Thailand were around the 50 per cent mark.[6]

None of this would be possible, or even desirable, in democratic India. Rich Indians do not want the rupee to be undervalued, hampering their purchase of imported goods, increasing the cost of their children's tuition in colleges abroad and making foreign vacations more expensive. It is probably not even possible to do so. To keep foreign capital from flowing in and elevating the exchange rate, India would have to maintain persistently low interest rates. That would upset our middle-class savers. Workers and their unions would also protest quickly about below-productivity wages.

Furthermore, the land acquisition needed to build infrastructure is extremely costly and difficult in crowded India: Land ownership is still murky in some regions, with property boundaries not clearly marked and who actually owns the land unclear. Political parties and the judicial system are ready to side with those whose land is acquired if there is any hint of coercion, and prominent citizens are quite willing to lend their voices to this opposition. On this last point: naturally, no one wants a highway running through their fields or in front of their apartment, even if the benefits for the community are significant—India's nightingale, Lata Mangeshkar, played a critical role in ensuring a congestion-relieving Mumbai flyover that would have passed outside her flat was not built.[7]

The overarching theme here is that any attempt by the government to run roughshod over citizens' concerns will provoke protests. Democratic but still developing India has a first-world civil society, without the first-world government capacity to address its concerns. Consequently, while it takes a long time for the government to acquire the land for a new highway or power station in Europe, in India it can take still longer.

Could India have become a democracy too early in its development path? The United States and the United Kingdom experienced steady economic growth since the early nineteenth century, and also had steady democratization, with universal suffrage granted only after they had reached upper-middle income by today's standards. The Asian tiger economies embarked on their accelerated development path decades after World War II. Nevertheless, Korea stayed autocratic for longer in terms of development time—it became a full democracy only when it was richer than the US and the UK.

China and India are the clear exceptions in very different ways. China grew explosively after liberalizing its economy in the early 1980s, with little change in its autocratic one-party system. India was unusual in that it started as a democracy even when it was poor. Arguably, India may have democratized too early—perhaps strong manufacturing growth in its early years required an authoritarian hand to remove the obstacles in the way of development.

Of course, democracy has intrinsic benefits, and many authoritarian countries have stayed poor, plagued by cronyism and corruption. So we cannot conclude that democracy was a mistake in India's early years, only that it was unusual. We will argue that, going forward, the developmental path India should take requires more democratization, not less.

Are There Other Reasons Why India Has Not Built a Manufacturing Base?

Prior to the early 1990s, India, like many other developing countries, attempted an import substitution strategy, where high tariffs (that is, customs duties) kept out imports, leaving the domestic market entirely to Indian producers. The problem was that the Indian market was typically too small for the producers to acquire scale and manufacture efficiently, and the lack of competition, especially in areas like auto manufacturing, where only four firms were licensed to produce, gave producers little incentive to innovate or improve. Indian growth was slow. The import substitution strategy, a key component of the Licence Raj, or Permit Raj, ensured India stayed poor.

India embarked on reforms in the early 1990s and finally liberalized its high-tariff, uncompetitive economy, adopting a more open export-oriented strategy. Average tariffs came down from 125 per cent in 1991 to 13 per cent in 2014.[8] The lowering of tariffs increased domestic competition—for instance, three auto manufacturers shut down, while the fourth, Maruti, remade itself with foreign collaboration. However, even with liberalization, India was not able to take full advantage of global demand for manufactured goods. India did not, and sometimes could not, address the impediments we have discussed. But there were other impediments too.

Some were self-imposed. India's labour laws and regulations get more onerous as firms increase in size. Labour laws therefore act as a tax on scale and productivity, ensuring far too many manufacturing firms remain small and unproductive.[9] For instance, workers are granted tenure, or, in local parlance, 'become permanent' (and therefore harder to motivate or let go), once they have been employed for some time. So labour regulations incentivize employers to keep most workers on temporary contracts, firing them periodically so they do not become permanent. Most workers thus have precarious temporary work, with firms hesitant to invest in their skills since these workers will have to be let go soon.

Another impediment is India's haphazard negotiation of trade treaties, as well as its frequent and unpredictable use of tariffs to protect influential intermediate goods producers. This has left Indian manufacturing perversely wide open to finished goods imports while tariffs on intermediate inputs make manufacturing in India excessively costly. For instance, the global clothing market (finished good) is hugely dependent on cloth made from man-made fibre such as polyester (intermediate good). An important ingredient in making polyester is purified terephthalic acid (PTA). Even while the production of this input by two large producers within India declined, severe import restrictions were imposed on it in 2014.[10] Domestic PTA prices shot up, increasing the input costs for Indian polyester textiles manufacturers, making them globally uncompetitive. As a result of such own goals, Bangladesh, Vietnam, and even the Netherlands and Germany have taken up, to a greater extent than India, the global market share that China has given up in textiles and apparel.

Despite impediments to manufacturing, India has had a number of areas of success, where it produces competitively for the world. These include auto ancillaries, two-wheelers and generic pharmaceuticals. We will argue that India's strength in incremental innovation and engineering helped the Indian presence in these industries. But the broader environment that is required to make manufacturing the base of growth never fully materialized in India. Consider the once-promising story of Punjab.

What Happened to Punjab?

Among Indian states, Punjab best illustrates the phenomenon of premature deindustrialization. Punjab's wheat production made it India's breadbasket after Independence, while the 1960s Green Revolution—the dramatic increase in crop yields because of better seed varieties, irrigation, fertilizers and credit—tilted it towards rice, and it became the rice bowl of the country too. Punjab's influence was perhaps most visible in its pop culture—poetry, music, dance and films, which didn't just spread across the country but, through the Punjabi diaspora, to the rest of the world too.

Many factors came together in Punjab's agricultural success. Post Independence, the construction of canals and dams, such as the Bhakra Nangal Dam, which Jawaharlal Nehru praised as one of the 'temples of modern India' spread irrigation through historically fertile land. The Punjab Agricultural University system, initiated by Chief Minister Pratap Singh Kairon, produced leading-edge research on seeds and farming practices, and helped take them to the farmers. Agricultural credit was ramped up to support the investments farmers had to make. Farmers were assured of government grain procurement at preannounced minimum prices, thus reducing the already-low risk in wheat and paddy production.

Politics also played a part. Indian policymakers, such as agriculture minister C. Subramaniam, dialled up the need to achieve food security after US President Lyndon B. Johnson started delaying food shipments, retaliating to India's criticism of US handling of the Vietnam war. India was vulnerable when it lived from ship to mouth, and India's leaders were determined to change this. The Green Revolution, ironically with significant US technical support, made Punjab rich.

As farmers grew wealthy, their surpluses set in motion a minor industrial revolution. Ludhiana was locally called the 'Manchester of the East'. By the early 1980s, it was producing farm implements, hosiery, hydraulic motors, sewing machines, textiles, auto parts, bicycles and more. Jalandhar made sports equipment (Raghu remembers the fine cricket gear that came from there in his teenage years of gully cricket). These were not being produced simply for domestic sales; a significant quantum was also exported.

One of Punjab's big successes was Hero Cycles, which made reliable, sturdy, popular bicycles. Hero's owners, the Munjal brothers, focused on incremental engineering and productivity improvements, not path-breaking products. They paid relentless attention to costs and kept inventories lean. This was Japanese-style manufacturing, long before it became popular practice. A key element was to build close relationships with dealers and suppliers. It started early on, when the first batch of cycles developed cracks, and Hero bought them all back, compensating the dealers fully. Hero paid suppliers promptly on Saturdays, something unusual in India, where getting paid can be an ordeal in itself.

The miracle, of course, was that Hero thrived in pre-liberalization India. It was aided by Chief Minister Kairon, who, much in the manner of Chinese mayors, lobbied the Centre to relax oppressive production caps. Hero achieved adequate scale domestically, since even a relatively poor country had a robust demand for cycles. As Hero competed with other domestic manufacturers, like Atlas and Tube Investments, a thriving cycle industry emerged. (Raghu's first cycle was an Atlas, and the second a Hero; Rohit's first was a Hero, and he became a loyal customer.)

By 1975, Hero was the largest manufacturer of bicycles in India, and had started exporting to much of the world. Its success mirrored Punjab's industrial success. At the turn of the century, Punjab was the richest state in India in terms of per capita income. Unfortunately, today it doesn't feature in the top fifteen. What happened?

Once again, it was a combination of circumstances. Perhaps the most important was competition, both from other states in India but also from foreign goods as India reduced tariffs and liberalized its economy in the early 1990s. Punjab had a fundamental disadvantage as a location for goods production—given the impaired relations with our neighbouring countries. Remember, access to larger markets increases scale, productivity and hence income. Amritsar, one of Punjab's most important cities, is just fifty kilometres from Lahore in Pakistan, and the distance between Ludhiana and Kabul in Afghanistan is two-thirds of the distance between Ludhiana and Bhopal in central India. As a landlocked northern border state, with little trade across the border, Punjab is not close to other markets. Consequently, as competition started heating up, Punjab's higher freight costs started to bite.

Another problem was the dominance and profitability of rice farming and its hold over the political establishment. Agricultural subsidies kept the economic value of growing paddy and wheat artificially high, which prevented a natural transition of small and marginal farmers out of agriculture. The state government further distorted economic choices by offering farmers free power to draw out groundwater, which depleted the water table. Eventually, smaller farmers, who could not afford the big pumps that were needed to draw water from the depths it had sunk to, were hurt. Farming surpluses started diminishing—it would have made sense for farmers to switch to other crops than paddy, but the low risk of growing paddy combined with the substantial government supports meant they were trapped.

The government subsidies to, and focus on, agriculture raised costs for industry. In addition to making labour harder to find as fewer farmers left agriculture, power, too, got expensive. Since power supply to agriculture was largely free, the government had to charge higher prices elsewhere to make up for the losses, and industry bore the brunt.[11] Other taxes, such as VAT (Value Added Tax), were also set higher in Punjab than in surrounding states, to pay for the transfers to agriculture. With Punjabi firms facing more competition from imports and from manufacturers in neighbouring states, and higher costs, their profitability fell. This reduced their ability to undertake the research and product development that might have kept them competitive. One measure of the political apathy towards industry was that between 1960 and 2010, barely 10 per cent of the state assembly debates focused on industry; the main obsession continued to be agriculture.[12] Perhaps not coincidentally, the Hero Group decided to move to Haryana when it set up its motorcycle manufacturing plants, and now is the second-largest motorized two-wheeler manufacturer in the world.

Punjab has had more than its share of misfortune too. The trauma of Partition, followed by wars with neighbouring Pakistan in 1965 and 1971, and the politico-religious extremism that enveloped it in the 1980s, would have challenged any state. But the inability of successive state governments to adapt to changed circumstances has contributed to this decline. Far from supporting industry, as neighbouring states of Haryana and Himachal Pradesh have done, powerful politicians in Punjab reportedly pressured industry to contribute large sums to party coffers.[13]

As industry has either closed or fled to other states, the state government finances have deteriorated, making it even more dependent on taxing the industry that remains. According to a Reserve Bank of India (RBI) report on Indian states, Punjab has the largest value of debt to total economic output among all Indian states. 'We have no money left to invest in the education and skilling of our youth,' a senior bureaucrat lamented to us. 'How will you get industry if you don't have any labour skilled enough to work in it?'

In recent years, Punjab's youths, unable to find options outside agriculture, have started migrating abroad. Among those who have stayed behind, substance abuse has become commonplace. The vicious cycle of deterioration continues.

Punjab needs to turn the situation around before it becomes irredeemable. Thoughtful Punjabi agriculturists tell us that there is a need to diversify farming away from wheat and paddy through a better allocation of subsidies, and to invest resources to support other sectors of its economy. Indeed, as climate volatility increases, Punjab's privileged access to snowmelt-fed rivers and its reserves of groundwater can once again become an essential element of India's food security, so long as water is not sucked up in paddy cultivation. Whether Punjab will regain its prominence in industry is an open question. But it can do much better.

Interest-group politics has played an important role in Punjab's deindustrialization. Economic policies, initially introduced to benefit the large farmer, are hard to change even when circumstances change, since the beneficiaries of those policies have become politically powerful. Visionaries like Pratap Singh Kairon are in short supply. A democratic push for change from those who have lost out over the years will be a first step towards reclaiming Punjab's past glory.

What happened in Punjab is reflected somewhat in India more broadly—manufacturing's share of jobs has been stagnant for decades. However, it is not just the aggregate numbers that are worrisome. The Economic Survey of India 2016–17 estimated that within manufacturing, the number of jobs generated for every investment of Rs 1 lakh (that is about $1200) in apparel is twenty-four, in leather and footwear it is around seven, in the auto industry it is 0.3, and in the steel industry it is 0.1. Alarmingly, the news portal Moneycontrol reported that for twelve out of the twenty-three categories of manufacturing products that make up the Index of Industrial Production, the index was lower in June 2023 than in June 2016.[14] Prominent among the shrinking categories are low-capital-using and low-skilled-worker-employing sectors like textiles, apparel and leather.

But what about services? Could they be a pathway to India's development?

3

The Transformation in Trade and Services-Led Development

Services have traditionally not been as supportive to economic development as manufacturing for important reasons. Manufactured goods such as toys can be exported to richer countries, where demand is large and easier to sustain, thus accelerating growth. In contrast, services, like haircuts or retail shops, are intensely local—it is virtually impossible (as yet) for a barber in Delhi to cut hair in Los Angeles. It is equally hard for the barber to store haircuts—he needs to cut hair in real time. Many services must be in the same place where the demand resides and coincident in time with that demand, which has meant that service producers within a country have not been able to cater to global demand. They have been constrained by the needs of the local economy, which, as we have argued, grows slowly in a developing country absent exports.

Productivity in services has also typically grown slowly, in part because scale and innovation are hard. The barber in the United States uses pretty much the same tools (and techniques) as the barber in India—a combination of electric clippers, comb and scissors. Given human heads are not standardized, it is hard for one barber today to tonsure many heads at the same time without doing substantial damage to the customers' looks or to their heads. We have not managed to find labour-saving equipment that would substantially increase services productivity in such occupations. But the world has changed in other ways.

Global Supply Chains and the Transformation in Trade

New technologies have changed the nature of goods trade and, interestingly, the tradability of a variety of services. Standardized containers, which are easy to load and unload off ships on to railway wagons and trucks, as well as improvements in logistics and tracking, have reduced the costs of transportation and improved its timeliness. Low tariffs have reduced the cost of goods crossing country borders. At the same time, communications technology enables the production of parts in a manufacturing plant in Thailand to be tracked in real time from Chennai, and the firm's management to foresee and address production interruptions.

This means that the supply chain for a product no longer needs to be close together in one place. It can be sliced up and placed across the globe, with every segment done in the place where it is the cheapest to produce. The idea of a smile curve has become popular in representing the value added in each segment of the supply chain, as one goes from beginning to end. Much of the value in a product is created at the initial stage, as R&D and design go into conceptualizing the product. Then the product is manufactured, with each part produced in the region where it is most cost-competitive to do so. Sub-assemblies go back and forth across borders. The final product is then sold in the target market, with a whole range of high-value services, like advertising, marketing, financing and content provision, accompanying it. The idea of the smile curve is that most of the value addition in a product is at the beginning and the end of the supply chain, where services are embedded in the product. Today, the manufacturing portion, where moderately skilled workers across emerging markets compete to reduce costs, accounts for far less value than it used to.

We mentioned the iPhone in the introduction. A variety of business-oriented services, like software programming, research and development or product design, are also embedded in more traditional goods. According to one estimate, over 10 million lines of programming code went into General Motor's 2010 car, the Chevrolet Volt, accounting for over 40 per cent of its value. In comparison, software constituted just 5 per cent of the value in the 1980s.[1] Therefore, as electric vehicles become more like mobile phones, even that most traditional of manufactured exportable products, the automobile, will consist of largely embedded intermediate services.

So one reason services have become more tradeable is that they are embedded in tradeable goods. A second reason, however, is that services can now be provided at a distance. Both combine to increase the tradability of high-value services.

Services at a Distance and Scale Economies

In our introduction, Professor Erali from WIMWI delivers his services in real time to the global market. So do Samia, his technician and all the teaching assistants who make his course successful. There are also the programmers who create the software that allows students to read or watch preparatory material before class. Others train the chatbots that will tutor students or create and correct assignments. All of them are essentially embedding their services into the course before it starts. So they do not need to provide their services in real time.

Many high-skilled services are now liberated from the tyranny of space and time. For instance, a consultant only needs to make a final presentation to the client in real time, though even this can be done at a distance through videoconferencing. Moreover, the consulting team can do its analysis offline. Its work is embedded in the final advice to the client, but it need not be done either where the client is or in real time.

Some high-skilled business services also enjoy scale economies, reducing costs and enhancing productivity as their output grows. Programming for the Chevrolet Volt is a fixed cost, so the more such cars General Motors sells, the lower the cost of programming in each car and the higher the profits. Such fixed costs abound. Samia, the technical support person, will not only help Professor Erali but also many other professors at WIMWI to reach a global audience. Each of those professors will also use the costly technical equipment in the classroom. The more the number of professors, the lower the per-professor fixed costs of personnel or equipment, and the lower the cost of services provided by each professor. Thus, there are scale economies even in services, allowing service providers to benefit from a larger global market by producing more cheaply.

Service enterprises can also scale up through branching or franchising—that is, replicating successful small establishments manifold. McDonald's and Starbucks have multinational reach because these firms have a common efficient modus operandi for their franchisees, developed through years of experience, as well as efficiencies acquired through common purchasing, financing and marketing platforms. For instance, an Italian Dark Roast Americano coffee has a similar taste across the world in every Starbucks franchise, because it is made the same way, using a common recipe, ingredients and equipment. This allows an international customer base to know largely what to expect when they walk into a Starbucks anywhere and allows Starbucks marketing to work for every franchisee. Interestingly, Rohit prefers north Indian masala chai, while Raghu prefers south Indian filter coffee, and neither finds a drink exactly to their taste in these international franchises—the awkwardly named Chai Tea Latte at Starbucks does not quite hit the spot. There may well be room for Indian chains to go multinational!

In sum, services can be traded either because they are embedded in goods or because they can be delivered at a distance. Scale economies in some services can be significant, encouraging firms, franchises, networks and platforms to grow based on exports, and in doing so create more jobs. Such scale also incentivizes innovation. If a Starbucks coffee can be made with less energy consumption and every franchisee deploys the same new technique, the firm will collectively generate enormous cost savings.[2]

Is Scale Always Necessary in Services?

At the same time, scale can be less central to the productivity of services than for manufacturing. If fixed costs and capital investment requirements are low, scale is not necessary. Perhaps the most important recent example of productivity without scale is the advent of cloud computing.

As Ramana Nanda of Imperial College London has argued, when Amazon Web Services started offering cloud computing in 2006, it immediately lowered the costs to small start-ups of providing Internet-based services. No longer did such companies have to buy enormous quantities of hardware and software before starting up; they could simply rent the resources they needed to provide Internet-based services from Amazon. Not surprisingly, this led to an explosion in Internet-based companies, like DoorDash and Uber. It also led to the meteoric rise of Amazon, which is now one of the most valuable firms of our time. Not many realize that the largest profit generator in Amazon today is its web services, not its retail business.

Networks and platforms also offer the possibility for small firms to access some of the benefits of scale without growing big themselves. For instance, a small bank in India can allow its customers to pay anywhere through the RuPay (or Mastercard or Visa) card network, or through the Unified Payments Interface (UPI). It does not have to have a branch in every city.

Similarly, digital platforms allow service freelancers and small manufacturers to find customers across the world, without the need to advertise in every local market. We will later see the example of

Moglix, which provides warehousing, logistics and procurement services for businesses. But for now, consider Tilfi, which sells Banarasi saris around the world, thus popularizing and enhancing the value of a traditional handicraft.

Tilfi: Selling Banarasi Saris to the World

India has myriad high-quality arts and crafts, many of them passed down from artisan to artisan over hundreds of years. Yet these have not been able to achieve large markets despite their beauty, and despite the many handicrafts boards and cooperatives that governments have set up. Since the life of an artisan can be precarious and uncertain, youths are no longer attracted to these crafts. Aditi Chand and Udit Khanna, co-founders, along with Ujjwal Khanna, of the emerging brand Tilfi, asked a question that has always puzzled us: Why doesn't India have brands of the kind the Italians and the French do in fine clothing, accessories, furniture and other such luxury crafts?

Tilfi started out in 2016, with the classic Banarasi sari as its flagship product. Udit's family had been in the sari business for five generations in Varanasi, and Udit, like any small-town boy who had fled to the city, swore never to return to the trade and 'sell saris'. Aditi, an army kid, and Udit met in college in Delhi, fell in love, got married and were on their own career paths—Aditi in investment banking and Udit running a start-up teaching English as a foreign language in England.

On frequent trips back home to Kashi (another name for Varanasi), they would meet artisans, who would complain about the dying demand for their fine products and about their low incomes. Udit would encourage them not to give up and keep the craft alive. In response, they would ask why he had abandoned the business. This question stayed with the couple, and after attending business school in Europe, they decided to devote themselves full time to creating a robust brand and a deeper market for Kashi's fine crafts.

Aditi and Udit identified two salient problems. First, a substantial amount of risk was being borne by the weavers and other craftsmen. Typically, the artisan would deliver the finished product to a wholesaler, who would then pass it on to a retailer. If the product was not sold, it went back through the supply chain to the artisan. This meant there was little incentive to innovate and try newer designs. Consequently, there was a sameness and tiredness in the designs, but also a lot of cheaper me-too products of dubious quality. So the first step would be to insure the weaver against the risk of products that did not sell.

Second: How could a customer trust the quality of the product? Is this 'really' a handmade Banarasi sari that took three months on the handloom? How do the best craftsmen consistently start commanding the sort of prices these products deserve? If you are willing to pay $3000 (approximately Rs 2.5 lakh) for a decent (not even the best) bag sold by the French brand Louis Vuitton, shouldn't there be a globally recognized Indian brand that commands a good price in the international market for a finely crafted sari or scarf?

Aditi and Udit believed the answer was to create a brand, Tilfi, for fine saris and other crafts of Varanasi. They would bring together a network of designers, graphers, punchers (these translate the designs into cards that weavers rely on) and weavers, not just to produce traditional designs but also to try new ones. They would provide the raw material and take the risk away from the weaver—once the product was woven, the risk would be Tilfi's, and the artisan would be paid even if the product had defects or did not sell. Of course, Tilfi had to identify defects and ensure quality control to build trust in its products, so that customers did not ask, 'Is this really handwoven silk?' As their sales grew, customer confidence grew. But then, the pandemic struck. Fortunately, pre-orders for their products took off. Pre-orders significantly reduce risks all around. Tilfi was pleasantly surprised when this trend of pre-ordering a design persisted after the pandemic.

Brand creation is a long-term project, so the couple had to be patient and learn along the way. Aditi is quick to point out that you will not find their products on Amazon or any other online retail store. They want their own web page and social media handles, for they want to control the narrative. The website and social media pages help them build awareness of the products they sell and of the stories behind them. This is key for building a market for luxury products, especially for a generation that is increasingly rich but has little awareness of India's heritage. Udit adds there are no special sales or wedding season offers either—you are buying a high-quality product, and that is that. They assert enthusiastically that their weavers are not labourers looking for charity; they are artisans paid for creating objects of beauty.

Being online allows them to internalize feedback quickly—not only do they learn what the customer wants, but they can try and influence consumer taste. The business has built a cult following. From 300 artisans in 2016, they now work with 2000, and half their sales are outside India. They opened a store called the Tilfi Experience Centre in Varanasi, and locations for new stores in Delhi and Bangalore are being scouted. Interestingly, they can sell more intricate and sophisticated designs at the store—customers are willing to pay a premium when they can see, touch and feel the product before buying it. As with Lenskart, which we will encounter later, Tilfi sees the value of online assisted commerce, online to build awareness, and the physical store to clinch the deal.

Tilfi works with the traditional system of apprenticeship, where a master weaver trains younger artisans. The master weaver must be challenged with complex designs. These may not be the most profitable for Tilfi, but it keeps the master's creative juices flowing. Younger designers are brought in to marry fresh ideas with the ancient craft. Tilfi has also trained and employed their first woman weaver on the outskirts of the city, where attitudes are less traditional.

Tilfi has now started expanding to other Kashi products—clothing, of course, but also furniture and sculptures. There is great talent in Kashi temple art; for example, in metal work. This is easily transferable to luxury furnishing. Tilfi wants to build a truly Indian luxury brand, with Indian roots and ethos but global appeal. The model could potentially be applied to the plethora of fine arts and crafts all over the country.

When Scale Is Less Important

The bottom line is that while scale could help in certain services, in others, productivity can grow even without scale increases, unlike in manufacturing. This phenomenon of a rise in productivity without scale matters because the average service firm in a country like India starts small—typically a *kirana* shop with three employees. It only doubles in employment size over six years. In contrast, manufacturing firms start larger (around thirteen employees) and triple in size over the same period. But because scale matters less in services, productivity differences between the smallest and the largest service firms are smaller than in manufacturing.[3] Indeed, in developed countries, there is little variation of productivity with service firm size.[4] Put differently, a freelance design consultant may make as much income as any of the many partners in a design consultancy. Huge demand is not needed for the freelance consultant to earn a good living!

Furthermore, service firms (apart from multi-establishment retailers like Smart Bazaar, formerly called Big Bazaar, or franchisers like the Delhi Public School that both Rohit and Raghu attended) tend to grow at a slower pace, but this does not mean that the service sector as a whole creates employment slowly. There is more churn in the service sector, with many new businesses being created and some exiting.[5] Think of how many restaurants started in your neighbourhood recently and closed down. On net, employment creation in services can be substantial, but many will be in small and medium enterprises, or even informal freelancing.

A final point: Since scale is not necessary for productivity in every service, such services don't necessarily have to be export-oriented to be productive; they can also cater to domestic demand alone.

Categorization of Services

India already has a huge presence in high value-added services that are either delivered directly (think of India's software industry, and the growing number of consultants, legal analysts and accountants who provide services from India), or embedded in manufactured or service products that are then sold to global clients. For instance, the global bank Goldman Sachs's largest office outside New York is in Bengaluru, where it employs over 8000 people, building systems for everything from trading to managing risks.[6] Engineers have helped develop a trading system called Atlas for Goldman's quantitative-investing-oriented clients, and a commodities platform called Janus, which provides data analytics. Increasingly, companies like the aircraft engine maker Rolls-Royce and turbine maker General Electric are doing original research in their India-based GCCs, supplementing the research centres in the United States or Europe. Other GCCs are supporting finance, advertising and marketing out of India, with the pandemic boosting such activities.

From India's perspective, one concern is that a significant portion of the value added by these workers is captured as profits by the firms that employ them, which often are foreign-owned. A Goldman Sachs has instant recognition with foreign clients, can anticipate client needs, can scope out the project and can therefore provide the front-office function that generates the projects Indian engineers work on. Because Goldman is a trusted intermediary between clients and engineers, it keeps much of the value added as profits. Over time, Indian engineers will recognize they can disintermediate Goldman and go directly to the client, much as Indian software firms like TCS and Infosys discovered, and as some of the start-ups we will describe are discovering. At that point, the profits too will migrate to India.

Another concern is that the demand for highly skilled Indian employees is huge, but, as we will describe, the supply is limited. As a Siemens Healthineers executive puts it, the employability of new graduates 'is still a challenge. Till they're trained and retrained and many times trained, they don't become employable.'[7] So salaries are bid up for those who make the grade, but many more college graduates could find employment if they had better-quality education. We will describe in detail later the challenge of higher education and skills more generally, and how it can be addressed.

This does not exhaust the job potential in services. Moderately skilled workers can also contribute to trade—think of truck drivers, railway workers, ship workers and dock hands who support goods trade, as well as waiters, hotel clerks and tour guides who cater to tourists. Both these categories of services are 'traded' in the sense that they can be sold to foreigners, benefit from external demand and generate valuable foreign exchange.

And finally, perhaps the largest number of jobs lie in domestically oriented services, ranging from highly skilled jobs, like professors and surgeons, to moderately skilled ones, such as domestic help, drivers, security guards, shop assistants, laundry operators, construction workers and workers employed by local governments, such as Anganwadi workers who run rural childcare centres.

The perceptive reader can fit most jobs in these categories. For instance, S.S. Rajamouli, director of *RRR*, a film that enjoyed global popularity, is probably a highly skilled creative worker, selling creative content to both India and the world. The broader point is that service jobs can cover the spectrum between the very highly skilled and the very low skilled. Most can contribute to exports, though the highest incomes will be generated by the highly skilled. But there will also be plenty of domestically focused service jobs.

Are All Service Jobs Equally Beneficial for Development?

It is easier, of course, to turn an agricultural labourer into a kirana shop worker or a construction worker (readers might recall the movie *Peepli Live*) than into a software programmer or a Professor Erali. The productivity gains from the greater transformation are, of course, much greater, and so is the addition to the worker's income. Unfortunately, unless the agricultural labourer has had sound schooling, or is extraordinarily intelligent, so that she can compensate for her inadequate preparation, the easier transformation is the more likely one.

If we cannot create enough software programmers out of workers leaving agriculture, and enough jobs for software programmers, should we give up on services? Certainly not!

With an excess of workers dependent on a shrinking quantum of arable land, agricultural productivity is very low. So moving excess workers from agriculture to even low-paying service jobs, such as those in construction or urban waste management, adds value. The ubiquitous street sweepers in every Indian city are probably being more productive than they would be as surplus labour in agriculture. Indeed, a study estimates that about one-third of growth comes from such reallocation between agriculture and more modern sectors.[8]

Income growth need not stop at the street sweeper using her broom to sweep the streets. With a mechanized vacuum-equipped sweeper truck, she could do the work of many, with far less effort and less risk to her health. Similarly, apps and programs can augment the productivity of a relatively unskilled worker significantly. For instance, the Ola taxi that brought Erali to WIMWI is part of a ride-sharing platform. It connects an ordinary car driver to a vast market of customers, making the driver an instant entrepreneur. Some platforms do everything from giving the driver driving directions to billing the customer and depositing the proceeds in the driver's bank account. In some cases, the app company can finance the car and even maintain it. All the driver needs to know is how to drive.

Higher incomes also create the demand for more services. WIMWI's green gardens that Erali loves so much are tended by a host of ground staff, and the security guards stationed at the gates keep the campus safe. Professor Erali himself has a personal cook and cleaner, at home. Every high-income service job aimed at the global market, that is, a traded service job, creates a number of supporting domestic service jobs. A recent study found that a 10 per cent increase in the tradeable service jobs in an Indian district results in a 4.2 per cent increase in other services employment. Since these other service jobs are significantly more in number than traded services jobs, the multiplicative effect on job creation of these traded jobs is significant.[9]

There are other aspects of the dynamics that are even more encouraging. Even though many newly created service jobs require modest skills and will barely lift the worker's family out of poverty into the ranks of the lower middle class, the job usually is in an urban area with better government schools than those in rural areas. Better schooling for the worker's children can equip them for much better jobs. When Raghu served as governor of the RBI, one of his most enjoyable experiences was the annual party for the RBI drivers, cooks and waiters and their families at his home. These workers proudly introduced their children—one a software engineer, the other an officer working for a multinational bank. These families had made the jump from lower middle class to upper middle class in one generation, in part because the RBI had employed someone in the family in a low-paying but steady job with decent housing and health-care benefits.

Of course, not all urban jobs offer the security that an RBI job does. Consequently, many urban migrants, typically male, leave their families in the villages. Reforms that make labour contracts less precarious, create affordable urban housing and offer migrant households an urban safety net will allow more families to migrate to cities and enable the kind of social mobility that we see with the children of RBI employees.

As alluded to earlier, one must also not underestimate the desire for self-improvement that the availability of high-quality jobs creates. The allure of obtaining good jobs is very apparent at every income level in society. A study finds that the opening of an IT-enabled centre servicing global markets, such as a call centre, results in enrolment in nearby English-medium schools going up by 7 per cent.[10] Interestingly, enrolment in schools where instruction is in the vernacular languages does not budge, suggesting that parents are motivated to put their children in schools that will lead to the world-facing jobs that they see are now available.

Another study finds that when young women in villages are exposed to recruiters who explain how to get jobs in call centres, they are, not surprisingly, more likely to find work in such centres. Interestingly, they are significantly more likely to enrol in computer courses or English language courses, have better health outcomes and are less likely to have children quickly.[11] Importantly, the availability of white-collar service jobs in a safe environment can do much to improve the employment of India's women, an issue we will return to later.

Services Driving Manufacturing: Lenskart

We now turn to a start-up that is tackling a very important Indian need, eyesight, with what one might term service-driven manufacturing. Over half a billion Indians have problems with their eyesight, which can be corrected with eyewear. Lenskart has set itself up to make it easier for Indians, and eventually citizens of the world, to get the eyewear they need easily and at an affordable price. In the process, it has also branched out into contact lenses and sunglasses.

After a boyhood in Delhi, Peyush Bansal, co-founder and CEO of Lenskart, studied engineering at McGill University in Canada, and then went on to work for Microsoft in Seattle. He reminisces how, as a reward for good work, he was invited to meet Bill Gates at his lake-shore mansion in Seattle. Hearing Gates's vision for the foundation he was setting up, Peyush felt the desire 'to do something that touches people's lives in a big way, like building Microsoft or the Gates Foundation'.

Those who use Microsoft Word may notice the command 'Save as Adobe PDF'. Peyush worked diligently with Adobe, which owns PDF technology, to create it. 'It might look trivial on the outside,' Peyush remarks, 'but it cut a lot of steps out for the customer and made it easy for them to save their Word files as PDF.' Motivated by the idea of simplifying matters for consumers using technology, he returned to India, for 'this is my land, and this is also where transformative changes needed to happen'.

He started first with a company that matched college students to apartments around campus. It was reasonably successful, with over 1500 colleges covered, but Peyush soon realized it had limited potential, both in terms of the scale it could achieve and the problem it was solving. He shifted focus to eyecare, which, given the number of Indians with deficient eyesight, seemed like a problem worth tackling.

Unlike buying a watch or a mobile phone, eyewear has more steps built into the purchase. First, the customer has to get their eyes tested. Many don't realize they have a problem, even though they edge closer and closer to the TV or monitor to see clearly. So lack of awareness is the first problem. The second is access. With only about 50,000 eyewear shops in India, most people do not have a shop near them. And the final problem is affordability of the eyewear.

Lenskart has been chipping away at each of these. It is spreading awareness about the need to test children early for vision, as also the importance of testing adults more frequently, given rising screen times. It is trying to make eyewear purchase easier through web-assisted commerce. Its website allows you to try on frames virtually. Few, however, buy prescription eyewear online. In the 'fun' physical store, of which there are now 1500, you can get your eyes tested for free as well as try the frame you saw online. Alternatively, Lenskart also sends employees to visit potential customers at home, where they test eyes and show sample frames. Once the order is taken, the eyewear is with the customer in two days, a commitment that requires a significant logistical effort.

Initially, Lenskart manufactured frames in a factory in China, a natural choice, for, as Peyush remarks, 'they have entire towns there which only make glasses'. There is little match for China, he believes, in commoditized manufacturing. The level of discipline in following set tasks and the consequent efficiency gains make China a formidable manufacturer.

But as Lenskart became more confident in its own product and moved from standard frames to a variety for every occasion, it shifted more manufacturing to its factory in Gurgaon. India, in Peyush's view, can compete in areas where manufacturing is more customized, and needs constant incremental engineering fixes or innovation. The abundance of engineering talent makes this viable in India. 'We have different kinds of *jugaad* [fixes],' Peyush exclaims enthusiastically. 'It is important to understand what we in India are good at.' It is not that quality Indian engineering talent is moderately priced, Peyush explains; it is that it now has years of experience in building large scalable systems that work across layers of software and hardware, using automation to overcome constraints.

In fact, Lenskart has not just implemented in India what it learnt from producing in China, it has also automated further. After all, given the scale of orders—50,000 frames a day—automation has to underpin everything Lenskart does. Indian labour has been trained to work with these machines, which induces high productivity and is more affordable than Chinese labour (Peyush differs here from other Indian manufacturers we spoke with). So Lenskart manufactures highly standardized lenses from its China factory but does most of the customized eyewear from the Gurgaon factory—the need for quick delivery also undoubtedly plays a role here. In addition to India, Lenskart now operates in South-East Asia and the Middle East, and is taking baby steps in America.

Lenskart represents a form of service-driven manufacturing, with services contributing significantly to the product. It starts with one of the fifty designers developing a frame model—one of the 5000 that Lenskart carries. It continues with one of the 10,000 store employees testing the customers' eyesight and helping them choose a frame. A number of employees are involved in the logistics of moving the frame from warehouse to factory to store, another group in architecting and monitoring the systems that keep everything on track, and yet another in trying to improve the customer experience, first by remote optometry and eventually by embedding eye tests into the mobile phone. About 2000 employees are directly involved in production.

Peyush feels that Lenskart is still at the beginning, even though it has an annual turnover of Rs 5000 crore. Demand still needs to be worked at, with the need to create much more awareness and access. The company also wants high-end spenders to start treating eyeglasses as a fashion accessory—a different pair for office, sports, holiday, family visit and a night out, all in an affordable way. There is much to be done, but Peyush is already touching people's lives in a big way.

AI and Services

We have argued for the importance of service jobs. Yet, an important recent concern is whether artificial intelligence, as embodied in generative AI, may displace services. A large language model that underlies generative AI, such as ChatGPT, is basically an algorithm that has encapsulated the structure of a language, say, English or a computer language. It does this by processing myriad pages of text, getting a sense of what words fit together and how they follow one another. Given a prompt, then, the AI can respond with a sentence, or a paragraph, or even an essay, based on the billions of pages of text it has processed. What is interesting is that when trained on sufficiently large data sets, and with a sufficiently large set of parameters, the responses start making sense and are logical—as if the AI is actually thinking, even though it is simply constructing sentences based on the text it has absorbed. Essentially, these AI models seem to reason based on text completion and exhibit astonishing properties.

For instance, GPT-4 passed the American Uniform Bar Examination, designed to test lawyers' skills, at the 90th percentile of test takers. This has many worried. Could generative AI replace lawyers? More generally, could generative AI write code and replace programmers? Could it replace customer service agents, foreign language translators, even (shudder!) professors like us?

Fortunately, not yet, at least not in full measure. One lawyer tried to use ChatGPT on behalf of his client while suing Avianca Airlines (his client had suffered a knee injury when struck by an airline cart). When Avianca asked the judge to throw out the case, the lawyer submitted a ten-page brief, citing more than half a dozen relevant court decisions, such as 'Martinez vs Delta Airlines', and so on.[12] There was only one hitch: none of the court decisions actually existed, ChatGPT had made them up!

There are other problems with generative AI. Its output comes from a process that no one really understands—in geek land this is called the problem of interpretability of AI. This may create built-in biases that human beings would not have, or this may, in fact, reinforce human biases. For instance, suppose the language about a particular community is unusually derogatory in the text the AI algorithm is fed. It may then treat members of that community unfairly when it encounters them as customers, which is termed algorithmic bias. Relatedly, since norms and ethics are not programmed into the AI, it may choose paths that violate considerations of decency, regulations or even laws.

It is early days in the use of generative AI. While it is obvious that it cannot replace humans fully as yet, some of these glitches will be fixed over time. What seems clear is that it can be a valuable aid to service providers. For instance, a study of customer service agents working for a Fortune 500 firm providing business processing software found that the number of problems an agent could successfully resolve in an hour went up by around 14 per cent when the agent was aided by AI. Typically, it gave real-time suggestions on how the service agent should respond to a problem or offered links to the relevant internal technical documentation.[13] The AI tool was most useful for new agents. Since the industry had around 60 per cent agent turnover a year, this was beneficial in improving their quality as well as aiding their learning. For more experienced agents, AI was of little benefit.

So should India be worried? Certainly, India should not fall behind in the race to use AI, since the technology seems to increase the productivity of services considerably. But if productivity increases, the price (say, per unit of software code written, a prime beneficiary of AI) falls, and there is thus more demand for the service. So if the cost of programming falls, it could well increase the overall demand for it. Similarly, we should not assume that artificial intelligence will displace service workers big time. It may actually give a new lease of life to workers like the entry-level customer service representatives in the study just described, who are now better equipped to fix customer problems right from the get-go. Many journalists have argued that an initial draft of an article prepared by AI can then be developed and made much richer by a human—AI can take the drudgery out of writing, much as a worksheet has taken the drudgery out of calculations. We ourselves used AI to help us with different versions of this book's title, though the final version was, like it or not, our own.

Indeed, AI can make existing services much better. For instance, we have Professor Erali's teaching assistants helped by chatbots, which are essentially individualized tutors that can help each student get up to speed. Imagine how this would improve the quality of our schools, with students who are falling behind identified by chatbots and then helped with individual tutoring.

Of course, AI will displace some jobs. Yet the pace of job losses due to technological change can be overstated. In 2013, two Oxford professors estimated that 47 per cent of US employment was at risk as a result of computerization.[14] At the time of our writing in 2023, labour force participation in the United States is at a twenty-year high, and unemployment at a two-decade low. So clearly, the professors were mistaken, at least about the pace of change. The pace of change is usually slower than we think. It takes a substantial amount of time between the early prototypes and mass adoption—in part because the technology needs to be made easier to use and also because most people, including regulators, want to see error rates come down. Even when change takes place, humans figure out how they can add value to the technology, so that humans and machines do much better than either of them alone. This means that technology displaces fewer workers than one would imagine. Finally, by raising productivity and lowering prices, technology adoption raises demand, which again reduces the direct effect of technological change on job losses.

Regardless, the advent of AI increases the urgency of improving the human capital of our labour force so that we can occupy the creative end of the job spectrum. Such jobs are at the frontier where there aren't enough data to train AI, so they are likely to be the last jobs to be threatened by AI. Fortunately, AI also offers us new tools to improve education and other services, as just discussed, and we should make full use of them.

The Future Model of Indian Growth

We must not think of manufacturing exports-led growth as the only way to develop fast. Services, either delivered directly or as embedded in manufactured goods, now offer an alternative means of exports. It is possible to achieve scale (though scale is not always necessary for productivity). Globally, services have been less exposed to competition, so these activities can still be very profitable. Moreover, India already has a substantial presence in such areas, suggesting some proof of concept. India also has a large domestic market for services, especially services like education and health care that can improve its human capital, allowing it to climb the value-added ladder for services.

Does India need to choose between manufacturing and services? Both are highly intertwined today, as Lenskart's example suggests. Services are an increasing input to manufacturing, and vice versa, so perhaps the distinction is less meaningful today than it was in the past. But we still have to make choices on where we want to devote resources—in people or on things.

4

Where Should We Place Our Hopes?

With a per capita income of around $2400, India is now on the verge of entering the ranks of middle-income countries. At even a very respectable per capita income growth rate of 4 per cent, per capita income will reach $10,000 only by 2060, which is lower than China's level today.

We must do better. Over the next decade, we will see a possible 'population dividend', that is, a rise in the share of our population of working age, before we, like other countries, succumb to ageing. If we can generate good employment for all our youth, we will accelerate growth and have a shot at becoming comfortably upper middle class before our population starts ageing. Can India become rich before it becomes old?

To do this, we need a sense of urgency. The unfortunate reality is that very few of the fast-growing developers have escaped the middle-income trap, South Korea and Taiwan being the rare exceptions. Brazil, Malaysia, Mexico and Thailand have yet to break through. What will it take us to get to $10,000 per capita more quickly, and go on from there to the more rarefied $30,000 club within our lifetimes? If we want the journey to be short, we need to know where we are going. For that, we must cut through the hype and examine our weaknesses and strengths with a clear eye.

Why Is the Manufacturing Ladder Harder to Climb Now?

Can India catch up with globally competitive manufacturers around the world? Foreign manufacturers are siting some production in India, if only to access the growing domestic market. For instance, the Danish wind turbine manufacturer Vestas now assembles parts in Sriperumbudur in south India. It was attracted to that place, in part, by the heady projection that India will soon be the second-largest market for turbines made by Vestas.[1] Some heavy manufacturing—such as the composite 260-foot-long wind turbine blades made by American contract manufacturer TPI Composites—is also coming readily to India because the costs of transporting from elsewhere to the Indian market warrants it.[2]

Today, most goods are produced by global supply chains, criss-crossing through many countries. The supply chains have exploited labour arbitrage so that little is produced by expensive workers in industrial countries, unless they are aided by significant automation. Instead, Indian labour will be competing with labour from Vietnam or from China, which has still not fully exhausted its supply of cheap labour, especially in its less-developed Western provinces. Unlike the situation for early developers decades ago, Indian workers, adjusted for quality, will not be much cheaper than their competitors. Therefore, the gains from labour arbitrage will not pay for other deficiencies.

And India has important deficiencies. For a product such as a fan motor to even be assembled competitively in India, border tariffs have to be lowered to rock bottom. Importantly, they have to be lowered not just on the imports into India of intermediate inputs, such as motor parts, but also on Indian fan motor exports to other nearby countries through which the supply chain snakes. Moreover, non-tariff impediments, such as differential safety standards and border inspections, have also to be addressed to make exports seamless. But that requires India to be a part of regional trade agreements. Unfortunately, India has been resistant to signing those.

Indeed, without accounting for tariffs, a report by the Swiss bank UBS finds little difference in costs between India, China and Vietnam in the low-skill task of assembling and shipping a fan.[3] However, Vietnam is a signatory to many more regional trade agreements, and can import or export its products virtually duty free. No wonder global supply chains go through Vietnam, and much less so through India. In fact, the share of global value chain-related manufacturing output for India rose only slightly from 14 per cent to 16 per cent between 2007 and 2021, whereas for Vietnam this same share grew from 35 per cent to over 56 per cent in the same time period.[4]

We will explore why India is so reluctant to sign regional trade agreements later, but let us also caution that India's signing international agreements has not always benefited Indian industry.

Cipla and Intellectual Property

Consider the very successful Indian generic pharmaceuticals industry, which exported around $25 billion in 2022–23. One of the most prominent figures in this industry is Dr Yusuf Hamied of Cipla.

Hamied's family owned a small pharmaceutical company, which got underway producing medicines for India during the Second World War, when imports were difficult. But after the war, multinational firms again resumed their dominance in India because their drug patents prevented anyone else from making drugs without an expensive licence—India followed the strict British Patent Act of 1911.

Hamied worked on a PhD in chemistry at the University of Cambridge in the late 1950s, studying under Professor Alexander Todd, who would later receive the Nobel Prize in chemistry.[5] After his return to India to join the family company on completing his PhD, Hamied started campaigning against the patent act, arguing that India needed more freedom to produce drugs.

The campaign succeeded in 1972 under interesting circumstances. Cipla introduced a generic version of a drug, Propranolol, in India.

The multinational ICI, which owned the patent, sued. Hamied sent a message to the then prime minister, Indira Gandhi, making the case that the generic drug would save millions of lives and should not be denied to Indians. In response, the Indian government changed the patent law so that the end product, the drug, could not be patented, but the process by which it was made could. So if an Indian company found another way to make the final drug, it could do it legally. Cipla had freed itself from the patent law!

Many multinational firms left India at this time, seeing little profit in competing with generic manufacturers like Cipla and Ranbaxy. This then opened the door for the Indian generic pharmaceutical industry, which started manufacturing the active pharmaceutical ingredients (APIs) that go into drugs and the drugs themselves.

The new patent law played to the strengths of Indian pharmaceutical companies. Finding new processes to make drugs is a form of incremental innovation, which Indian scientists did very well—much as Indian engineers incrementally improve productivity. Indeed, Hamied argues that even large multinationals do very little fundamental or concept innovation in pharmaceuticals. Much of that is done by the US government-funded research in universities, and then the patent rights are acquired by the multinationals which do the incremental research to enable production and commercialization. So, in a sense, India's new patent law only made the fruits of US government-funded research more widely available in a country that did not have such a well-endowed government!

There is a broader point here. Domestic firms in developing countries primarily consume intellectual property as they try to catch up, and their ability to do so, as well as to innovate incrementally, would benefit from fewer protections for intellectual property. Josh Lerner from Harvard University has found, after examining the patent policy of sixty countries ranging over 150 years, that an enhancement in patent protection in a country is associated with more patent filing by foreign firms while reducing filings by domestic firms.[6] This phenomenon is particularly pronounced in developing countries.

Cipla's international claim to fame, however, came with the treatment of AIDS. In early 2001, a cocktail of three antiretroviral drugs came to be accepted as the most effective treatment against AIDS. The prevailing price of the cocktail from multinational drug firms at that time was $12,000, which put it beyond the reach of many poor countries in Africa, where the disease was rampant. Dr Hamied offered it to the NGO Médecins Sans Frontières for $350 a year, that is, less than $1 a day. The offer made the front page of the *New York Times*, and Cipla started leading the fight against AIDS, which today is no longer the death sentence it used to be.

In the meantime, multinational pharmaceutical companies started recognizing the threat generic producers posed to their profits and worked with the US government and the World Trade Organization (WTO) to change patent laws across the world. By signing the Trade Related Intellectual Property Rights Agreement (TRIPS), negotiated under the auspices of the WTO in 1994, India agreed to long periods of patent protection even in areas where intellectual property rights protection is controversial.

Dr Hamied argues that not only did the Indian government sign a bad deal, thus foregoing India's natural advantage in generic drugs, but it also betrayed the Indian pharmaceutical industry by agreeing to backdate enforcement to 1995, not 2005, as he claims was promised. With Indian pharmaceuticals now having to pay hefty royalties on drug production, their pathways to growth became more limited.

All countries start by expropriating intellectual property, either by outright theft or by weakening the enforcement of patents, as in India's case. However, once the country has built a base in R&D, it eventually starts enforcing patents strictly, so that its own firms have the incentive to do research and produce original patents. Was 2005 the right time for India to start enforcing product patents? It is too early to tell, but we have not seen an outpouring of Indian pharmaceuticals research since then. Dr Hamied argues that with his profit margins, he really has no ability to invest in cutting-edge research. Perhaps in the longer run, Indian pharmaceutical firms will participate in concept research, certainly with Indian universities but also with US universities, and start selling the drugs they have patented. Rather than turning the clock back on patents, this seems the better way to go. Towards this goal, research in Indian universities will have to be strengthened, and we will suggest ways to do so. For now, it seems the generics pathway to growth will have much diminished returns.

Globalization Backlash

The current inward turn in the West, a retreat from globalization, is driven partly by the Chinese dominance in manufacturing and the associated loss of middle-income manufacturing jobs in the West. But it is accentuated by the geopolitical concerns raised by China's possible dominance in sunrise industries, like 5G, artificial intelligence, battery technology and electric vehicles (EVs), drones and so on, which are capable of both commercial and military uses. In fact, despite agreeing on little else, both President Donald Trump and President Joe Biden seem to agree on rolling back free trade.

Is Nearshoring an Opportunity for India to Get on the Manufacturing Bus?

The expanding conflict between the United States and China for geo-economic supremacy suggests a possible opportunity for India. In case the two superpowers apply wide-ranging sanctions on each other, or enter into overt conflict, Western corporations fear supply chains running through China will get disrupted and production choked off. They have already experienced such disruptions during the pandemic. So they are looking to diversify. Many multinational Western firms are developing their 'China+1' strategy, that is, for every segment of the supply chain that is in China, they are looking for an alternative producer in a country that is likely to remain friendly to the Western bloc. Some global supply chains are looking to India as their China+1 producer, especially given the growing attractiveness of India's domestic market.

Yet, as they choose, they also see reasons why India is not the obvious choice. These include, of course, all the reasons we have listed earlier for why manufacturing in India is difficult, including still-high tariffs on inputs.

Even if these are addressed, there is the issue of physical distance. Regional trade has always accounted for far more of a country's trade than flows to and from distant lands. Roughly speaking, there are three big regional trading blocs. About 70 per cent of European trade is within Europe, 50 per cent of East Asian trade within East Asia and 40 per cent of North American trade within North America.[7] The preponderance of trade with nearby countries is a regularity that economists refer to as the gravity model of trade. India is surrounded by relatively poor countries, with the exception of China. If a US company wants a cheap production locale that is not subject to as much disruption risk as China, it might prefer Mexico, while a European company might prefer Romania. These 'nearshoring' alternatives are connected by a variety of land routes and are near, so they are harder for war, climate or pestilence to disrupt. They are also part of low-tariff regional trade agreements.

For industrial countries, the most fail-safe way of eliminating any supply-chain disruption, as well as to deal with the political pressure to create manufacturing jobs, is to bring back the entire supply chain within the country—what is called 'reshoring'.[8] Rich countries know that by reshoring, they will lose access to cheap labour elsewhere. So reshoring is being accompanied by frenzied efforts at automating the production chain to minimize the use of workers. And, of course, machines can never down tools or protest.

In sum, India, on current patterns, is not necessarily going to be a huge beneficiary of the global trend towards friend-shoring and nearshoring production, other than from firms seeking access to the Indian market or where transportation costs are a small part of value.

Can India Succeed through Renewed Protectionism?

India could avoid global supply chains and produce everything in-house, so long as the final goods it exports do not attract tariffs at their destination. But this requires it to match the most efficient producers in the world in every segment of the supply chain—we have to be better at research than the United States, at design than the Italians, at manufacturing than the Germans, Chinese and Vietnamese, and so on. Put differently, global supply chains have been optimized, as a result of which the prices of final manufactured goods have fallen steadily over the years. Each country that dominates some segment of the supply chain not only has a natural advantage in that segment, it has also honed it by years of learning and skilling. Consequently, it is difficult for a country to compete in global markets against global supply chains, relying on an entirely home-grown supply chain.

India's domestic market is larger now. A manufacturer that caters simply to the Indian domestic market can achieve some scale, learn by doing in a relatively familiar and proximate market, and reach a reasonable level of productivity even without embarking on exports. If so, India could close off its market by erecting protectionist tariffs so as to give uncompetitive domestic producers a chance. Indeed, it seems to be on this path—since 2014, India's average import tariffs have been raised steadily from 13.5 per cent to nearly 18.1 per cent in 2022.[9] One sector that has benefited is domestic steel producers. But while this makes the domestic market much more attractive for the producer, operating behind high tariffs, they typically become uncompetitive globally. Clever policy design, such as stating tariffs will be removed once the industry has had breathing space to recover, rarely works. Once used to tariffs, industry will lobby to maintain them. Furthermore, if manufacturers know the government is amenable, every manufacturer will start clamouring for tariff protection so as to enjoy an easier life.

Furthermore, the argument that the Indian domestic market is large is true only for mass-market goods that everyone consumes—for instance, bicycles. However, India's upper middle class—equivalent in per capita purchasing power to the middle class in industrialized countries—is still small, so to achieve scale in areas like passenger electric vehicles or high-end electronics, there is still no alternative to exports. If our producers are reliant only on the domestic market, they will also suffer higher costs from production at inadequate scale. Consequently, growing protectionism will slow our rate of growth, force our households to pay high prices for shoddy products, thus favouring inefficient but well-connected businesses, and keep us poor.

All this is not idle theorizing. It is exactly what happened the last time we went protectionist during the Licence Raj. The world was not nearly as competitive then, so we got a chance to remedy our errors when the economy was liberalized. This time will be harder.

Will Subsidies to Manufacturing in Addition to Protection Offset Our Weaknesses?

What if we abandon the illusion that our firms are mature, take the position that they are still infants and add subsidies to the protection? It is not that the Indian government is unaware of the difficulties of manufacturing in India. The government says, for example, that the electronics sector suffers a competitive disadvantage of around 8.5–11 per cent on account of factors such as the lack of adequate infrastructure in India, high cost of finance, inadequate availability of quality power, limited design capabilities in industry and its neglect of R&D, and inadequate skills of Indian workers.[10]

Since addressing these weaknesses will take time, the government wants to offset these disadvantages through production subsidies. The Production Linked Incentive (PLI) scheme, first introduced in mobile phone production, works as follows.

Starting in 2016, the Indian government started raising tariffs on imported mobile phone parts, and in April 2018, it imposed a 20 per cent tariff on the entire mobile phone. Over and above the increased tariffs on imports, starting early 2020, the government essentially pays manufacturers in India—whether Indian or foreign-owned—a sum of 6 per cent of a phone's invoice price, coming down to 4 per cent in the fifth year for every incremental unit produced in India. In addition, state governments offer tax incentives, and power and land subsidies, for setting up production in their state.

At face value, the scheme seems to have worked. In the period from April 2017 to March 2018, imports of mobile phones amounted to nearly $3.6 billion, while phone exports were a measly $334 million. Net exports were thus −$3.3 billion. By the end of the 2022–23 financial year, phone imports were down to $1.6 billion, while phone exports were up to nearly $11 billion. Net exports were thus $9.4 billion, a turnaround of $13.1 billion from 2017–18.

Yet the details are far less impressive. Exports of final goods is not a useful metric if we are subsidizing manufacturers to finish in India then export. What matters for manufacturing prowess is how much value is being added in India. Apparently, very little! India has become a mass assembler of mobile phones, the least value-added part of the supply chain, accounting for only a few percentage points of the total value of the mobile phone. Most of the parts, including the most sophisticated elements, such as logic chips, are imported. Indeed, it is not even clear if the value added in India exceeds the subsidies that are offered.

When this was pointed out, government ministers admitted that India was only assembling but reasoned that this was a stepping stone to manufacturing higher-value-added parts. Clearly, countries have followed such a path in the past. But is it a likely path today? If the cost of transport is small, and it is for tiny mobile phone parts, why would Xiaomi increase part manufacturing in India if it is cheaper to manufacture elsewhere? So are we going to offer PLI schemes for each part also? Put differently, there is an assumption that assembly at scale will lead to production at scale. While this may have been true in the past, when logistics were more difficult, it is not obvious that it will be true going forward.

Korea is often cited as an example of a country that aggressively promoted an 'infant' domestic industry through protectionism and subsidies to help it achieve scale in global markets.[11] But we have to be clear on what worked. Korea's early industrial policy, in the 1960s and 1970s, was almost entirely exports-driven, and not sector-specific— whoever exported would get a subsidy. With the government not picking winners, there was pressure on Korean industry to pick areas where it could become globally competitive. Korean policy did become more directed or sector-specific, but only for a brief period in the 1970s, when credit was disbursed to six important sectors at cheap rates.

Korean President Park Chung Hee was a big believer in industrial policy. After his assassination in 1979, these sector-specific benefits were withdrawn and the economy was largely liberalized. Korean companies were forced to contend with market forces. Therefore, industrial policy in Korea was introduced in a focused way: first with explicit export incentives and then subsidies for a limited time in certain priority sectors, and then liberalized to encourage competitive performance. Even when Samsung, which started off as a vegetable trading company, wanted to go big in electronics, Korean banks helped only to the extent of cheaper credit, but Samsung was still expected to compete in the global market from the outset.

To succeed, industrial policy of the Korean type needs to be ruthless and dispassionate; it cannot harbour favourites or stay protective. Instead, the Indian PLI policy starts with an opaque selection of sectors to favour, with little public debate or transparency on which sectors are favoured and why. Only a subset of firms is given subsidies, which puts all other firms at a disadvantage. We don't know if subsidies were needed to get firms to invest, or if subsidies are a free gift from the nation. We don't know what the metrics of success are or even when the subsidies will be withdrawn—in some sectors, the duration of the subsidies has already been increased in response to lobbying by beneficiaries.

The real problem is that the PLI scheme is a policy shortcut, an attempt to substitute for the harder task of fixing the impediments to manufacturing in India. It is not even clear if it is a useful short-term policy tool to crowd in initial investment. Net foreign direct investment into India has fallen from $44 billion in FY 2021 to $28 billion in FY 2023. PLI also cannot substitute for real reforms—after all, if we have not remedied our weaknesses, won't those who came in to produce in India leave as quickly when subsidies end?

There is some sign that with the building of infrastructure— better roads and ports, and more efficient railway freight haulage— transportation logistics costs are coming down in India and getting nearer globally competitive levels. But despite this, India still believes it has to offer subsidies to attract the most competitive segment of the global supply chain: low-skilled manufacturing. If every segment of the global supply chain is optimized, does that not mean there is not much point paying to 'own' low-skilled assembly, since it gives us little advantage in conquering higher-value-added segments?

Are We Chasing a Chimera?

What is the alternative? How do we go about breaking the mould? Why not work on reducing the impediments to job growth, whether in manufacturing or services, or some combination of both, so that we can get investment and job creation without offering huge subsidies?

Improving Capabilities

Today, despite India's large and young population, the constant refrain we hear from employers is that their existing employees are fine, but they cannot find adequately trained new workers. We have to improve the capabilities of our workforce significantly so that global manufacturers come to India looking for them, and our workers can move up the jobs ladder. This requires improved population nutrition, education and health care at all levels.

Services and Services for Manufacturing

History has gifted us an advantage that neither China nor Vietnam has: the ability to speak in the global tongue. We have adopted the language of our former colonial power, English, and made it our own. This is now playing out in interesting ways. For example, almost 60 per cent of global websites are in English, which gives artificial intelligence algorithms based on English a much greater database to train on.[12] Most of the world's textbooks and scientific papers are published in English, and ad hoc translations are rarely as easy to read. More prosaically, while real-time translation by bots will come, perhaps soon, the ability to converse in a common language with the world will be an advantage in providing real-time services, and in business transactions, for years to come.

We also need to increase the numbers of our best-educated and trained professional workers—doctors, engineers, consultants, lawyers and professors—who could provide services directly to the world, even as they serve the domestic market. They will also create many lower-skilled support jobs.

These professionals could also provide services for manufactured products, which some are already doing as employees of GCCs. Because they provide services at a distance, they can bypass the tariff and other barriers that are impeding the flow of goods. As services have not been central to regional trade agreements, India's lack of membership in those agreements will matter less. The opportunity is enormous and growing. Digitally delivered service exports have nearly quadrupled between 2005 and 2022, accounting for 12 per cent of global trade today, while goods exports have increased only about 2.5 times, even though this period accounts for China's great expansion in goods exports.[13]

But all this requires that we raise our aspiration levels. Instead of bringing mobile phone assembly to India, we need to design the phones and chips of the future, and the associated software and app platforms, thereby profiting from the truly value-added parts of the global supply chain. Phone assembly coming to India would also be nice, the added cherry on our value-added cake, but not if we have to pay enormous subsidies for it.

Entrepreneurship

We must also create the conditions for better-educated workers to be entrepreneurial, for them to be able to start new small- and medium-sized ventures of all kinds. There is a sense that entrepreneurship only means high-tech innovation, yet the bulk of new businesses, even fast-growing ones, don't require significant innovation. What is important is to recognize a need out there, have the risk appetite to try and address it—including giving up an existing job and the associated income—and have the organizational capability to set up a functioning enterprise. As we have seen, even the idea of selling fresh idli batter to households across India can employ many and add tremendous value. Prosperous India will need thousands, if not lakhs, of such companies.

India has not succeeded in commoditized manufacturing, where low cost is all that matters—if you want cheap umbrellas or clay Ganeshas, India is not your natural supplier. Nor has it excelled (thus far) in businesses that require a great leap in product innovation. No global bestselling drug or social media phenomenon, such as Twitter or Facebook, has emerged from India. Instead, India has found its niche in businesses where incremental innovation or engineering to ensure product reliability, product customization and affordability are necessary. Indian businesses have drawn on India's pool of engineering and scientific talent, developed in good undergraduate universities, to address such applied challenges. Thus far, such incrementalism has played out more in India's export of services like software. As more manufacturing employs services as an intermediate input, India, if it prepares itself well, stands to gain a leg up in the new-age industrial revolution.

Thinking Bigger

But we cannot be satisfied with the status quo. We must embrace a truly ambitious path to development, where India comes up with world-beating ideas and products, and companies or organizations to deliver them globally. No developing country has taken this path before, but India can. Remember, no large developing country had skipped the standard route, jumping from agriculture straight to high-skilled services, but India did. Now it has to reinvent itself once again.

Instead of making generic pharmaceuticals, we should turn to finding new cures for the diseases that plague our people and sell those new medicines to the world. Instead of buying expensive 5G technology from a vendor in an industrial country, we should create a cheaper version in India and sell it to the emerging world, assuring buyers that India will create no backdoors through which it can snoop on them. It is important to recognize that India has the foundations on which it can build to fulfil these aspirations. But it is not there yet.

For instance, we have only a few top-quality research institutions, like some of the IITs, the Tata Institute of Fundamental Research and the Indian Institute of Science. To move from incremental innovation to path-breaking innovation, we need to raise many more of our universities to global standards, and encourage and fund innovative research, as well as business–academia collaborations.

In sum, while we should create the conditions for more manufacturing in India, export-led, low-skilled manufacturing no longer offers the most effective path to becoming a middle-income nation. This is especially true for a country like India, which is so different from the East Asian countries that embarked on this path. While services can also expand to provide the foreign exchange and jobs India needs, the emphasis should be on new firms, ideas and products, whether in manufacturing or services, that can allow India to leapfrog.

Our Democratic Advantage

Citizens benefit intrinsically from democracy—the dignity that comes from being able to vote, the right to express your opinion through it, having freedom of thought and expression more generally, being treated fairly, enjoying the rule of law and so on. But there is also an instrumental reason why we should strengthen our democracy.

In the early stages of development, the focus is, as we have seen, on catch-up growth. The ideas and know-how needed for development are already out there, discovered by some other country and its businesses; they simply have to be imitated or licensed.

The development path we suggest will depend far more on our people having innovative ideas and being creative, pushing the intellectual frontier out. Growth at the frontier requires debate and argumentation, which an authoritarian government rarely tolerates. It is not that authoritarian countries cannot innovate to some degree—the Soviet Union had a flourishing military–industrial complex. But authoritarian governments want to direct research and innovation, which ensures they are limited by the imagination of those directing it. If these are apparatchiks from the government, research and innovation will be very limited indeed, especially if the apparatchiks interfere constantly because they worry these directions may not be consistent with the views of the supreme leader.

By contrast, innovation in a democracy does not have to respect the existing power structure and its beliefs, and can be really path-breaking. Chip technology in the Soviet Union was behind that of the United States because the Russians simply could not innovate in that area.[14] So they always tried to steal the intellectual property when it became widely available, which always put them behind.

China's political system may have been ideal for catch-up, infrastructure-led growth. Arguably, it is much less so as China approaches the technology frontier. For instance, China has imposed requirements that artificial intelligence essentially respect the primacy of the Communist Party.[15] This could limit the extent to which firms can explore what artificial intelligence can do, for fear they might inadvertently cross regulatory boundaries. Scholars have argued that China's ability to make major scientific breakthroughs will depend 'on whether researchers have the space to think critically and creatively'.[16]

Careful studies by economic historians have addressed the relation between creativity and economic and political freedom over the long run. One study looks at the consequences of the French occupation of German cities after the French Revolution in 1789. Among the key reforms the occupying French implemented was abolishing local guilds (an early form of business cronyism or Licence/Permit Raj). The French also brought in their civil law, under which the judiciary was made independent from the local administration and all citizens were treated equally before law. The study finds that cities that were occupied for the longest period, and thus where these French reforms took greatest hold, had 2.5 times the patents per capita almost a century later, in 1900, than cities that were not occupied.[17]

A related study looks at which cities in Europe saw a rise in births as well as the immigration of notably creative people between the eleventh and nineteenth centuries. The researchers find that independent cities that assured their citizens political freedoms were most likely to see a rise in the presence of such people, because the city environment fostered creativity and also because such cities attracted creative souls.[18] All this also suggests that the argument made by some relatives at the dinner table—that all will go well in India if only we have an iron-fisted leader—is just silly. Today, such an authoritarian leader can only build more roads and monuments, running roughshod over people's rights, but cannot allow the environment of free thinking and speech that India needs for innovative ideas and products. For such a liberal environment will open the door to criticism of all authority. By trying to control debate, the authoritarian leader will make it hard for our researchers to be innovative, attract free thinkers from the diaspora or retain our youth, who are unhappy with the status quo. An authoritarian leadership is certainly not what India needs today.

Is Manufacturing Needed for Security?

Before ending this chapter, we must ask an important question: If we do not have a strong manufacturing base, will our national security be impaired?

Take, for example, the global race to get into the manufacture of advanced logic chips. Both the United States and Europe are trying to bring more high-end chip fabrication to their shores, while China is trying to upgrade its existing facilities as the United States bans the sale of high-end chips to China. Should India also fabricate chips?

Start first with the obvious point, that if short-term disruptions in chip availability are the concern, as during the pandemic, the solutions are simpler. We could have larger inventories of critical chips, even possibly a national reserve. We could source chips from multiple countries and companies. Our firms should build flexibility around production processes so that products can be redesigned to replace the chips in short supply with the chips that are available. All this is much cheaper than manufacturing chips domestically, given that even a plant making chips that are a few generations behind the current technological frontier will cost tens of billions of dollars in subsidies.

If the longer-term concern is that we might face sanctions from potential enemies, the solution is to have a wider and more diversified set of friends. It is hard to imagine that democratic India will take a course of action that will make the Euro area, the United States,

South Korea, Japan and Taiwan all want to sanction it. But what if the unimaginable happens and the democratic world turns against India?

If so, simply having factories making older chips will not be enough. India will need to make state-of-the-art chips (that is, the kind that goes into mobile phones and AI machine learning processors); it will need to make the machines the make the chips (firms that make those machines, such as the Dutch company ASML, will also apply sanctions); and it will have to make every part of the chip supply chain, starting from the silicon wafer, all of which requires speciality processes and chemicals that India does not have. Put differently, unless India brings the entire manufacturing process for chips into India, there will always be choke points that run through other countries. Total self-sufficiency is nearly impossible, even if we are prepared to invest hundreds of billions of dollars. And logic chips are just a small part of what India will need if sanctioned.

In short, India cannot obtain security with a toehold in chip manufacturing. Chip manufacturing, unless more carefully thought out, could be like the prestige-project white elephants that we have had plenty of in the past. Should we spend tens of billions in subsidizing chip manufacturing when the world has periodic gluts of chips, or should we devote those tens of billions to opening tens of thousands of high-quality primary schools, thousands of high-quality high schools and hundreds of top-notch universities? Are we better off dominating chip design with the tens of thousands of additional engineers and scientists we will produce, and starting firms like Nvidia, Qualcomm or Broadcom, none of which fabricate their chips, or do we want to imitate China, especially when we have much better relations with the chip manufacturing world? Once again, rather than imitating others blindly, we need to look to our own advantages.

Some argue that we need chip fabrication so that we can build strength in chip design or other parts of the supply chain. There is no evidence that this is the case—witness Nvidia in the United States or ASML in the Netherlands. That other countries or regions are jumping to subsidize chip fabrication is good for India; it will increase our choice even if we do not produce, especially when the periodic glut emerges.

That is not to say we should never enter chip fabrication. As the current frenzy of subsidies dies down, investment in the industry will, eventually, be worthwhile. India's trained engineers and designers will have the human capital to participate in the innovation that is so crucial in this industry. We should not hesitate at that point. Nor should we hesitate if anyone wants to invest in India without massive subsidies. But it does not seem wise at this moment to enter this ruinous subsidies game—we are better off investing in India's human capital to produce ideas and creativity.

Fitting with the Emerging Political Economy of Trade

While ideas and creativity should be our main vehicle for growth, there is a reason why services and manufacturing-related services may be easier for India to expand in than manufacturing. China's dominance of manufacturing, and the consequent loss of middle-income factory jobs in industrial countries, has made the West wary of opening the way for any other entrant that may turn out to be another China. Protectionism in manufacturing is rife, as is competition for the remaining shrinking pie. Services, however, are still relatively virgin territory. For instance, an Indian consultant still costs a fraction of what a US consultant costs, with pretty much the same capabilities, albeit a somewhat different base of experience. This is why many global service firms are looking to India even without any subsidies.

As the world grows richer and older, it will expand its use of services, but climate change suggests additional urgency. The world has to slow the growth in its consumption of goods if it is to mitigate climate change. This offers one more reason for India to be mildly biased towards services and manufacturing-related services, even while emphasizing that our thrust should be on ideas and creativity, wherever these apply. In sum, the premature deindustrialization that Professor Dani Rodrik of Harvard worries about need not be a bug but a feature of our growth path.

PART II

GOVERNANCE, CAPABILITIES AND MORE

Prelude: Governance and Structures

'The struggle of man against power is the struggle of memory against forgetting.'

—Milan Kundera, *The Book of Laughter and Forgetting*

A truly Indian way has to start by improving governance, which is so necessary for guiding us as we embrace a different path. Why start with governance? Because it touches everything else. The pandemic stress tested governance systems across the world. No system was perfect, but in some respects, India's was found more wanting than others.

The Pandemic and Its Aftermath

The second wave of the Covid pandemic, which hit India in February–May 2021, was truly disastrous in its impact. The dreadful pictures of bodies floating down the Ganges that were on the front pages of newspapers around the world, as crematoria and burning ghats became overwhelmed and firewood ran out, were a testament to the sheer unpreparedness of the government at every level.

What went wrong? Almost surely, it was an overconfident government apparatus that had fooled itself into thinking that the pandemic was over, because the data and analysis it based these judgements on were deeply flawed. Prime Minister Narendra Modi declared in January 2021 at the Davos World Economic Forum that through its preparedness 'the country has saved humanity from a big disaster by containing corona effectively'.[1] In February, the ruling Bharatiya Janata Party (BJP) passed a resolution thanking the prime minister for 'defeating' the pandemic, lauding the 'able, sensitive, committed and visionary leadership' during the Covid pandemic.[2] While some of this may be passed off as usual political posturing, it cannot be denied that these views, emanating from the top and internalized by the state everywhere, left India unprepared for the terrible second wave.

For even as other countries continued taking precautions, knowing that the virus could mutate into deadlier forms, India not only dismantled the facilities it had set up but also allowed cricket matches, election rallies and the Kumbh Mela, a massive gathering of pilgrims from all parts of the country. While many countries contracted well in advance with vaccine manufacturers for supplies, thus also giving manufacturers the funds to invest in expanding production facilities, India, home to the largest vaccine producer in the world, the Serum Institute of India (SII), did little.[3] That meant a minuscule per cent of the population was fully vaccinated with two doses when the second wave struck.

Why was India so complacent? Part of the problem was that India had undercounted deaths from the first wave, which peaked in mid-September 2020, by a factor of two or three.[4] Moreover, since the leadership emphasized Indian exceptionalism—that Indians, aided by a very effective medical system, were less susceptible to Covid—studies that questioned it were discouraged or suppressed.[5] There were exceptions. Some local governments, such as Mumbai's municipal commission, were better prepared because they resisted this narrative. And tireless medical personnel, voluntary organizations and brave individuals filled the hole left by the state. We all heard heart-warming stories of selfless members of our communities and the medical fraternity fighting the virus against incredible odds. Eventually, the second wave ebbed.

The government vaccination campaign then took on a measure of urgency. It was not without hiccups, but vaccinations are something the Indian state has experience with. In October 2021, India administered its billionth dose of the vaccine.[6] The rapidity of the eventual vaccination roll-out suggests that institutional memory built over years of administrative learning from past campaigns does pay off, especially when the government decides to act based on expert advice. Unfortunately, though, the successful roll-out of vaccines reignited triumphalism.

According to Indian official numbers, India suffered around 5,30,000 deaths during the pandemic—a fraction of the deaths suffered by the United States as a share of its population. The World Health Organization's own estimates are that the excess deaths in India (relative to the normal number) could be around 5 million, making India the largest outlier by far in undercounted deaths.[7] Other scholarly work comes up with similar numbers.[8] Of course, some of these deaths could be because medical care was simply harder to access during the pandemic, but these deaths are still pandemic- and health-care-related.

Yet India is unwilling to revise the flawed official death toll, for it would reflect badly on our Covid management. This, then, prevents us from learning from our mistakes. India has instituted no official inquiry into how it handled Covid: What's the need when the official data says India managed so well? Indeed, in a striking example of bad data justifying worse policy, the Indian finance ministry's Economic Survey of India 2021–22 points to the sudden and devastating complete lockdown in 2020 as the reason India suffered so few (officially admitted) deaths.[9]

Governance and More

It is too easy to point to the leadership as the problem. The leadership in other countries made mistakes, but their systems contained their worst instincts. What systemic changes does India have to make to get the governance and outcomes it needs for the twenty-first century, no matter who the leader in power is?

In Chapters 5 and 6, we will describe the government we need, one that decentralizes, is willing to experiment and learn, and ultimately, is democratic in that it keeps the electoral playing field level, and empowers the citizenry and keeps it informed. The needed government reforms are not insignificant, but they deepen our democratic ethos, thus they are *anukool* (with the grain) rather than *pratikool* (against the grain).

Then we turn to our people's capabilities. In Chapter 7, we discuss early childhood nutrition and education, in Chapter 8 higher education and in Chapter 9 health care. In Chapter 10, we will examine aspects of economic and social inequality, and how to reduce it so that development can be inclusive and fair. Our proposals will draw on the previously discussed governance reforms that enlist the energy of our people to effect change, but also on digitalization. Specifically, we will explore how new technologies can come up with better solutions than in the past. We will also go beyond the tired debate on whether public services should be provided by the private sector or the public sector. What matters is that the embedded incentives achieve the desired outcomes, that the cat catches mice, not whether it is black or white, as Deng Xiaoping famously said.

Finally, we turn to how we can expand the opportunities for our people to flourish as their capabilities improve. In Chapter 11, we will focus on our engagement with the world; then, in Chapter 12, on how we can get the creativity and ferment, the buzz and excitement that will make India an innovation nation.

5

Governance for the Twenty-First Century: Structure

The aim of government should be to govern well and in the best interests of the people over the longer term—that is the proverbial 'Ram Rajya'. Staying in power should be a consequence of good governance, not the primary aim. Unfortunately, this is an idealistic view of government. Often, it is not clear what policies are optimal, there is no consensus among the governed on the most preferred alternative, so what is politically convenient dominates.

In arriving at the right decisions, a good government must be aware of what it does not know and be willing to learn. It must seek advice from all kinds of politicians, technocratic experts, experienced bureaucrats, businesspeople and civil society organizations to map out the contours of what is feasible. It should decentralize decision-making where necessary, formulate policy with a deep sense of empathy towards the people whom its decisions will affect, build a consensus around the decisions it finally takes, and use data, public debate and criticism to correct course periodically. By contrast, if the leadership is overconfident of its own capabilities, centralizes decision-making, is disdainful of consensus, and willing to suppress inconvenient data and criticism, even a seemingly strong and decisive leadership can turn quickly into an unprepared and disastrous one. This is why governments in liberal societies are hemmed in by checks and balances, so that they do not stray too far from a reasonable path. These allow society to be vibrant, and innovation and creativity to flourish, in addition to improving governance.

Aren't periodic elections sufficient to bring about thoughtful, empathetic decision-making? Unfortunately not! There are varieties of democracies, and not all of them place restraints on impetuous or oppressive leadership. Both Russia and Venezuela are democracies, as is Turkey, but few would argue that their systems impose sufficient checks and balances on their leaders. The state of these countries is a warning about giving strong elected leaders free rein.

Economists Ajay Chhibber and Salman Anees Soz, in their excellent book, *Unshackling India*, ask whether India is an 'electocracy' rather than a democracy. That is, it has regular elections which are free, but once elected, a government with a significant majority has few checks on its leadership. Why has our democracy evolved in such a way, especially when what happens between elections is also important?

How Did We Get Here?

Our founding fathers chose to give every adult the vote when India became independent, even though this was unprecedented for a country at India's income levels at the time. It was an audacious choice. In the horrendous aftermath of Partition, it was not clear if India would survive as a country, let alone a democratic one, or whether the provinces of British India and the princely states would be welded together, whether their peoples would feel a sense of national unity and purpose that overcame differences of religion, caste, language and income. Gandhi rightly feared that India would get the Indian elite's version of political freedom, with the Brown Sahib simply replacing the White Sahib to lord it over the largely poor and illiterate masses.

Against all odds, India developed many of the traditions and institutions of a robust democracy. People grew into voters and voters into citizens. We were blessed that our early leaders were largely committed democrats, who set and then strengthened democratic traditions and practices. Consequently, they were able to correct course and did so repeatedly. Democratic dialogue functioned as a safety valve, managing and mediating pressures that emerged from our vast country. A collateral benefit was that our fledgling democracy gave us soft power internationally. We were respected as the idealistic voice for developing countries, even though our economic footprint was minuscule.

The passage of time did raise concerns about our initial design. First, our constitutional structure, perhaps influenced by the calibre of the governing leaders of the time, was too trusting of the government's good intentions. Maybe this bias was necessary when the nation's unity was uncertain and the instruments through which the government could exercise power untested. Insurrection and secession were ever-present threats—Tamil leader C.N. Annadurai dropped his demand for an independent Dravida Nadu only after the outbreak of the Sino–Indian war in 1962. So an overly powerful Central government was deemed a lesser evil than a potentially weak one.

Yet, allowing the government substantial leeway to set its own powers against the citizen was problematic, especially since the entire government machinery could be suborned by a single powerful individual who wanted to hold on to power at all costs. As Dr Ambedkar, chairman of the Drafting Committee of India's Constituent Assembly, admitted, '. . . if things go wrong under the new Constitution, the reason will not be that we had a bad Constitution. What we will have to say is that Man was vile.'[1] Yet there were insufficient constitutional guardrails against this possibility.

These fears were realized in 1975, when Prime Minister Indira Gandhi suspended democratic rights after the judiciary found her guilty of misuse of official machinery during elections. She declared a state of internal emergency, which was permissible under the Constitution. Every constitutional check and balance on government power gave way in the face of a determined and popular leader—the President approved the Emergency, as did the cabinet and Parliament, while the Supreme Court, with notable exceptions, caved. The 42nd Amendment to the Constitution gave Parliament (then dominated by Mrs Gandhi's Congress party) virtually unchecked power, allowing it to amend the Constitution thenceforth as it thought fit.

India could well have turned into a dictatorship, but for reasons that will remain shrouded in history, Indira Gandhi ended the Emergency in 1977 and called for an election. Mrs Gandhi and her Congress Party lost, and the 43rd and 44th constitutional amendments then reversed many of the measures in the 42nd Amendment. Yet that episode suggested that India's key institutions could not stand up in the face of a determined government leader. BJP leader L.K. Advani famously berated the Indian media for its behaviour during the Emergency: 'You were asked only to bend, but you crawled.'[2] Unfortunately, not much has changed.

Today, there is no serious existential threat to India emanating internally. We have a million small mutinies at any moment, but none that is threatening to tear the country apart. Indeed, an authoritarian brook-no-dissent government wielding the *lathi* is perhaps a greater danger, for it often provokes yet more protest. We have achieved administrative integration (through the all-India civil services, the judiciary, the defense services and paramilitary services), legal integration (through a common set of laws), political integration (through national parties, Parliament and national elections), economic integration (through interstate trade, investment, employment flows and national companies), social integration (through national welfare schemes and all-India educational institutions with national admissions), integration of national sentiment (through national sports teams and national entertainment media) and integration through interstate migration and intermarriage.

The fear of the framers of the Constitution—that India, the nation, would be torn apart—is no longer a primary concern. So, on balance, we must now strengthen checks and balances on government. These can also push the government to do more for the people, which will be necessary if we are to embark on the ambitious path we have outlined. An authoritarian government that is in power and already accustomed to pulling the levers of state machinery for its political benefit is unlikely to forgo them. One possible hope is that a coalition of Opposition parties, knowing the damage that such unbridled power acquired by any single party can do, will commit in its manifesto to changing the status quo. This is precisely what the Janata Party government, which was elected after the Emergency, accomplished with the 43rd and 44th amendments to the Constitution.

Business and Press Pliability

Private business in India rarely stands up to government. The problem is so systemic that it is unlikely it is because of the weak personalities of business leaders. Instead, it is probably because the government, since Independence, has steadily acquired enormous ability to appoint, reward and punish, which allows it to influence those who might serve as an institutional check on it.

For instance, the government places large quantities of government advertisements in pliant newspapers. Criticism then costs a publisher serious money. Karan Thapar, a noted independent journalist who has worked for a variety of top media institutions, indicated there are many other pressure points. Media houses make a lot of money off conferences. The government can undercut those by not sending any representatives to conferences organized by disfavoured media houses.

Media sponsors can also be directly 'persuaded'. When the sponsor of Thapar's show went to meet a senior government official, the official dropped a veiled hint that the government was not happy with its sponsorship. A while later, when the sponsor went to meet the official on a business matter, the official first asked what had happened to the sponsorship. The sponsor got the message and stopped funding Thapar's show.

The government, of course, has stronger weapons. When asked in an interview in June 2023 about the pressures he had received from foreign governments during his time as CEO of Twitter, Jack Dorsey said, 'India is a country that had many requests of us around the farmers protest, around particular journalists that were critical of the government, and it manifested in ways such as "we will shut Twitter down in India," which is a very large market for us; "we will raid the homes of your employees," which they did; "we will shut down your offices, if you don't follow suit," and this is India, a democratic country.' The government accused Dorsey of lying.[3]

More generally, even business houses that may not have any particular fondness for the government can be persuaded to toe the line with their media properties, given the vast array of carrots and sticks, such as contracts, permissions and tax raids that the government can use. The rarity of critical business comments on government budgets or policies is a good barometer of how submissive business is to the government of the day.

If a publisher is foolish enough not to rein in critical journalists, business houses that are close to the government can be persuaded to buy the publisher out. Given these powers, which undoubtedly some governments misuse more than others, it is no wonder that habitual critics in the mainstream media are fired from their jobs and end up in niche online sites. To be a government critic in India one has to be brave and have an independent income, or be willing to endure economic hardship. Many naturally choose to be cheerleaders for the government regardless of their convictions.

It is impossible to legislate backbone. In countries where the norm is independence, punitive government actions against critics are called out by the free press, and independence is maintained. But where the norm is pliability, it is the independent critics who get their head handed on a platter, and no one dares to notice or at least discuss it publicly.

What we can do in India, apart from lauding those who have shown independence, is to limit government discretion to reward or punish to only where truly necessary, and even there require substantial transparency. For instance, few developed countries have the plethora of frontpage advertisements extolling the accomplishments of national and state political leaders, paid for by the government. This is political campaigning, effectively funded by the taxpayer, and gives a tremendous advantage to the incumbent party. Why not require that all government advertisements should have a public purpose— for instance, persuading people to get vaccinated—and carry no photographs or names of leaders? Furthermore, why not require that the ads be placed in outlets in proportion to their circulation? That will eliminate an enormous and distortionary government carrot.

Of course, no incumbent has an incentive to change this state of affairs, irrespective of who is in power. Change requires a concerted and persistent civil-society campaign that exposes this compromised media model and shames leaders who waste taxpayers' money in aggrandizing themselves.

The Right to Debate, Appoint, Reward and Punish

India has a diverse population in terms of ethnicity, caste, language, religion and culture. When there are large differences between the people in a country, decision-making has to be sensitive to different interests and mediate them. Democracy allows mediation, for the aggrieved to blow off steam and be pacified. It is better that India experience small mutinies every day than these coalesce into collective anger. For this, India needs a functioning Parliament with a functioning Opposition, where concerns are aired and debates take place. In recent years, governments with overwhelming majorities have suppressed critical discussion, while unhappy Opposition parties have prevented Parliament from functioning.

As legal scholar Tarunabh Khaitan points out, while the leader of the Opposition should not be seen as part of the government, they should be seen as a part of the state.[4] The leader should be kept informed of the working of the government and have the power to request briefings from defence chiefs, intelligence chiefs and bureaucrats. This will instil in the defence forces and the bureaucracy a greater sense that they owe their loyalty to the state, not to the personalities or the party that is in the government. Another worthwhile suggestion from Khaitan is that the leader of the Opposition should also have the right to schedule discussions one day a week when Parliament is in session. The deputy speaker, a member of the Opposition, should chair these sessions, where no votes will be allowed or taken, but where critical feedback can be aired, and the government is not shielded by an overly loyal speaker.

We also need our institutions to have more independence. One such institution that sometimes serves as a check on the government is the judiciary, especially the Supreme Court. The constitutional expert Professor Granville Austin points out that the Constituent Assembly realized the importance of an independent judiciary and devoted more time discussing this issue than any other. Yet, as various law commissions noted, the procedure the Constitution laid out for the appointment of judges was not immune from government influence.[5] Perhaps the most notable act of government interference was in the case of Justice H.R. Khanna. His was the lone brave vote against the majority Supreme Court judgment in the ADM Jabalpur case, which sided with the government in allowing citizens' fundamental rights to be suspended during the Emergency. Justice Khanna was then superseded when the position of chief justice became vacant. The message to the judges was clear.

Subsequently, through a series of judgments, to detail which would take us too far afield, judges have wrested the power to appoint from the executive. Appointments are now done by a collegium of judges headed by the chief justice, and the serving justice who is most senior at the time the seat of the chief justice becomes vacant fills the post.

Governments have attempted legislation to seize back some of the power to appoint, but the Supreme Court has protected its privilege. Arguably, the Supreme Court now enjoys too much power and really is accountable to no one. That is never good in a democracy. But until there is a transparent appointment process that cannot be subverted by the executive, perhaps the country has to live with a lesser evil.

An independent appointment process does not, of course, assure independence. Chief justices, once appointed, have tremendous power.[6] There are thirty-four judges when the Supreme Court is at full strength. Supreme Court cases, depending on their constitutional importance, are heard by a varying number of judges, ranging from two to nine. Judges have different proclivities—one will always uphold the death penalty while another will always commute it. So the chief justice, who decides which judges will sit on which cases (also called the roster), can sometimes effectively decide the case.

There are many other powers the chief justice has. Given their range, it becomes very tempting for the government to try and influence the chief justice with carrots—a post-retirement Rajya Sabha seat or the chairmanship of a commission—or sticks—an investigation into possible past misdemeanours. Since not every chief justice is immune to such persuasion, the concentration of power in the chief justice becomes a key source of vulnerability for the Supreme Court.

It would be futile to attempt to eliminate all the ways the government can try and influence the chief justice. Instead, perhaps the focus should be on reducing the chief justice's discretion. For instance, former finance minister and Supreme Court lawyer P. Chidambaram has advocated breaking up the Supreme Court into a constitutional court, which hears only constitutional matters, and five courts of appeal, for cases that come up from lower courts.[7] A narrower definition of what comes before the Supreme Court could also reduce the incentive of the Supreme Court to intervene beyond its remit and reduce the backlog of cases before it. Another possibility is to set the roster by lottery rather than have the chief justice do it.

The broader point is that making the government's power to appoint, reward or punish more transparent and much less discretionary can allow national institutions more independence, enabling them to maintain checks and balances on the government. At the same time, we should guard against unchecked concentration of power in those institutions too.

There will be a need for differentiation. Some institutions, like the Reserve Bank, have to be operationally independent. For instance, the RBI should be allowed to take whatever steps it deems necessary to fulfil its mandate of keeping inflation and the risks of financial instability low. However, it also has to cooperate with the government on a number of development issues, such as expanding access to finance for the poor. Total independence is neither necessary nor even desirable in these matters. The government could have a reasonable role in appointments of the top leadership in such institutions.

But when it comes to agencies like the Central Bureau of Investigation or the Enforcement Directorate, which can be, and are frequently, weaponized by the government in power, and agencies like the Central Information Commission, which serves as a check on the government, appointments of top officials should be determined by a committee that is more independent of the government. It could comprise independent eminent citizens with domain expertise, nominated in equal measure by the government and the leader of the Opposition. Moreover, civil society should scrutinize proposals by the government to downgrade the rank of heads of independent institutions—more junior heads are often less influential, and themselves more susceptible to influence and pressure.

Finally, a vibrant society has a variety of institutions outside government that can help distribute power. Political parties can themselves be a check on their authoritarian leaders. The lack of intra-party democracy inhibits this. Perhaps every party registered with the Election Commission should be required to have regular intra-party elections in order to obtain its election symbol. A desirable aim should be that political leaders should not have such power concentrated in them that they come to dominate their parties, regardless of support, for prolonged periods of time.

Civil society organizations such as NGOs can also help, including by substituting for the government when it is weak or missing, as we saw during the second wave of the pandemic in March–May 2021. In India, such organizations need better legal protection from arbitrary government action, such as cutting off their flow of funds or tax raids if they do not hew to the government line. Civil society organizations add a richness to democracy and check on the government of the day, and this serves the country well in the longer run, even if it is inconvenient to the government. Being anti-government should be a protected status, being anti-national should not, the difference is important.

Decentralization

General Principle

India, despite its federal structure, is still fairly centralized. There continue to be disputes, sometimes even constitutional ones, about the relative power of the Centre and the states; for example, on the powers of the Centre-appointed state governors, and the status of Delhi and Jammu and Kashmir. The Centre also has the power to supersede state governments in a national emergency. Therefore, an independent Supreme Court is once again key to ensuring that an authoritarian Centre does not overwhelm states.

Even though India now has powerful regional parties, a dominating Central leadership has many levers of power in the normal course, not just over the Central government or the states its party controls, but also over Opposition states. These come through the Centre-appointed governors, the Centre's control over investigative agencies, and through the Centre's ability to make or withhold financial transfers and guarantees to the states. An authoritarian Indian government therefore also implies centralized decision-making, with few checks and balances on how those decisions are made.

At early stages of development, optimal government policies are relatively clear and have more of a one-size-fits-all character—for instance, build roads and railways or eliminate tariffs on imported inputs. Even so, as we saw with China, local authorities may need to interpret the centrally imposed rules flexibly so as to encourage local entrepreneurship. A centralized bureaucracy, as we have had in India, does not permit governance to be nearly as sensitive to local conditions.

Centralization becomes more problematic as economies develop, for the economic challenges in large, complex economies rarely have simple answers. Infrastructure buildout has to be sensitive to local needs. Too much, and we can get unsustainable overdevelopment. For example, many parts of the Himalayan town of Joshimath are sinking, and town dwellers blame the stresses created by development projects, including the public-sector firm NTPC's Tapovan Vishnugad hydroelectric project, and the Centre's Char Dham Pariyojana road-widening project.[8] At India's level of development, a more democratic discourse among local interested parties can arguably produce better solutions than one-size-fits-all solutions thrust down from the top.

From Centre to State

India's federal structure, where a Central government and state governments can be ruled by different parties, helps distribute power away from the Centre and closer to the citizen. As envisioned by the Constitution, several governance subjects (such as police, prisons and, interestingly, local government) are purely in the purview of states, and a larger number (such as defence) are exclusively for the Central government, while some (such as education) are in the concurrent list, where both state and Centre can pass laws and regulations.

One important dispute today surrounds funding. The Finance Commission, set up every five years to allocate tax revenues between the Centre and states, has typically devolved more and more funds to the states. While a determined Central government can reclassify revenues to withhold money from the states, and while there are ways it can favour friendly states, it is hard for it to go completely against the spirit of the Finance Commission's recommendations. This is why it is important that going forward, the Finance Commission be appointed in ways that ensure it is truly independent of the Centre or states.

Decentralization is not just about devolving power, it also gives every state the room to try out its own policies and share experiences about what works. For instance, the midday meal scheme, whereby children in government-run schools are provided a nutritious meal, was initially criticized as a freebie, a populist giveaway of little value. It has since been found to be immensely beneficial in bettering the health and nutrition of poor children, as well as in encouraging parents to leave their children in school.[9] The first state to try it was Tamil Nadu in the mid-1960s. It has now spread to every state and has even been endorsed by the Centre. Similarly, the popular National Rural Employment Guarantee Scheme was introduced, at a smaller scale, in the state of Maharashtra, and has since emerged as an effective means of providing a safety net at the national level.

The Planning Commission used to be criticized for thrusting one-size-fits-all schemes on states and discouraging such experimentation. It also, however, used to be a venue where the experience with programmes like the midday meal could be shared with the Centre and with other states. With the Planning Commission now defunct, India needs new venues for such dialogue. The Inter-State Council, chaired by the prime minister and with state chief ministers as members, meets infrequently and at too high a level to promote meaningful dialogue. However, organizations like the Goods and Services Tax (GST) Council, which is chaired by the Union finance minister and has representatives from every state government, allow for pointed dialogue and sharing of experiences. More such Centre–state councils covering different issues can only be beneficial for India.

From State to Local

The Constitution did not initially empower, fund or staff the government at the village or municipality level to any significant degree. While Gandhi extolled the virtues of the village republic, Ambedkar believed that the village was 'but a sink of localism, a den of ignorance, narrow-mindedness and communalism', and India could only be pulled into modernity if the more enlightened national and state governments took charge. Ambedkar's views won in the Constituent Assembly, and India did not have a constitutionally required third layer of government until the 73rd and 74th amendments to the Constitution in 1993 created the possibility of panchayats (for villages) and municipalities (for towns).

'Everybody loves decentralization, but only to their level,' economist Raja Chelliah wrote. And indeed, that has proved to be the case. The constitutional amendments compelled states to create a third layer of government and to ensure regular elections to these bodies, but nothing required states to transfer functions or funds to them (or to allow them to collect funds through local taxes).[10] Some states, like Kerala, have empowered local government, others typically have not done so to any great extent. As a result, local government functionaries are elected but typically do not have a lot to do, as portrayed in the popular web series *Panchayat*. Indeed, sometimes the state government will create a parallel board, such as a district development board or a water board, and withhold these functions from the local government. The decrepit state of many of India's towns, even though they generate much of India's income, is partly because city mayors have not been empowered by their state.

The concentration of power at the top in state governments is almost as concerning as its concentration in the Centre: devolution of functions, funds and functionaries to local government has thus become essential. States are getting too large to govern from the state capital. Today, the state of Uttar Pradesh has nearly 240 million people, about three-fourth the size of the United States, which has fifty states and thousands of counties and mayoralties. How can the government functionary in Lucknow possibly formulate policy for every remote village, and how will villagers hold that functionary to account?

Devolution allows for governance to be sensitive to local needs and for the governed to influence how they are governed. Rather than a large hydel dam, built by national contractors using company workers, empowered local government will rely on age-old methods of harvesting water in tanks and using the slope of the land to replenish the water table. The latter is more environmentally sustainable, uses local labour and local small contractors, and the quality of work is repeatedly tested by local beneficiaries, the people.

With every local government attempting its own solutions, much can be learnt from everyone's experience. When best practices are identified, shared and modified by each local government to its own situation, they can improve the effectiveness of governance tremendously, especially because policies are based on practical experience.

Prime Minister Rajiv Gandhi, who initiated the constitutional amendments towards local government, also believed that by bringing more people into fighting elections and representing electors, local government would prove a training ground for democracy. That certainly has been the case, and today, millions of elected representatives, including many hitherto underrepresented minorities, such as women, are finding their voice and their confidence. Also, much as the Chinese Communist Party promotes local functionaries with a superior record to higher office, once Indian functionaries have adequate funds and functions, they too can use their record to vie for higher office. Local government will thus be an effective training ground for higher political office.

One criticism made by those opposed to devolution is that local government will be both incompetent and corrupt. These are not new arguments and are not made only in India. While functionaries for local government are not recruited through an all-India exam (which would result in a much larger pool of applicants and thus a higher inherent aptitude of selected candidates), these functionaries have much more local experience and local knowledge of what works. Moreover, they can be held responsible for local results. Consequently, their decisions will typically be more aligned with the needs of the local people than decisions taken by a smart Indian Administrative Service officer, who, in her short posting, may not necessarily become attuned to local realities.

There is also no reason for the local functionary to be inherently more corrupt than the smart outsider. With both the state government and the local people watching her every move, the functionary may indeed be less corrupt. The key is for the local people to care, which means the functionary should actually have the power to help them, and the people should be informed about what the functionary does, including the funds she receives and how they are spent.

Data, Transparency and People Power

When It Works

What gets measured gets managed, as the saying goes. Think, for example, of the Chinese local government officials who were promoted for generating local growth, increasing their incentives to generate it. This could not happen if local growth was not accurately measured or was liable to significant manipulation.

Data also allow course correction. In the complex environments that prevail as economies develop, policies need to be fine-tuned based on data and feedback. Governments with authoritarian tendencies dislike data that might suggest weaknesses, or feedback that looks like criticism, for it suggests they are fallible. Such governments stop collecting any kind of data that might be unfavourable. As a perverse consequence, they are left to navigate in the dark, which makes it hard for them to correct course.

The more bottom-up case for data collection and availability has to do with empowering the people: if data on the effects of government action (or inaction) are made public, the people, including independent experts, can react. They can argue over the causes and consequences, including in the press and other media. The debate can produce ideas for improvement that the government can implement. If the government does not listen and segments of the public feel very strongly about the issue, they can organize to put pressure on the government. Non-violent protests by citizens, of the kind we see at Jantar Mantar in New Delhi periodically, are not an aberration of democracy, they are its very essence, something we were taught by the Father of the Nation.

One example of government-enabled people power, which actually reduces corruption, comes from Uganda.[11] The government of Uganda used to send money for school spending (other than salaries) to local governments. The average school received only 20 per cent of the funds, the rest being corruptly appropriated by the local government officials and politicians in charge of distributing the grants. To fight this, the Central government initiated a newspaper campaign: it published the grants that were sent to each district every month. Research found that not only did the average school receive more than 80 per cent of its grant after the campaign, schools that were closer to newspaper outlets and had head teachers who were more informed about the programme received significantly more. Student enrolments and student test performance also increased significantly. So better-informed beneficiaries (the teachers) could pressure local government officials once they had basic information on how much funds were supposed to flow into their district. People power works!

Technology has made everything in this ingenious approach more feasible. The Central (or state) government can post and access information online, and the local community can draw its members into monitoring and sharing their experience with the local government. This makes effective decentralization much more feasible today than it was in the past.

In Bangalore, a website, IPaidaBribe.com, encourages people to report situations where they had to pay a bribe, situations where they refused to pay a bribe as well as recognize honest officers who did not ask for bribes. The website, started by community activist Swati Ramanathan, also produces reports on areas and communities that are most prone to corruption. It has a network of retired senior government officials who help publicize and rectify the problems the website has uncovered from its analysis of citizen reports.

When It Does Not Work

Any link in this chain, if broken, makes it hard for people power to be exercised. Without accurate data on performance, people cannot know if their government did a good or a bad job. In many cases, they will give the government the benefit of the doubt, which gives governments the incentive to suppress information whenever it is particularly adverse. In that case, since few in the government will know the true position, the government may mislead itself—for instance, it may even disband medical facilities after the first wave of Covid, assuming that Indians are relatively immune to Covid.

Sometimes, the government does not even collect the data, making it unnecessary to hide it. For instance, India has not collected consumption data in the last six years, since the last report from 2017 was suppressed, perhaps because leaked versions suggested an increase in poverty.[12] The latest census data is from 2011, the new decadal round has simply been shelved. The infrequently collected data on employment is noisy, often not squaring with the lived reality of the citizenry. So the government policymakers or researchers are unable to use the employment data to understand the ebbs and flows of the economy, and act on what they learn. Once again, the absence of data may be politically convenient if peoples' consumption is falling or if few jobs are being created, but it makes policymaking much harder.

It is not enough for the government to collect and release data publicly. Sometimes, the freedom to criticize can be shut down, for instance, under the pretext of limiting hate speech. It is commonplace nowadays to see the police filing cases against those who criticize a government leader, such as the prime minister or a state chief minister, because someone (usually from the leader's party) felt their sentiments had been hurt by the criticism. While these cases rarely result in conviction, the process here is the punishment. A few days in jail while the critic is being bailed out is enough to quell criticism. Of course, government leaders can criticize others however much they want, without being arrested for 'hurting sentiments'. The problem with the judicial system reacting to 'hurt sentiments' is that those in power can define what 'hurt' means, which results in injustice. Better for the system to not react at all unless the speaker actually calls for violence.

More generally, our system allows for the arbitrary use of power against the citizenry without appropriate checks and balances. For instance, the Unlawful Activities (Prevention) Act allows the government to designate individuals as terrorists without following any judicial process. The accused are then afforded very few protections such as bail. The Prevention of Money Laundering Act allows the attachment of a suspect's property at any stage of the investigation, potentially subjecting innocent people to undue hardships. In many of these cases, people sometimes spend decades in and out of detention, even though they are finally cleared.[13] Of course, the aim to chill any form of protest is then achieved.

When debate and protest are suppressed, public perceptions can further quell dissent. Political scientist Timur Kuran coined the evocative phrase 'preference falsification', which is the act of misrepresenting what one believes, perceiving public pressure to do so. For instance, a substantial portion of the population of the Soviet Union was unhappy with the state, but many feared sharing their views openly. It was only when the Soviet state collapsed, weighed down by decades of misgovernance without effective feedback, that people realized others, too, thought the same way. Because these views were never shared, the government was never aware of the scale of dissatisfaction.[14]

We must examine every link of the chain, from independent and accurate data generation to the room for protest, and improve it. Police and investigative agencies need better training, so they don't need to use blunt colonial-era laws against our own citizens. Many of those laws giving the government draconian powers should be repealed, for they do more harm than good. Commendably, the central government has initiated a process of reviewing much of the legal code but some experts fear the end result may be even more draconian laws.[15]

Courts have started penalizing officers and government agencies that do shoddy, biased work. If done in a measured way, this is a good trend. More broadly, for governance to work effectively, it has to understand where it is going wrong and, occasionally, have that pointed out when it simply refuses to listen. We need far more effective governance in the years to come, which is why we cannot afford to suppress criticism.

Government Capacity

That leads us to the last issue in our discussion of structure: government capacity. Political scientist Devesh Kapur has argued that the Indian state is too small, especially at the local-government level. This may come as a surprise to those who have grown up with the belief that India has a bloated bureaucracy. It is perhaps bloated, but in a specific way.

Kapur estimates that the number of Central government employees, including its public-sector enterprises, such as the railways and the banks, was about 4.5 civilian employees per 1000 people in 2014, down from 8.47 in 1995.[16] The US federal government had 8.07 such employees per 1000, down from 10.4 in 1995, even though public-sector employment is smaller there. Of course, rich countries tend to have bigger governments since they perform more services, including administering a strong safety net, but this suggests that India's Central government is not excessively bloated in terms of personnel.

In fact, what is particularly understaffed is local government. Kapur cites data showing that in the United States and China, two-thirds of public employment is in local government. In India, that number is only 12 per cent. Similarly, local government spending in India is only 3 per cent of total government expenditure, while it is 27 per cent in the United States and 51 per cent in China.[17] Of course, the classification of spending is not uniform, but the difference in numbers is stark. So India has too few government employees, taking all levels of government into account, even for a country at its stage of development, and the number is shrinking. Indeed, the share of the public sector in overall salaried employment fell from 26 per cent in 1999 to 11 per cent in 2020.[18]

Economists Chhibber and Soz agree that the number of government employees is relatively small but find that Indian government spending, including tax and non-tax revenues as well as the large budget deficits, is on a par with that of rich countries. So, in part, India does not spend its revenues well and has a tendency to offer government employees generous pay and benefits. For example, in 2019, the average secondary school teacher's salary ratio to GDP per capita was 0.76 in China, it was around 1.1 in countries in Asia, but higher than 1.7 in India. For government schools, the number for India is approximately 3.[19] So a government secondary school teacher in India was making more than three times the average income in the country. Similarly, the Institute for Strategic Studies reported that 53 per cent of India's 2023 defence budget spending goes towards salaries and pensions.[20] This leaves little room for defence procurement and investment in infrastructure. In contrast, according to the Peter G. Peterson Foundation, this number in the United States is much lower, at around 24 per cent in 2022.[21]

The high government pay also means that India does not have a problem attracting quality recruits to government service. In 2021–22, nearly 3 million people took the central civil service exams and 3559 were selected for appointment, about one in 850. Back in 1950–51, 24,680 applications were received, and 2780 candidates were recommended for appointment, suggesting one in nine were selected.[22] How today's civil services aspirants, whose travails are vividly portrayed in the recent web series aptly titled *Aspirants*, would love such a ratio!

What is surprising, though, is that despite so many knocking on the door, a large number of vacancies exist at every level of government, especially at the local level. For instance, in a recent survey conducted in 160 districts spread across the country, more than 40 per cent of posts in Block Development Offices, the key local administrative body, were found to be vacant.[23] In part, this may be because of a lack of funds, given that the government prioritizes other spending (every tier of the Indian government runs budget deficits); and in part it may be that despite the large number of applicants, not enough can meet the acceptable level for recruitment, especially in specialized positions, such as development administrators, doctors, teachers and regulators.

The consequence of all this is that local officials are often capable but overloaded. So they focus on what is most immediate and measured. Disasters are, of course, both immediate and closely followed by the media, so the government has become more effective on disaster management and relief. Similarly, time-bound events/programmes— like organizing the gigantic logistics of the Kumbh Mela, or the Covid vaccination rollout to a billion people, or even targeted monitored schemes, such as the building of toilets in the Swachh Bharat Abhiyan (Clean India Mission)—are done very effectively, once set in motion. However, longer-term programmes with hard-to-measure outcomes, such as good primary education or effective health care, are not delivered well, as we will discuss shortly.

A final point: as India deals with more complex issues that a modern economy at the frontier faces, it will need more specialists. Trade negotiations are best handled by those who understand trade economics and have spent years in the weeds, getting to know WTO rules and studying trade agreements. Corporate fraud investigations are best handled by an investigator who has a background in forensic accounting, and when the case comes to court the judge should have an intimate understanding of corporate law and finance. Lateral entry of specialists is very difficult, since those who have spent years in the system resist such entry. (Raghu knows, having brought in lateral entrants both at the finance ministry and the RBI.) But it should be tried and persisted with, since India needs such experts. An alternative is to send those in the system for training, not as a boondoggle to be enjoyed but as preparation for their next career move.

6

Governance for the Twenty-First Century: Process

Thus far, we have discussed changes in the structure of government that would make it far better positioned to guide India through the twenty-first century. But what should the government actually do? Our intent here is not to be encyclopedic and offer a laundry list of reforms—there already are some excellent books outlining them.[1] Rather, our goal here is to outline some basic principles for governance, so that most, if not all reforms, can fit under these fundamental themes.

Among the needed changes is a shift of focus from subsidies and transfers to providing for public services, such as quality education and health care. We also need to improve the environment for business, including start-ups in frontier industries, by creating enabling frameworks that help businesses flourish. Regulations are an important element of the environment, and how to steer between the twin dangers of over- and under-regulation will be a challenge. In new areas, regulatory experimentation may also be useful in determining appropriate policies as the economy gets more complex. One area that needs constant attention is competition, to ensure the playing field allows for new entry and innovation, and does not give private or public incumbents an unfair advantage. And finally, to minimize crony capitalism, an ever-present danger in India, we need transparent election funding.

Public Services versus Targeted Benefits

India has focused historically on targeted interventions with clear short-term outcomes. With regard to people, this implies transfers of money, grain, laptops, or reserving seats and jobs for targeted groups. Let us term these 'targeted benefits' in that they offer immediate benefits to favoured groups. They should be contrasted with the tasks of improving public services like education or health-care delivery, which have longer-term beneficial effects on the citizenry and the economy. With regard to business, every budget is preceded by meetings with industry representatives, where each sector seeks special privileges, subsidies and tariff protection (or reductions if it is an importer). Few push for improving the business environment, which would work for all sectors of the economy. Consequently, the budget, instead of being a broad statement of intent, typically has a preponderance of benefits catering to the industry sectors that have been most persuasive in the weeks before the budget. Why so short term and why so specific, whether the government is focused on helping households or business?

It may simply be that India became a democracy when it was poor. Political scientist Devesh Kapur argues that 'precocious' democracies like India prioritize targeted benefits over delivering public services.[2] When India became independent, the politically dominant upper-caste land-owning class might not have believed field workers or their children needed education, as Myron Wiener suggested. Perhaps workers also did not feel it would help since there were few jobs outside of agriculture at that time. Once budgetary allocation were made initially, they became rigid, partly as a result of inertia, partly because they were defended by interest groups that benefited from the existing allocations. So, with slow economic growth in the early years and government budgets limited, there was little demand for educated workers, and reallocation of government funds to education, especially primary education and vocational skilling, was very difficult. History matters!

This led to vicious circles. With government primary health care initially underfunded and of poor quality, the middle class typically turned to private clinics for their needs. If the vocal middle class uses public services, it can be a major force for quality improvement. An angry businessman or accountant can berate the government doctor for not showing up on time at the health centre in a way that the poor agricultural labourer would not dare. With the middle class not using public services, their quality stayed low—as economist Larry Summers says, services only for the poor are poor services.

Furthermore, as the middle class saw few benefits coming their way from the government, their incentive to pay taxes also diminished. In some countries, tax evasion is shameful, something you hide from your neighbours. However, when the government is seen to do little for the taxes that it collects, evasion becomes more socially acceptable, even something to boast about. Lower tax collection constrains spending, making the government capable of even less.

With limited resources, and a state electorate divided by caste and religion, there are further disincentives for politicians to provide public services. At the state level, resources will be spread too widely and thinly to make a difference to one's favoured voters, certainly in the limited time before the next election. Also, any effort at improvement has to work through many layers of government, with overextended officials having to contribute their energies.

Quality improvements in education or health care at the state level are also hard to measure and even harder to communicate. Improvements in patient health outcomes, for example, take a long time to be discernable. It is easier, of course, to see repainted, cleaned and well-stocked government dispensaries, as well as pharmacists present in the government pharmacy whenever it is supposed to be open. But these are largely visible locally, and much harder to capture or communicate in state or national statistics.

So instead of public services, an Indian politician prefers to provide their favoured voters immediate and visible benefits, which the politician can be identified with and be rewarded for. Once benefits such as grain procurement at above-market prices are granted, beneficiaries see them as a right, and they become hard to change.[3] Indeed, one of the underlying fears in the recent farmer agitation against the proposed farm law reforms was that the government might stop procuring grain at the official above-market support prices, once a large segment of politically influential farmers sold their harvest to companies and private traders.[4]

Interestingly, incremental improvements in the system can entrench the bias towards targeted benefits further. In the past, benefits distribution did not work well—the manager in the government's ration shop skimmed off the grain intended for the poor customer. In despair, the poor would appeal to the local politician, who would put pressure on the ration shop operator to treat them fairly. In return, the local politician hoped to gain their vote. Ironically, as technological advances have improved delivery of targeted benefits—better data on delivery and sales allow for better monitoring of the ration shop operator—the local politician is no longer 'needed'. The top leadership in the state or national capital can now identify themselves with the delivery of a specific benefit such as cash transfers, toilets, food grains, gas cylinders or education loans, and directly build a personal rapport with the voter. So, the new Indian welfare state is cleaner, but it aggrandizes political leaders more, and for this reason they may have an incentive to skimp even more on the delivery of public services and tilt towards targeted benefits.

The greater skill and education intensity required for available jobs though has increased the public's demand for high-quality public services. A strong, empowered local government tier would help here; a sarpanch could claim credit for making the local primary health-care centre better. Her electorate could see the change with their eyes and experience the benefits, and the sarpanch would be rewarded in the next election. Arming people with better data and information on the quality of public services—for instance, a school's test scores—can also help increase pressure on local public officials to provide better services. And, of course, while we are sceptical of in-kind direct benefits, such as unlimited free power, direct cash transfers can empower the very poor by giving them the money to choose private-sector service providers over government ones. Competition will discipline public providers. Taken together, these actions can improve the quality of public services that are delivered, especially to the very poor.

Enabling Frameworks Rather than Directing Outcomes

For far too long, the government has tried to determine the sectors that the Indian economy should pursue, the size businesses should have, the nature of the capital equipment they should operate and how firms should be owned. Today's intervention takes the form of tariff protection plus production-linked incentives, which are applied by the Central government to large firms in specific sectors without a transparent articulation of which sectors ought to get protection and subsidies and why. India's past experience suggests government is not good at making these choices.

Rather than influencing outcomes through corporate freebies (of course, every benefiting corporate leader will swear to their value), government should create enabling frameworks. For instance, the government could improve the quality of available workers (through public services like education and skilling), make available competitively priced power, water, broadband, speedy logistics and other relevant infrastructure. Business also needs moderate and predictable taxes and tariffs, and clear and relatively stable regulations and laws, preferably light but effective ones. Development, including of critical physical infrastructure such as affordable housing, would be easier if land were demarked clearly, ownership clarified, and land acquisition and re-zoning were fair, transparent and straightforward. Put all these together and we create the ideal conditions for the emergence of new firms and competition between businesses, which is the greatest spur to improving productivity and growth.

None of this requires the government to champion manufacturing or services, or specific sectors within manufacturing. While the government will have to make choices about the allocation of its scarce resources, it should spend in a way that is broadly agnostic about what will work, letting the energy of India's businesspeople figure out what sectors to focus on for themselves. Of course, certain sectors may need specific policy or infrastructure support that only the government can provide. Consider, for example, a truly effective government-created public infrastructure: the India Stack.

The India Stack

In 2009, the United Progressive Alliance government in India was voted back into office. Along with Abhijit Banerjee, who later won the Nobel Prize in Economics, and C.K. Prahalad, a world-renowned management guru, Raghu, who was then an economic adviser to Prime Minister Manmohan Singh, wrote a letter outlining some of the steps the government could take in its first 100 days. One of the suggestions made was that the government should roll out the much-discussed unique ID programme, which had got stuck in bureaucratic red tape. Whether that letter made a difference, we do not know. But in a stroke of genius, Dr Singh persuaded Nandan Nilekani, a founder and one-time CEO of Infosys, one of India's largest software services firms, to drive the project.

Nilekani was not content with rolling out the largest ID programme in the world. He and his team wanted it to be the basis of a digital revolution in India, and hence they wanted to design an enabling framework that would support the revolution. This is important, for far too often government programmes are overly narrow and prescriptive, and do little to harness the energy of our people. In fact, they often do not achieve their aims because they have an overly rigid view of how citizens will respond to the programme. When citizens, as is their wont, respond differently, government programmes fall short because they are not designed to be adaptive.

The India Stack, as the framework is called, is different. It has three layers. An identity layer assigns a unique digital ID to each individual—the Aadhaar number essentially links an individual to their biometric data, such as fingerprints or iris scans. Since biometric data are unique, and supporting data, like name, address and passport number, can be layered on, this identity layer has many uses. It can certainly authenticate an individual and allow them to obtain a bank account or cell-phone account. For example, with the help of Aadhaar, mobile giant Reliance Jio onboarded over 100 million customers within its first six months.[5] But the stack can do much more. With the simple requirement that an individual's tax ID be linked to the individual's unique ID, the tax authorities can eliminate the many fraudulent tax accounts created by unscrupulous individuals to evade their tax liability.

The second layer is the payment layer. Commercial transactions often have to be completed with payments. The Unified Payments Interface (UPI) allows anyone to pay anyone else via an app, knowing only the recipient's chosen alias (such as rohit@econ) or QR code or their mobile number, with transfers taking place in the background from one's bank account to the other's account. It was launched when Raghu was RBI governor in 2016. Little did he imagine that one day, street vendors across India would receive payment via UPI, with over 10 billion transactions taking place in August 2023.[6]

The third layer, the data layer, allows individual data histories tied to their ID to be shared with whomsoever an individual chooses to give their consent to. Intermediaries known as account aggregators can allow individuals to see all their accounts at one go, but also give others consent-based access. For instance, a street vendor might want to share data on all her incoming customer payments with a bank, so that the bank can lend against the revenues she is generating. In the past, because her transactions were in cash, there would be no record of them, and she would not be able to borrow money to expand her business because she had no collateral to pledge. Today she can. Researchers show that after the implementation of UPI, households in districts where lead banks adopted UPI early tend to have 5.8 per cent higher income, 1.45 per cent higher levels of business ownership and 19 per cent higher business income than households in districts that adopted UPI late.[7] Households reliant on self-employment benefitted in particular.

Many businesses have been started based on the India Stack. For instance, Zerodha and Upstox, zero-commission brokerages that are the largest in India by market share, use the identity and payment layers of the India Stack to onboard users quickly, which enables them to start trading with their mobile phones.[8] India needs many more of its people to invest in shares, providing risk capital to businesses, while also benefiting from their success. By reducing the costs of equity investment to investors and easing access, the India Stack offers that opportunity to many more.

The technology underlying the India Stack is not complicated. What is new is that it is designed to be easily accessible, modular and interoperable. Ease of access is not just about whether any device, including ordinary mobile phones, can be used to tap easily into it, but also about the cost of that access. Competition is key here in keeping down the cost to the consumer. One important decision Raghu's RBI had to make on UPI was whether to restrict usage to the banks. These were then the dominant payment providers, and they were lobbying to keep it that way. The alternative was to open it to non-banks too, such as fintech companies. Persuaded by Nilekani that competition was essential to the design, the RBI allowed non-banks to offer payment services on UPI. Today, nearly 95 per cent of UPI transactions go through non-banks such as PhonePe, Google Pay and Paytm, so much so that restrictions on them are being contemplated to allow banks to compete! There is a larger point here. Rather than a framework favouring one or the other party, ideally it should create a level playing field, where the most efficient emerge on top.

The modularity of India Stack allows a variety of apps to be designed and plugged into its various layers. Applications that were probably not dreamt of when the stack was designed can be created. For instance, medical records can be stored and selectively shared. Finally, the requirement of, and constant focus on, interoperability ensures that no one can lock customers in. Every provider's system has to be able to work with other providers' systems and with the stack. In many other countries, privately provided digital ecosystems ensure the customer cannot shift their business and data to some other provider's ecosystem. This locks the customer in and allows the provider to charge enormous fees over time. Because the India Stack is a well-designed digital public infrastructure, it is much more difficult for businesses to lock customers in digitally, creating the much-needed competition that spurs growth and productivity. The India Stack offers a great example of an enabling framework.

Pruning Old Laws and Creating New Frameworks

India has a plethora of laws and regulations covering every conceivable aspect of life, many dating back to colonial times. Far too many tomes have been written about the need to streamline them, to reduce red tape and the associated corruption, for us to have anything new to say. But there may be additional ways of making navigation easier.

The RBI has a process by which all the regulations covering an activity are gathered together in a master circular, which is updated periodically. This allows regulators to understand what they require of the regulated and to eliminate inconsistencies. It also allows the regulated to know what is expected of them, not always an easy task. Master circulars could be created for every government-regulated activity. Periodic pruning of the master circular to eliminate unnecessary regulations as well as translation into user-friendly language—if you want to open a restaurant, here are the steps you must take—would improve the effectiveness of regulation.

One of the ironies of bureaucracy is that, while in office, the bureaucrat, aided by assistants who can call up other assistants and get their personal work done, never gets to see what a nightmare bureaucratic regulations create. That becomes clear perhaps only after retirement, when the assistants are gone and the retired bureaucrat must face the full weight of the bureaucracy on his own. If the policymaker understood the unnecessary weight of the regulatory state, maybe change would be easier. At the RBI, Raghu believed customer regulations would become more user-friendly if one day every year senior officers were given some task to carry out at a bank—such as opening a trust account—without using their assistants and without revealing they were RBI officials. He termed the programme 'Retired for a Day', but somehow his staff never managed to set a date for it. Raghu wonders why!

While we need to prune many existing regulations, we also need new ones. For instance, the data collected by the India Stack, despite controls, can be abused. In the landmark Puttaswamy case in 2017, the Indian Supreme Court rejected the government's stance that there was no fundamental right to privacy, and instead held that under the Constitution the right to privacy was 'an intrinsic part of the right to life and personal liberty'.[9] Since then, the government has enacted a law requiring companies to respect the privacy of their customers.

What it has not done is to enact safeguards against the potential misuse of data by an intrusive government. The possibility that a government may require companies to reveal the data they have collected on their customers may make data-intensive service exports hard. There is growing opposition in the United States to allowing a Chinese-owned company like TikTok to operate freely in the US and acquire enormous amounts of data on ordinary Americans.[10] The US authorities fear that TikTok will not be able to refuse a Chinese government request for sensitive data on US citizens—data that could be used to potentially brainwash or trap their citizens, or even blackmail them into spying. Might they fear an Indian government exercising sway over an India company if the law allows it?

Foreign companies may also feel uncomfortable approaching Indian consulting, tax or legal firms for services if we don't have strong data protection laws. What if the Indian tax authorities, who are not shy or always correct in their tax demands, go on a fishing expedition, looking through privately shared data for potential violations of tax laws? Under Indian law, even illegally collected evidence can be used by the government against an accused.

Strong data protection, with government intrusion being limited to the rarest of rare cases and requiring prior approval by an independent panel, say, of judges, might finally give Indians the full privacy they deserve and foreigners the confidence they need. As of now, intrusion only has to be blessed by a panel of bureaucrats, who have little incentive to limit government actions.[11] This is particularly worrisome as new cyber tools allow government agencies to spy easily on anyone, including leaders of the Opposition. Even if the agencies can resist pressure from government ministers to engage in political espionage (as distinct from spying for reasons of national security), there are few restraints on rogue officials using such tools for corrupt or perverse purposes. As legal scholar Gautam Bhatia argues, India has to move from a culture of authority (where the state's actions are seldom questioned) to a culture of justification (where the state's actions have to be justified).[12] The government would then work better for our people. It is also essential for our future growth.

Regulatory Enforcement

Aside from new enabling legislation in areas from fintech to artificial intelligence, India needs to strengthen regulatory enforcement. We referred earlier to India's success in manufacturing generic drugs, with drug exports amounting to $25.4 billion in 2022–23. Yet, India's regulation of pharmaceutical drugs leaves many gaps.

Regulation is partly in the hands of the Central government, which approves new drugs and drug imports, and partly in the hands of state governments, which enforce regulations. And enforcement focuses more on testing the produced drugs rather than inspecting the production process. And even when violations are uncovered, the data are not easily shared across jurisdictions, nor are penalties swift. So violators find ways of continuing to operate.

Western countries have understood this. The Food and Drug Administration (FDA) of the United States, not trusting the Indian regulatory process, uses its own inspectors to inspect the factories of Indian exporters to the United States. In 2011, drug manufacturer Ranbaxy paid a huge fine to the US Justice Department for violations in its production processes, but its troubles continued, and its products were banned again in 2014.[13] This is an embarrassing reflection of the need for India to step up its own regulation, if nothing else, for the safety of our citizens.

Unfortunately, poorer developing countries do not have an effective layer of their own regulation to compensate for India's deficiencies. In 2022, the WHO warned that cough syrup made by an Indian manufacturer was responsible for seventy deaths of children in the West African nation of The Gambia.[14] The syrup were found to have excessively high amounts of poisonous diethylene glycol and ethylene glycol. Worryingly, the company had previously been flagged for substandard products by the state of Kerala and by Vietnam, with the Indian consul general there even highlighting the damage to India's reputation done by the manufacturer. In contrast, though, the initial reaction of the controller general of drugs in India to the child deaths was to avoid responsibility, saying that the medicines had been tested by a government laboratory and no toxins were found. Instead, he blamed the narrative promoted by the world media. Eventually, Indian authorities raided the production site and closed it down, but the damage had been done—as one disconsolate Gambian father lamented, '. . . now her twin sister always asks where her twin is.'

More generally, even as we prune regulations in every area, what is left on the books must be enforced strictly. When violations are proven, violators must be strictly penalized. That also means measuring the performance of regulators and holding them to task. Else business will suffer the burdens of regulation without the benefits, with a few rogues bringing the whole system into disrepute.

Experimentation

On the new path we propose, it will be important for India to encourage the emergence of creative new firms and new sectors. With new sectors, there is the twin risk—of regulating excessively early on and killing innovation, or waiting too long and finding that huge risks have built up in the system. For instance, with cryptocurrencies, the Indian approach was to ban them early and drive them into the shadows, while the US approach was to let them flourish without regulation until they became a $3-trillion problem. An intermediate approach, of allowing experimentation at a small scale or in a specific region, with the permission, and under the watchful eye, of the regulator—what is sometimes called the sandbox approach—might permit innovation without the system taking on too much risk. We will have to do more of this.

A similar approach is needed for momentous policy decisions. Should decisions be sudden and bold, or should they be slower, contemplative decisions, based on consultation and evidence? Sudden decisions can unsettle vested interests. Yet by their very nature, they occur without much consultation, are often based on short-term political calculations and can have unintended effects, especially in large, complex modern economies. Arguably, the 1969 nationalization of banks and the 2016 demonetization both fall in this category.

The Chinese had a way of describing their reforms—crossing the river by feeling the stones. Essentially, they felt the next stone in the bridge of stones across the river to see if it was stable before stepping on it. Put differently, rather than taking huge untested steps, reforms used to occur incrementally and after experimentation. Often the reform was tested in a few localities or in a specific sector to learn what its effects might be and to iron out any teething problems. Then, as the authorities gained confidence that the reform worked, it was rolled out nationally. Again, we use the past tense since it is no longer clear that China under President Xi Jinping operates this way.

In India, some of that experimentation takes place naturally because we have a variety of state governments with different reform programmes, but experimentation should be an active part of any reform proposal wherever possible. If India's Goods and Services Tax had been rolled out only after it had been debugged by asking a few districts or states to operate the system in parallel with the existing system, perhaps the 2017 rollout would have been less fraught with difficulty. As the economy gets more complex and governance more difficult, experimentation, evaluation, consultation, redesign and rollout may become much more effective than bold but not fully thought-out action.

Ensuring Competition

The lifeblood of a modern dynamic economy is competition. Key to competition is a level playing field—the government should support everyone equally, not favour large firms over small firms, public-sector firms over private-sector firms or vice versa, or encourage domestic monopolies under the guise of creating national champions.

Form should not dominate over substance in assessing competition. For instance, it is sometimes assumed that holding a public auction is sufficient to ensure that the bid is competitive. Auctions can be rigged; detailed minimum qualifications of who is allowed to bid in the auction, sometimes unnecessary to achieving better outcomes, often rule out many worthy bidders—and sometimes that is the intent. Once the winning bid is announced, winners with clout will renegotiate the terms of the deal so that their all-too-low bid, intended solely to beat the competition, is viable. And in some auctions, unscrupulous powerful players threaten to punish anyone else who places a bid, ensuring they win easily. Transparency in government actions and public scrutiny of procedures is therefore essential.

Almost surely, though, powerful players will find ways around such checks and balances. The United States has historically developed a practice whereby a single firm or sector that gets too big is broken up, so that it does not exercise excessive economic or political power. Hence Standard Oil, AT&T, IBM, Microsoft and now the tech giants have come under regulatory scrutiny, and have sometimes been forced to break up or to abandon monopolistic practices. The US banking sector was required to separate commercial from investment banking by the Glass–Steagall Act of 1933, which gave us J.P. Morgan and Morgan Stanley. While corporate lobbying is still rife in the United States, it would be hard to argue that any firm has unlimited political clout in the United States. Cronyism exists, but crony capitalism does not dominate the political dialogue.

While India's Monopolies and Restrictive Trade Practices Act (MRTP), 1969, aimed to limit concentration of wealth and control over production in India, its limits on firm size were set too low. Successful conglomerates found it hard to expand, and MRTP became an integral part of the oppressive Licence/Permit Raj, placing enormous discretionary powers of approval in the hands of bureaucrats. It was deservedly repealed in 2009, and its objectives delegated to the Competition Commission of India (CCI). While the website of the CCI is replete with orders against bid-rigging, the key question is whether it has succeeded in maintaining the competitiveness of Indian industry and prevented the excessive enlargement of a few players. The answer, unfortunately, is not reassuring.

In an important study published by the Brookings Institution, Viral Acharya of New York University and a former deputy governor of the Reserve Bank of India shows that by 2009, private conglomerates were the largest five non-financial groups by assets in the economy.

Perhaps because of the slowdown induced by the global financial crisis, and perhaps because of the initial zeal of the CCI, the share of assets of the top five groups subsequently fell. Since 2015, however, with the current government's accent on creating national champions, the top five private conglomerates own a larger and larger share of each industry sector's assets. Acharya argues that this is partly because of India's reversion to protectionism, which has kept out foreign competition; India's average import tariffs in 2022, at 18.1 per cent, were fifth highest in the World Trade Organization's records, only behind Sudan, Tunisia, Algeria and Uganda.[15]

It may also be because of the CCI's passivity. Acharya shows that the share of mergers and acquisitions by top five conglomerates more than doubled from 2014, while the share of the next five by size remained relatively flat. Since the CCI is primarily responsible for evaluating the effects of mergers on industry concentration, it certainly has allowed the growing asset concentration.

The Competition Commission should oppose mergers that lead to excessive concentration. This may require it to be more independent. And the government needs to move away from freebies for specific industries and from favouring specific groups towards improving conditions for all businesses. Rather than privileging national champions, it needs to give all firms a fair chance, whether public sector or private sector, small or large. A critical part of every enabling framework has to be free competition.

Election Funding

One of the breeding grounds for business–government cronyism is opaque election funding. An estimated Rs 55,000–60,000 crore was spent in the 2019 Lok Sabha election; the Centre for Media Studies called it the 'most expensive election ever, anywhere'. There are widespread worries that such massive spending is neither cleanly nor transparently funded.

Concerned that 'political parties continue to receive most of their funds through anonymous donations which are shown in cash', the late finance minister Arun Jaitley argued that 'an effort, therefore, requires to be made to cleanse the system of political funding in India'.[16] To do so, electoral bonds were introduced in 2018. Anonymous cash donations were capped at Rs 2000, while electoral bonds in denominations ranging from Rs 1000 to Rs 1 crore could be bought by Indian citizens from the State Bank of India and donated to any political party of their choice. Over the past four years, more than Rs 12,000 crore's worth of bonds have been issued.

Unfortunately, electoral bonds in their current form are no solution to cronyism and probably exacerbate it. These bonds do not improve transparency. The name of the donor is hidden from the public and other political parties. According to the Association for Democratic Reforms, over 90 per cent of the amounts issued so far are in the Rs 1-crore slab, which must come from very rich individuals and corporations. The public simply cannot judge whether these donations were made out of goodwill or there was a quid pro quo, even pressure, involved.

For instance, if the public saw that companies from sectors that benefited from tariff protection, from state subsidies, from the auction of public assets or from public-sector bank loans, donated more, they could put two and two together and vote in a more informed way. This is not possible under the current system, which makes it fail the test of cleanliness that Arun Jaitley talked about. No wonder the Election Commission objected to the bonds.

Such bonds also may be misused by the incumbent government. Since bonds are issued by public-sector banks, an unprincipled government might apply pressure on officials to learn the names of donors and recipients. Knowing this, and given the carrots and sticks at the government's disposal, few individuals or corporations would risk donating large sums to the Opposition through these bonds. Any donations would have to be made through the now-illegal, but hidden-from-government, cash route. But then, the ruling party can use investigative agencies to target unaccounted-for cash, which Opposition parties may be forced to use disproportionately. Election-time raids on Opposition leaders will invariably reveal cash hoards, allowing the ruling party to label them corrupt. Without defending illegality, it is easy to see how the system may be skewed towards the incumbent who gets the lion's share of legal bond donations.

Our objective should indeed be to make all electoral spending clean, even while minimizing incumbency bias. While making the list of donors public will help, we would also need to ensure that those who donate to the Opposition are protected from government harassment. Other possibilities include funding parties with public money based on their share of vote in prior elections, with an upper limit on such funding so that no party gets an extreme advantage, and limiting the amounts any individual entity can give.

Change from Within

There is much that can be done to reform government to make it nimbler and more attuned to the needs of Indians on the road ahead. Government is a leviathan, and it is hard to imagine that change will happen easily or quickly. But there are many idealistic and capable government officials who are looking to change. Indeed, one person can make a difference. Few would dispute the idea that T.N. Seshan, chief election commissioner between 1990 and 1996, cleaned up Indian elections significantly and gave the Election Commission a stature it had never held before. Before his tenure, 'booth capturing', whereby armed thugs took over polling booths and marked all votes for their patrons, was common. After his tenure, it became a rarity.[17] The coming challenges will make it imperative that India's institutions find more Seshans, who strive to achieve the objectives of their institutions by asserting their independence.

7

Capabilities: The Childhood Challenge

One purpose of economic development is to enhance the capabilities of our people, which will give them the health to live longer, more energetic lives and the education to make their lives more fulfilling. But enhanced capabilities themselves are also the key to better jobs, higher incomes and, thus, economic development. As we reimagine India's economic future and take the less-travelled path, it is the education, skills and health of our people, that is, the quality of our human capital, more than our bridges and airports, that will determine how rapidly we ascend the development ladder. Human capital will be essential, whether our businesses choose to focus on manufacturing or services, for the space for low-skilled or unskilled labour is shrinking rapidly today.

India's challenges start early, with maternal and child nutrition. Many of our children are born underweight and then continue to be malnourished well into the first few years of their lives. In schools, primary education has cracked the problem of enrolment, but learning outcomes for our kids are poor. This combination of poor early health and learning constrains our children's growth, cognitively and physically, and limits how much they can absorb later in life.

Over the last couple of decades, researchers from across the world have studied Indian data to propose solutions—some went on to win the Nobel Prize along the way. Indeed, India's National Education Policy, put out in 2020, is both brief and offers clear proposals, many of which we agree with it. The roadblock often has to do with implementation.

Raghu recalls a joke that the South Korean executive director at the International Monetary Fund (IMF) told him when Raghu marvelled at how much South Korea had achieved, even though it had been as poor as India in the 1960s: The Indian finance minister was once on a trip to Seoul. In the Korean finance minister's office, the Indian minister asked him the secret of Korea's success. The Korean minister pointed to a set of thick black tomes lining the shelf behind. 'It is all in there,' he said. The Indian finance minister went closer to read their titles, laughed and said, 'Why, these are our Five-Year Plans!' Pat came the response: 'Yes, but we implemented them!'

What hinders implementation? We have already argued that the political establishment, both at the Centre and at the state level, is much less concerned with providing public services, focusing instead on providing targeted benefits and freebies. Decentralization will help change this dynamic. Experimenting with different approaches, learning what works by gathering data and rigorously evaluating them, engaging people by empowering and informing them, using technology wherever possible and addressing incentives, including the vested interests in the system that resist change, will be key elements of the approaches we will suggest in this and subsequent chapters.

Nutrition

A child is deemed stunted—too short for its age—if it falls below two standard deviations from the median height-for-age of the World Health Organization's Child Growth Standards. In 2020, after more than three decades of strong growth, an unacceptable 35 per cent of our children younger than five years old were stunted. Many poorer countries in Sub-Saharan Africa, such as Tanzania, Liberia and Senegal, do better.

Some have challenged this metric, arguing that Indians' genetics give them a different growth, that is height-for-age, pattern. Yet Sri Lankans, who presumably come from similar gene pools, have a much lower level of stunting than Indians, and studies have found that South Asian children in the United States and the United Kingdom approach the mean height of their peers within one generation;[1] so it is not entirely 'genetics'. We are simply not feeding our pregnant mothers and children well enough!

Even within India, the heterogeneity is stark. If you take a train from the north of the country to the east, stopping in small towns, as Rohit did sometime ago, you will clearly notice how the average height decreases steadily from Punjab and Haryana to western Uttar Pradesh (UP) and then eastern UP and Bihar. Our people are simply less nourished in UP and Bihar than in Punjab and Haryana. According to the National Family Health Survey 2019–21, stunting in Punjab is 24 per cent, and in Bihar it is 43 per cent; moreover, 12 per cent of women in Punjab have body mass index below normal, and it is 25 per cent in Bihar.

Sustained childhood malnourishment can reduce an adult's intellectual and work capacity significantly, and make them more prone to diseases and heart conditions.[2] In other words, if we want healthier, more productive citizens in the future, our most urgent task is to combat malnutrition. Unfortunately, for too many Indians, it is already too late.

A host of factors contribute to malnutrition. Clearly, poverty reduces access to food, but abject poverty has been on the decline, and the government has various programmes to distribute food to the disadvantaged. Eating patterns and habits, especially of the pregnant mother and then of the newborn, are also important. Many women in the childbearing age in India are anaemic and hence more likely to give birth to nutritionally weak children. If a family has dietary restrictions, such as vegetarianism, it is all the more necessary that vulnerable members get a planned and balanced diet.

Poor sanitation and disease contribute to all this. If a village lacks clean drinking water and a child has chronic diarrhoea, she may be unable to absorb key nutrients even if these are fed to her regularly. Open defecation distributes faecal matter in the soil, contributing to such diseases—the positive impact of government's campaign to install toilets in every home and stop open defecation should soon start showing up in the statistics. Finally, social norms also matter. Traditionally, adult males and sons among children are fed better than adult females and daughters. While these norms are changing, their effects still cast a shadow today.

The Integrated Child Development Scheme (ICDS) is the government's flagship programme to tackle child malnutrition. Under the ICDS, the main intermediary between the state and the mother and child is the Anganwadi worker, typically a middle-aged woman. She is trained in, and tasked with ensuring, the nutrition of pregnant and lactating mothers and young children in their communities. There are about 1.5 million Anganwadi workers in India. Fundamentally, the system works, but there is significant heterogeneity—it works better in India's south and west, and less so in the north and east.[3] Where is it going wrong?

To start with, the Anganwadi worker is not paid a full salary and does not have access to the usual benefits that come with a government job. Many studies have mentioned the lack of pay, motivation, training and infrastructure for the Anganwadi worker as potential impediments. In an audit done by the Comptroller and Auditor General of India in 2013, it was found that 61 per cent of the Anganwadis did not even have their own building and many did not have basic weighing machines. The Anganwadi lacks human resources, funds and even bureaucratic support, and workers lack status and recognition.

Even though the system is spread too thin, the best way to move forward is to bolster the Anganwadi's capacity and supplement it with outside programmes. If the Anganwadi gets a physical location near a primary school, its charges could also get the midday meal prepared for schoolchildren and benefit from the added nutrition.

Over 85 per cent of a child's cumulative brain development occurs before age six, so it is important that Anganwadis, where 66.8 per cent of three-year-olds are enrolled, be upgraded with facilities for 'play-based, activity-based, and inquiry-based learning'.[4] Studies show that adding an extra worker who is focused on education to an Anganwadi can improve the preparedness of the children for primary school, as well as improve their nutrition, since it frees up the primary Anganwadi worker to focus on health.[5] If a young mother could help play-teach children while the Anganwadi worker focuses on the nutritional elements, there could be significant improvements in child preparedness for primary school.

Statewide, and nationwide, we need a more concerted publicity campaign, on par with the campaign against polio, informing the public how eating habits and social norms are contributing to stunted growth in children. Decentralization will also help, for what must be done in the Anganwadi will vary from area to area. For instance, in richer communities, women may not come to the Anganwadi but may benefit from nutritional advice. Local administrators should tailor the activities of the Anganwadi to their area's needs. Currently, workers' salaries are set at the state level because the funding comes from both the Central and state governments. Local administrators could have some leeway in setting the Anganwadi worker's pay and targets, and they themselves could have targets for stunting in their areas. A different agency could measure stunting in these areas, so that there is a separation of effort and evaluation.

We can learn from global success stories. Peru cut its stunting rate by over half in less than ten years, from 28 per cent in 2008 to 13 per cent in 2016, and it is not the only country to do so.[6] Peru had tried to tackle malnutrition for years, without much success. It had focused, much like India at present, on increasing food outlays and spending. But despite urbanization, increased literacy among women and better access to clean water, the stunting persisted. Starting in 2007, Peru changed tack: it made stunting not just a developmental issue but, through pressure from civil society groups, also a political one, so successive governments wanted to work to reduce the numbers.

In terms of policy, Peru shifted to a more localized system of outcome-based rewards for workers.[7] At the outset, the yearly resources devoted to the national nutritional strategy were also doubled. A results-based budgeting system was implemented to ensure that money was being spent judiciously, directed at achieving the results that politicians had promised. Regional governments were also provided with monetary incentives, encouraging them to offer more and better nutrition services. Cash incentives, through a conditional cash transfer programme known as Juntos (Together), were given to mothers, requiring them to take toddlers for growth monitoring and check-ups at health centres, and to ensure that their older children attended school. Peru also emphasized the communication and dissemination of information, so that the 'invisible problem' of stunting became 'visible' to parents.

While India needs to increase resources devoted to the problem, it also needs to redesign interventions based on what works, adopt creative incentive schemes based on outcome data and train local staff well. Instead of sweeping the shameful statistics on stunting under the carpet, political leaders should highlight them and mobilize society to eradicate stunting once and for all.

Schooling

Turning to education, India has laudably cracked the first step, which is enrolment in primary education. In 2002, the 86th Amendment to the Constitution finally made free and compulsory education to children between six and fourteen years a fundamental right. Subsequently, under the Sarva Shiksha Abhiyan (programme for universal education), new schools were opened in habitations that didn't have any schools and existing schools obtained additional teachers, teacher training, classrooms, toilets, drinking water and school improvement grants.

Other factors, such as the Midday Meal Scheme and the offer of free bicycles to girls for attending school, as well as the growing need for education and skills in the job market, led many more parents to put their children into school. One estimate suggests that India has close to 1.5 million schools and around 8 million teachers, and the enrolment rates are more than 95 per cent in the early years.

But learning outcomes, unfortunately, have lagged enrolment considerably, as the Annual Status of Education Report statistics cited in the introduction to this book suggest. The pandemic has taken an additional toll, with learning outcomes deteriorating further.

Why is learning performance so bad? With very imperfect means of measurement until the tenth- or twelfth-class external board exam, principals and parents evaluate teachers on whether they have finished the set syllabus. The typical curriculum requires that the teacher maintain a fast pace. Add to that the high teacher absenteeism in government schools—studies find that teachers are absent from government schools 25 per cent of the time across India, more so in poorer states. Consequently, the teacher has to rush through rather than ensuring that all or at least most students in the class learn.[8] Also, since there is no time for deep explanations or discussions, the system incentivizes rote learning as opposed to creative thinking.

Worse, it damages many students. For students come into a class with differing degrees of preparation and different speeds of absorbing the material. Unfortunately, even the most diligent of teachers has little time to ensure that everyone is following, as they have to complete the curriculum by the end of the year. As a student falls behind in class, she understands less and less. And if she is promoted without acquiring all the skills meant to be acquired in a particular grade, she is even worse off in the next grade. When she cannot read well, how will she go through her history textbook, let alone understand why Siraj-ud-Daulah lost the Battle of Plassey?

Karthik Muralidharan, an economist who studies education, has an interesting way of making this clear to an audience. He starts speaking in Tamil! In many parts of India, this language is, of course, incomprehensible to most of the audience. It effectively brings home the daily experience of a student who falls behind—lectures in class do not make sense and become really dull.

Parents who can afford private tuitions pay for it, often hiring the same teacher who fails to engage students in class. Nationally, the proportion of children in rural areas in primary and middle school taking paid private tuition classes was 30.5 per cent in 2022.[9] Those who cannot afford such luxuries, typically the children of the poor, drop out. The 2020 National Education Policy (NEP) reports that the gross enrolment ratio (the fraction of the relevant population in class) for classes 6–8 is 90.9 per cent, while for classes 9–10 and 11–12 it is 79.3 per cent and 56.5 per cent, respectively. The NEP estimates that 32 million children in the age group of 6–17 were out of school, and this was before the pandemic! In a recent survey in Bihar, after the devastation inflicted by Covid on student learning, half the schools surveyed reported that most students in classes 3–5 had forgotten how to read and write by the time schools reopened. Attendance was reported to be around 20 per cent of children enrolled, suggesting a massive dropout rate.[10]

In sum, too many students drop out, especially after class eight, and it has much to do with the difficulty they have in learning. The key school focus over the next decade should be on improving the quality of learning experience for all our children.

The Delhi Experiment

Delhi state's schools seem to have undergone a seismic shift. In 2019, for the first time, the government schools had a better overall pass rate (at 98 per cent) in the class twelve board exam than private schools (at 92 per cent). The system has been infused with a sense of optimism, and the satisfaction reported by teachers and parents seems to reflect that. The approach has been largely scientific, as experts have been consulted on what might work and policies have been scaled after modifying them based on results and feedback. Interestingly, perhaps because Delhi is effectively one connected community (albeit a large one) and the government effectively a city government, it has been able to put education (and health) front and centre of local politics.

The Boston Consulting Group (BCG) conducted a comprehensive study of the Delhi school reforms for the 2015–20 period.[11] They found that the allocations to capital expenditure went up from Rs 51 crore in 2014–15 to a yearly average of Rs 346 crore between 2015–16 and 2019–20. Better, freshly painted and clean school buildings, brighter, well-lit classrooms, new libraries and improved laboratories, and access to safe drinking water and clean toilets were visible improvements that drew students into the schools. The administration also set up specialist schools for the performing arts and for science subjects, thus catering to the especially talented.

The administration also focused on improving the working conditions of teachers—hiring more teachers to manage the workload, offering mentorship for underperforming and junior teachers and sending some, including headmasters, overseas for training.[12] More financial powers have been delegated to school management committees, giving teachers and parents a sense of empowerment.

Most importantly, the gap in learning outcomes for children below class eight has been recognized and taken head-on in designing curricula. In Mission Buniyaad (the word 'buniyaad' means foundation), the focus is on helping children read fluently, write without mistakes and understand basic arithmetic. This is an attempt to ensure that no child is left behind. Mission Buniyaad is supplemented with the Chunauti (challenge) initiatives, where students in each class are placed into small groups based on the skills they have and given different degrees of additional support.

The NEP stated, 'The aim of education will not only be cognitive development, but also building character and creating holistic and well-rounded individuals equipped with the key 21st century skills.' The Happiness Curriculum introduced by the Delhi government is targeted at some of these objectives. This is a forty-five-minute class every morning where students are introduced to concepts of happiness, framed by philosopher A. Nagraj as states of harmony and acceptance, where the self, family, society and the environment coexist without conflict.[13] Perhaps the Happiness Curriculum has helped in moving teachers away from a single-minded focus on completing the syllabus, and towards making classes more fun and inclusive. At any rate, school performance on traditional metrics does not seem to have been adversely affected.

Interestingly, the Happiness Curriculum gives way in classes nine and above to the Entrepreneurship Curriculum, which aims to inculcate an entrepreneurial mindset in students. The intent is that they should apply this mindset, along with skills of critical thinking, to career choices.

Before moving on, it is useful to highlight two additional features of Delhi's educational policies. First, the government deploys Anganwadi workers and volunteers to conduct door-to-door surveys of households to identify students who have dropped out and entice them back to the reformed schools. This is particularly important after the Covid pandemic, when so many more have dropped out.

Second, the so-called Delhi model has invested in a participatory process that engages and empowers all stakeholders—students, parents, teachers, headmasters and principals—in improving the condition of schools. Commenting on the restructuring of the school management committee (SMC), a parent, quoted in Hinglish in the BCG report, captures this succinctly: '*SMC hone ke karan ek "sense of ownership" aa gayi hai, kyunki humaare bachche bhi inhi schools mey padhte hai, toh jitna hum karenge utna unko laabh hoga* [SMCs have helped to create a "sense of ownership", because our children go to the same schools, so the more we do, the more they will benefit].'

As is always the case, not everything has worked on the ground as planned, and Covid dampened some of the early success. But much has worked. Both decision-making power and resources have been devolved to the local functionaries, and faith has been reposed in their judgement. Information has been made freely available in this participatory process, so changes can be calibrated to feedback. Finally, the top leadership seems to be available to address grievances.

While the Delhi government reforms are a good example of how favourable learning outcomes can be achieved when there is motivation and purpose from the top, there are questions of applicability and scalability. Delhi is one of the richest states per capita and can spend significantly more per school than most other states. It is also a small state, so it is effectively decentralized; the reforms have so far been applied to about 1000, mostly urban, schools; an average district in India has twice that number.

Nevertheless, the ideas of focusing, in initial classes, on universal foundational literacy and numeracy, so that the student can become a self-sustaining learning machine; bringing teachers and parents together at the heart of the learning process; using regular assessments to figure out which students need help; reducing curriculum overload; and going beyond conceptual understanding to encouraging creativity and critical thinking in young minds—all these are worth emulating elsewhere.

Other Possible Reforms

As with Anganwadis, many of India's primary schools can benefit from an additional worker who helps the teacher by taking care of the learning needs of a subset of students. All such a worker needs are sound foundational reading and arithmetic skills. Indeed, one educator who runs a large and effective NGO told us that this could be worthwhile employment for many mothers who have spare time because they are otherwise not working outside the house. Three birds—teacher assistance, parental engagement and greater women's labour force participation—would thus be killed with one stone.

Purist educators would shudder at the suggestion that untrained volunteers be used to teach children. The NEP even suggests that all teachers be required to get a BEd in education. There is little evidence that such degrees improve the quality of teaching significantly, over and above what can be learnt from experience. Given the magnitude of the dropout problem, we cannot wait till enough teachers have been trained. Moreover, employing only trained teachers would be extremely expensive.

Indeed, with an adequate screening process, perhaps schools can go beyond parents. Following the advice of an advisory committee that Raghu was on, the Tamil Nadu government ran an after-school remedial programme run by community volunteers for 60–90 minutes daily in the evening, called Illam Thedi Kalvi (Education at Doorstep). By June 2022, it employed approximately 2,00,000 volunteers, who were residents of local communities with high-school or college degrees but were not necessarily trained teachers. The programme provided supplementary instruction to 3.3 million students, led to a large increase in the instructional time for foundational skills. It showed positive measurable student learning results, within the span of a few months of operation.[14]

There is a broader point here. While we need to skill our people for the jobs they aspire for, we can also tailor the jobs according to the skills they have.

Failing Systems

We should not minimize the scale of the problem by focusing on well-run states like Delhi or Tamil Nadu. A recent report on the state of schools in Jharkhand suggests the scale of the problem elsewhere.

According to the reporter, eighty-eight pupils, the majority from the scheduled castes and scheduled tribes, study in two dingy classrooms in a school with a single teacher, without drinking water, functional toilets, a playground or a boundary wall.[15] The students, who have had no education for two years during Covid, cannot remember the last time they ate an egg in their midday meal, even though they are supposed to get it twice a week.

According to the report, 35 per cent of primary schools have a single teacher for all grades, half have no water supply, 54 per cent have no functional electricity connection and even those that have one have fans and tube lights missing. Teacher payments are delayed, as are funds for the midday meal, so much so that teachers sometimes use their own funds to pay for student meals. A recent survey further documented that in a majority of the primary schools in Jharkhand, 'most' pupils had forgotten how to read and write by the time schools reopened in February 2022.[16]

We can go on, but the point is that in poorer states, children, especially from weaker segments of society, are treated with a callousness that will jeopardize their future. If there is one priority for a reformist Central government, it should be to change this state of affairs, partly by supplementing state funds with its own funds, and partly by studying and spreading success stories elsewhere.

Restructuring Schools

Let us focus on one problem that is highlighted above. Since the 2010 Right to Education Act required that each child have a school within 1 km of their habitation, many small government schools have mushroomed. According to the responses given to a question in Parliament, around 8 per cent of all school students in India attend a school with one teacher; there is huge variation too—for instance, 40 per cent of the 2264 schools in district Alirajpur in Madhya Pradesh have one teacher.[17] Schools will fail to build foundational skills if teachers have too much to do. This is especially likely in the one-teacher schools that were set up to bring schooling to remote areas.

We need to consolidate such schools wherever ease of transportation allows, bussing in students to a common large school rather than having inadequate small schools everywhere. We must offer remote learning alternatives where transport is not easy. Where neither consolidation nor remote learning is possible, we must open well-managed boarding schools.

So, for instance, the role of the teacher in the one-teacher school in the Meghalaya highlands will be to see that all the students show up on time, log in to their lessons conducted by teachers in the state's capital and submit their homework regularly. She will provide assistance where needed and keep track of student assessments (done increasingly by chatbots), but her main role will be to oversee the student's holistic development rather than to teach specific subjects.

More generally, technology can be an aid in many ways even in the normal course of teaching, provided the teacher understands its usefulness as well as its limitations. She can point students to great lectures, documentaries and in-depth explanations of subjects touched on in class, such as those provided by Khan Academy. Class can even be inverted for the motivated students, with students listening to great lectures at homes, and discussing them or doing 'homework' assignments on them in class, with the teacher offering assistance where needed. Technology can also create regular assessments, which can be instantaneously graded. It can pinpoint the weaknesses of students falling behind and tailor lesson plans for them. Since such adaptive technology can be created at the Centre or state level, and then distributed to all schools, we have the possibility of genuinely distributed learning.

It is necessary, however, to train teachers in the use of technology, so that they use it as an aid rather than as a full substitute for their teaching. The engagement of the human teacher is important in motivating young students; even for mature, motivated students looking for professional qualifications, the completion rate of fully automated massive open online courses (MOOCs) is astonishingly low. Of course, for technology to be inclusive, all students should have access to the digital highway, for instance, with a laptop and an Internet connection. Since the costs of these have come down significantly, governments must help the poorest households to obtain them to further inclusive education. Orchids International School offers one example of scalable quality education.

Orchids The International Schools

Jai Decosta had a variety of experiences, including running *Femina* magazine's Miss India contest before he, along with other founders, started Orchids The International Schools in 2015. Orchids wants students to have a quality education at an affordable price. As Jai points out, India has venerable old schools, like Cathedral in Mumbai and St Columba's in Delhi, and they do charge an affordable price, but they are extremely hard to get into. How does one replicate their quality and scale up the numbers?

At the outset, Orchids' team, typically young professionals and subject-matter experts, deconstructed the school year into courses. Each course was then divided into forty-minute lesson plans, consisting of a few videos (none more than three minutes long, given the short attention span of students), presentations, problems and discussion segments, with each minute of the class accounted for. They developed 32,000 such plans, each of which is improved through trial and error.

Today, each of Orchids' 5000 teachers gets a lesson plan days before a class, giving them enough time to prepare. The school principal can check if teachers have accessed lesson plans in a timely fashion. Further, there is a CCTV in the classroom which records what teachers do, allowing course designers to get a sense of what needs fixing. The teacher and the principal can also do a 'postmortem' if the lesson falls short. After the class, the teacher sends a message to parents describing what was accomplished in class, thus keeping them abreast of what their child is doing in school.

Approximately every two weeks, students are tested, with multiple choice questions they turn in for grading, on the subject matter they have covered. Students that do not seem to have grasped the material are asked to come in on Saturdays for a refresher. Orchids sets a fast pace and emphasizes covering the lesson plan, but it does so in small digestible bits, and also identifies and helps those falling behind.

Orchids does incorporate a variety of other experiences in its classes, including public speaking in the English class, financial literacy in its mathematics classes, and hands-on projects in science and technology classes. It also emphasizes extracurricular activities like team sports and music—all students learn to play the piano, for example.

Teachers are evaluated on multiple dimensions, including by the students (though harsh student ratings are carefully investigated for bias). Underperforming teachers are let go. Orchids' management is also relentlessly focused on costs, renting premises from failing schools (typically schools teaching in vernacular languages) and buying everything in bulk, including pianos!

So the combination of micro-structured lesson plans delivered by teachers of reasonable quality, close monitoring of student and teacher performance, and the use of technology wherever possible produces a strong learning experience that is scalable across schools. While the student or teacher at an

Orchids school may not have the flexibility and freedom that might be available at a venerable old school, those old schools cannot be easily multiplied. Orchids' method deserves to be studied as one possible approach to India's schooling needs.

Orchids started with one school and 184 students. By 2023, it had 61,000 students in eighty schools spread over seventeen cities, and had licensed its methodology to a further 800 schools with 3,50,000 students. So if demand is the measure of success, it seems to be working.

Note that Orchids is not about rote learning but scripting the class better, so that average teachers can succeed and student learning be enhanced. In a careful study of Bridge International Academies, a chain of schools in Africa that follows similar methods, Nobel laureate Michael Kremer and others found that a student enrolled at Bridge for two years in primary school had test scores higher by about 0.89 additional years of schooling than students not enrolled.[18] For pre-primary students, the number was an even more astonishing: 1.48 years. Scripting seems to work!

Non-Solutions and Possible Ones

There are many non-solutions. As we noted earlier, Indian teachers, at least in government schools, are paid around thrice the per capita GDP of the country, enough to attract good talent.[19] A large fraction of our spending now on primary education is going into teachers' salaries, and evidence suggests that beyond a relatively low threshold, there is not much correlation between salary and a teacher's performance.[20]

In fact, recent evidence also suggests that low-cost private schools, which pay teachers much less and where teachers are less qualified than the teachers in government schools, produce similar or slightly better student performance than government schools in the same area.[21] One reason is that private schools often have smaller classes. Teachers are also better motivated and absent themselves less—the threat of losing their job is a powerful motivator.

Indeed, parents have been taking their children away from free government schools and placing them in fee-charging private schools, in part because private schools teach in English, and in part because their children learn more at private schools. The pandemic reversed this trend, perhaps because poorer parents could simply not afford the additional burden of school fees.

The bottom line is that from a resource-usage perspective, private schools are not doing worse and some could do even better if they had access to as many resources as the public ones. So simply throwing more public money at government schools is not the answer, nor is shutting down private schools.

The Right to Education Act, which came into force in 2010, had fundamental design flaws in the way it regulated private schools. For example, it demanded all private schools must have a playground and stipulated that all private schools admit 25 per cent students from economically weaker sections of society. Many good low-cost private schools did not have playgrounds (how do you find space for a playground in crowded Mumbai?), while the reimbursement promised them for admitting students from economically weaker sections of society wasn't paid on a timely basis. Diktats like these, while well-intentioned, have led to the closure of many private schools.

Perhaps it would be more useful to enable the poor to make an informed choice. The government should mandate that schools collect data on student performance, parental satisfaction and placements, and make the data public. Armed with that information, parents should have more freedom to decide which type of schools to send their children to.

If they prefer placing their children in the two-room private school with a motivated headmaster and loving teachers, over sending them to the free but indifferent government school, so be it. If enough parents vote with their feet, taking their children out of the government school, perhaps the government school should be closed after it is given a reasonable chance to reform itself.

It may also be time to experiment with more creative ways of engaging the private sector, without any presumption that the private sector is always better. Instead of expanding government schools even more, some systems could try out charter schools, others could attempt vouchers or direct benefit transfers (DBT). The charter school essentially has the government pay an annual amount for every student admitted to the school, but the day-to-day management of the school, including setting curriculum and hiring teachers, is left to the school. This has worked well in the United States.

The voucher system, on the other hand, allows those from economically weaker sections of society to access private schools, with the government paying the tuition fees or some portion of it. Given our digital infrastructure, this can be done through DBT. Vouchers could potentially be run in parallel with the mandate that all private schools admit 25 per cent students from economically weaker sections. Good private schools catering to the poor may actually be happy filling their classes with voucher-bearing students. Eventually, some combination of vouchers and the mandate may be most effective in giving the poor an equal chance.

Schooling happens as much outside the classroom as in it. Beyond tutoring, many children from disadvantaged backgrounds need role models and advisers who are successful in the world, in addition to the support given by their parents. Each one needs a 'Matthew Sir', something that the civil society in India can provide in a more organized way. Some children have an unsupportive, or even hostile, home environment. As we try and improve the learning experience of every student, we will have to create local safe spaces outside the school such as libraries and supervised homework rooms where such students can learn.

Post Independence, India's greatest failing has been its inability to give all its children a head start. Now that India is growing richer, we must correct this deficiency. It is our moral responsibility and will be a necessary foundation for economic growth.

8

Capabilities: Higher Education

The Indian educational system gave Abhijit Banerjee and Venki Ramakrishnan, both Nobel laureates, their educational foundations. It also educated, in large part, CEOs of companies such as Adobe, Alphabet, Chanel, FedEx, IBM, Micron, Microsoft and Starbucks, the current president of the World Bank, as well as university presidents, provosts and deans of prominent business schools and law schools across the world. This is, of course, looking at the cup as half full, for the other reality of India is that there are hundreds of millions Indians who are struggling to obtain basic skills and decent higher education.

Tanmay Mandal is a twenty-five-year-old college graduate from Bhopal. He paid around $4000 for a civil engineering degree, when his family income was $420 per month.[1] He told the news agency Bloomberg that he learnt almost nothing about the mechanics of construction because his teachers seemed to know little about the subject. He was unable to answer technical questions at an interview and has been unemployed for three years. Many of his peers, he said, are also sitting idle. He has now enrolled in a master's degree in another private institution, where he is yet again unlikely to learn much. But he claims this will at least boost his social status, because, while studying, he can escape the stigma associated with being unemployed, and one more degree may help distinguish him from his unemployed peers.

India has a few top-notch universities that have produced students who have gone on to achieve world prominence, but these are not the norm. Tanmay's story is sadly all too common. Too many of our youth do not have the skills for the jobs that are available. The most common refrain from employers is that even for the moderately skilled job of a factory worker, adjusting for how productive the worker is, it is not obvious that India's labour force is cheaper than China's or Vietnam's.

With few job openings in the formal private sector, educated youth look to government jobs, which are also too few to meet demand. The disillusionment with the small number of jobs on offer can spur protests, especially if the youth feel they have been treated unfairly in the already-limited recruitment for government jobs. Such anger was seen recently over short-service 'Agnipath' jobs in the Indian armed services. National resources are also wasted as millions of our youth sit for entrance exams for civil service jobs, year after year, until they become too old to qualify, and find that they have whiled away their youth acquiring unusable knowledge.

All these point towards a deep crisis of opportunities for our youth. The frustrations are then channelized in other ways: the fight over reservations in Manipur or the burgeoning substance abuse among the youth in Punjab. Clearly, the capabilities of our youth do not match the jobs on offer, and vice versa.

Education Funding

Indian Central and state governments budgeted about 4.6 per cent of GDP on education spending in 2020–21, up from 3.8 per cent in 2013–14.[2] Much of the increase came from the states, with the Centre's spending hovering around 1 per cent of GDP. The World Bank estimates that governments around the world spent about 4.4 per cent of GDP on average on education, so India is slightly better than the global average.[3] Of course, the global average contains many poor countries, and the India average contains many poor states that spend woefully little. Rich OECD countries spend about 5.3 per cent of GDP. Various Indian commissions have suggested that India should aim to spend about 6 per cent of GDP, and this certainly seems to be a reasonable aspiration level for the path we suggest.

Of the current spending, more public funds are spent on schooling than on higher education—the split for the Central government budget presented in 2023 was 61 and 39 per cent, respectively, and it broadly reflects the split for states also.[4] This is largely the right prioritization, given our past underinvestment in schooling. However, as we argued in the previous chapter, going forward our focus should be on improving schooling quality rather than quantity.

In higher education, though, public funding, targeting and the quality of education are all below par. India needs many more high-quality institutions of higher education. The system should fund the improvement of institutional quality partly through public funds and partly by charging reasonable fees to those who can afford to pay. We also need top-notch research institutions, supported with public and private research funding, to create the intellectual property that will seed our businesses.

Apart from the social benefits of a better educated population, a stronger higher education system will pay off in creativity, entrepreneurship and, of course, jobs. We must make it a political and societal imperative to bridge the gap between the skills of our youth and the skills a reimagined India will need.

The Great Jobs Hunt

As measured by employment, India is not doing well. Two large-scale datasets—the government's quarterly urban Periodic Labour Force

Survey (PLFS) and the Centre for Monitoring Indian Economy's Consumer Pyramids Household Survey—peg India's unemployment rate at around 7 per cent and 8 per cent as of March and September 2023, respectively. This means, around 3.5–4 crore Indians of working age, who are willing and able to search for jobs, can't get one.[5]

The unemployment rate only counts those who are unemployed and looking for jobs. If you are unemployed but not looking for a job—for example, a twenty-two-year-old preparing for civil services exams or a thirty-five-year-old who has given up looking—you are not counted. Moreover, five people manning a small retail store or tilling a small field, when only two would be sufficient, is disguised unemployment, but each one is counted as employed.

Digging deeper, the labour force participation rate in India—the fraction employed or looking for a job—is currently around 46 per cent. So, for every 100 Indians of working age, a staggering fifty-four are not participating in the labour force. To put things in a comparative perspective, in 2021, the labour force participation rate in Brazil was 58 per cent, in Indonesia 68 per cent and in all the OECD countries 60 per cent.[6] Moreover, and we will come to this in detail later, the gender break-up is more worrisome still. At around 20 per cent in recent times, the female labour force participation rate in India is even lower than in Saudi Arabia. Youth unemployment, those in the workforce who are aged fifteen to twenty-four years and without a job but actively seeking one, has also been increasing steadily—it stood at 22 per cent in 2019 (and was 28 per cent in 2021) as compared to 18 per cent in 2010. And, as noted earlier, in the last few years the fraction of the labour force in agriculture has increased for the first time in many decades— extremely unusual in a fast-growing developing country.

Vocational Training

Part of the reason we have too many graduates with unusable skills sitting for civil services exams is that there is a social aversion to working with hands, even though modern factories increasingly require a mix of brain and brawn. We need to create more space and status for vocational training.

Relatively few students transition from school education to vocational training. The twelfth and final Five-Year Plan for the period 2012–17 estimated that less than 5 per cent of the Indian workforce in the 19–24 age group received formal vocational education. According to the document, in the United States, the corresponding number is 52 per cent, in Germany it is 75 per cent and in South Korea it is 96 per cent.[7]

There are perhaps deeper social reasons for this state of affairs: while the *jati* (caste) system segregated society and limited opportunities for members of a jati, it also allowed skills to be transferred across generations. As the system of forced occupations rightly weakened in the modern market economy, nothing has substituted its apprenticeship system. Moreover, since an occupation that requires working with hands or exerting manual effort is lower in the traditional caste hierarchy than one that requires working with the mind, that is, white-collar work, higher education seems to be prized over vocational training. Of course, it is also the obvious pathway to that most prized of jobs: a safe government job with secure benefits.

About half of our college students are enrolled in three traditional courses: bachelor of arts, science or commerce, typically in small colleges.[8] Of course, a number of these students will go on to further professional degrees and qualifications, but if they stop, they have few alternatives other than sitting for various exams for government and public-sector jobs. Would it not be better if they were oriented in their final school years towards a career as a vet, a photographer, a sound technician, a clothes designer, an airplane mechanic or a master carpenter? For instance, despite its massive livestock and poultry population, 535 and 851 million, respectively, India graduates too few veterinarians, approximately 3000 per year. If we estimate the number of practising vets at approximately twenty times this number, India has one vet for nearly 10,000 livestock animals. Despite the cultural and economic importance of farm animals, this vocation attracts little interest and few resources.[9]

The National Education Policy recognizes the 'social status hierarchy' between traditional 'skill-free' bachelor's degrees and vocational education. As one educator told us, we need to change mindsets and expectations, right from middle school. The NEP proposes to have each child learn at least one vocation and be exposed to several more. Equally important is to create pathways for further skilling for those who leave school, including vocational courses for those who take traditional degrees. For instance, India will need a huge number of aircraft technicians in the years to come, and will need more technical schools teaching the necessary courses. Schools in traditional Indian crafts, with specializations taught by traditional craft workers, would also help pass on craft techniques, as would firms like Tilfi that support the apprenticeship system. And the judicious infusion of modern techniques and materials will create attractive new products and markets.

In all seriousness, a powerful way to change incentives to acquire vocational education today in India would be to include questions in one vocational area in the common part of the civil services exams and allow for more papers in the optional areas relating to vocational subjects, especially in state-level exams. Would a student trained in interior design, carpentry, plumbing or consumer electronics be any less capable than one trained in economics at being a local police officer or a town administrator? And if they don't pass the exams after many attempts, at least they have a marketable skill!

There is promising movement in students choosing vocational training. Enrolment in certificate and diploma programmes over the last few years has seen an uptick, from 1 per cent of total enrolments in 2005, they accounted for approximately 8 per cent of all enrolments in 2020.[10] Also, in a survey in 2019 conducted by the educational company Pearson, more than 70 per cent of Indian respondents in the working age group indicated that a vocational degree or certificate is more likely to culminate in a good job than a traditional university degree.

Business Apprenticeships and Training

Important destinations for those with vocational skills are businesses. Learning by doing actual work coupled with on-the-job training deepens and polishes an individual's skills. However, the reality in large parts of the country is distressing: Take a walk to a central market of a *kasba* (township) and you will find hundreds of youths hanging around to be picked up for *dehadi* (daily-wage labour). These are not the kinds of labour contracts that induce firms to train workers.

The culprit may be some of our labour laws, which protect workers that have spent more than a year or so in a firm from layoffs, regardless of the firm's needs or even the worker's performance. This incentivizes firms to hire only contract or casual labour. As the name suggests, such labour is hired for a short period of time and without benefits, and laid off before they become eligible for permanency. So the contract worker does not feel a deep attachment to the firm, and the firm, in turn, treats the worker as temporary and not worth investing in. Consequently, students with vocational skills have no natural place where they can hone their skills.

Many, then, work on their own, learning from no one. The International Labor Organization (ILO) estimated in 2017 that about one-third of Indian labour in the informal sector as 'own account workers', either as small entrepreneurs or workers who rent out their labour. This results in persistently low productivity.

India needs to reform labour laws so that workers can be hired for longer periods, accumulating more protection and compensation against layoffs over time, without becoming 'permanent'. States like Rajasthan and Karnataka are amending labour laws, in part to allow this.[11] Such changes will preserve worker incentives, as also the incentives of firms to train them. Firms will also be more eager to hire graduates of vocational training institutions if they align their courses better with the needs of local employers, perhaps by soliciting sponsorships, part-time teachers and advisory board members from possible employers.

As with much else that we have discussed, the dynamic can change quickly to virtuous cycles. Over time, labour-law reform coupled with the need for higher skills in the workforce will force businesses to give workers more on-the-job training, resulting in higher skills, better pay and more security. The government should set itself up as an active enabler in this regard by supporting digital labour exchanges, certifying skills, allowing online access to potential employers to check diplomas of those registered on exchanges and partially funding stipends for apprenticeships offered by reputable firms. The National Apprenticeship Promotion Scheme, which pays 25 per cent of the cost of apprentices, is an attempt in this direction, but it needs to be evaluated and modified on the basis of experience and after ascertaining if trainees do become employable.

We should also make use of the tremendous ingenuity of the Indian private non-degree education sector in providing coaching or training, whether it is in the English language, machine learning or preparation for the IIT entrance exam. The key here is to strengthen the consumer's hand and information about the provider's track record without dampening the vibrancy of the sector.

Higher Education

Our founding fathers were mostly learned men who were fascinated by science and learning. It is because of this scientific temperament that, despite being a poor country, we developed a few great universities, a system of surveys and national statistics, an atomic research centre and a space research organization. World-class institutions like the Tata Institute of Fundamental Research, the Indian Institute of Science and the first five IITs flourished. A poor country like India had little ability to absorb their students, and many migrated abroad, though many also stayed.

With the economic liberalization in the 1990s, the number of higher educational institutions expanded rapidly. This has had its downsides.

The problem is of maintaining a minimum level of quality—we have too many students in degree programmes that do not lead to marketable skills, and even in programmes like engineering, which are supposed to give students useful skills, many graduate knowing little. So even as India can finally use quality skilled personnel, it produces too few of them. Raghu used to see many IITians applying for PhD programmes at Chicago Booth business school because they did not find satisfying jobs. This is no longer the case, since they now find attractive jobs directly from campus, including in multinationals across the world. But while the well-trained are snapped up immediately, many of the poorly trained languish, unemployable. What happened?

In the last two decades, the number of universities and colleges in India has exploded. The number of universities quadrupled from 260 in 2001 to 1043 in 2020, and the number of colleges grew nearly fourfold, from 11,146 to 42,343. Devesh Kapur summarizes this acceleration pithily: India opened four and a half new colleges every day, including weekends, for the last twenty years!

'High access, low costs and high quality' are often referred to as the iron triangle of higher education. A low-income country (and perhaps even a high-income one) cannot achieve its desired outcomes on all three simultaneously—at least one of them must give. Since India is still a low-income country, in its quest to achieve scale and keep costs relatively low in the last twenty years, the quality of higher education has suffered tremendously.

Indeed, in our rush to meet public demand, we may have overreached. India's gross enrollment ratio (GER) of 27 per cent in higher education (that is, 27 per cent of those in the 18–23 age group are in college) is high for its stage of development, higher than that of China and even Japan, the UK and France, when they were at India's per capita GDP. In fact, the UK achieved a GER of 25 per cent at a per capita GDP of $16,000, almost eight times the income when India got to that GER.[12]

A host of demand factors have contributed to this anomaly—high societal expectations of the status associated with a college degree; the increase in skill premium, that is, the rise in wage differential between those who have acquired quality higher education and those who haven't; and India's choice of a service-intensive development path. But perhaps most important have been supply factors; the floodgates swung open without much regulatory oversight on the entry of degree-granting institutions.

The Higher Education Profit Machine

Take a drive on a highway out of a large city, especially in south or west India, and you will find impressive hotel-like buildings at regular intervals. As you approach more closely, you will find above the entrance gate a board announcing that the site is 'The Quicker Buck College of Engineering', or some such appellation. The business of higher education boomed in India at the turn of the century. With high profits to be made from the initially huge demand, most new colleges and universities, driven by individuals as opposed to trusts or endowments, adopted a low-quality, quick-profit-seeking model. Political scientist Rahul Verma writes: 'Outside the educational hubs of Tier 1 and Tier 2 cities, it is not professional educationists, but politicians and their supporters who own and run a large segment of private schools and colleges.'[13] The growth has been so rapid that according to the All India Survey on Higher Education conducted in 2020–21, 78 per cent of all colleges in India are private, and they account for more than half of the total enrolment.

Devesh Kapur explains how this model may have become viable, despite the limited incomes of even middle-class households. Some of these institutions benefited from the funding set aside for higher education in state budgets. Government data indicates that 36 per cent of all spending on higher education by state governments is transfers made to private colleges, and for the state of Maharashtra, the number is as high as 86 per cent.[14] Research suggests this money would be better utilized if it is disbursed directly as scholarships for the needy rather than direct transfers to private colleges, which are more prone to being diverted for non-educational purposes.[15]

In addition, students were also encouraged to take loans to pay fees—education loans from banks rose from Rs 3000 crore in 2000 to an aggregate outstanding amount of Rs 80,000 crore at the end of June 2022.[16] The most recent data reported by the Ministry of Education states that over Rs 17,000 crore's worth of education loans were disbursed in the financial year 2022–23 alone.[17] Add to that some portion of a household's hard-earned income devoted to seeing children through college, and we can understand how private education institutions' revenues are high.

The students and their families seem to get little in return. The pace of the boom ensured that there simply were not enough qualified teachers. While detailed studies on this are rare, anecdotal evidence and media reports all do seem to point to the fact Indian higher education institutions, especially in the private domain, have struggled to find good college and university teachers. The low quality of facilities other than the impressive building, coupled with the low calibre of the faculty, explains the kind of education received by Tanmay, whom we met at the beginning of the chapter. Unemployable graduates are the best evidence for the scant resources ploughed by unprincipled operators into higher education. If students are not employable, they cannot pay back their loans. It was recently reported that by the end of 2022, 8 per cent of all education loans in the twelve major public-sector banks had defaulted, a rate much higher than the average default rate for these banks. In short, the private higher education space needs a major clean-up.

Regulation

Clearly, the checks on quality did not work. 'Regulation of higher education,' the NEP admits, 'has been heavy-handed for decades; too much has been attempted to be regulated with too little effect.' The University Grants Commission (UGC) and fourteen professional councils, aided further by state councils, govern higher education. In the case of public universities, they control funding, accreditation and hiring of top leadership, and often even teachers, salary structures, scholarships, admission procedures for students, syllabi and more.

As of February 2023, only 38 per cent per cent of universities and 21 per cent of colleges in India had been accredited by the National Assessment and Accreditation Council (NAAC), the apex body responsible for this task.[18] Despite the plethora of regulatory bodies and overlapping jurisdictions, no entity has the explicit power to shut down underperforming institutions—so the unscrupulous thrive.

The opaqueness of the permissions process for private colleges and universities, inevitably leavened with corruption, has further kept quality low.[19] As with any system where low-quality operators thrive, higher-quality operators are a threat. Raghu was part of the not-for-profit group that founded the Indian School of Business, and he remembers how difficult it was for the school to get permission to start, despite the backing of the Kellogg School of Management and the Wharton School, as well as top Indian businesspeople.

At the same time, the old public universities, like University of Calcutta (home to the giants of modern Indian science, such as J.C. Bose, Satyendra Nath Bose, C.V. Raman and Meghnad Saha) or Delhi University or even the IITs, are deteriorating. They have been starved of funding by a government with other priorities, have not been able to charge the high fees private operators charge, often lack the emphasis on research that would keep the faculty on the frontier and attract business funding, lack autonomy from the government and are sometimes captured by political interest groups within the faculty or students. Earlier drafts of the National Education Policy in the public domain, before the final one accepted by the government in 2020, didn't mince any words in describing the compromised ethical standards of the appointment process for choosing the leadership to head some of these institutions.[20] What these institutions have going for them is the tremendous hunger of students for quality education at a reasonable price, some very motivated faculty; and consequently, they still attract many of the best and the brightest of young India.

The new public universities, on the other hand, such as the many new IITs, IIMs and AIIMS, have been trying to compete for the few remaining good faculty, with their hands tied by the necessity of keeping to civil-servant pay scales. They are overstretched and overwhelmed simply by teaching, and are unable to ensure quality.

Finally, there are a few new private universities, such as Ashoka University, Ahmedabad University, Shiv Nadar University and Krea University, which are trying to offer students a first-rate education but at a fee that would allow them to recover costs. While such universities do offer scholarships to help those who cannot pay, they can be expensive. Yet many upper-middle-class parents choose to send their children to these universities, for the alternative would be to send them abroad.

The Way Forward

Several committees appointed by the government and studies by researchers have opined on what needs to be done, with many sensible suggestions. Perhaps, as the Korean minister said to our finance minister in the anecdote we shared earlier, it is time for us to implement the proposed suggestions. Let us consider first an institution that has maintained quality over the years, suggesting that the quality challenge is not insurmountable.

The Indian Institute of Science: Leader of the Pack

The Indian Institute of Science (IISc) is the only institute of higher education in India that has regularly appeared near the top in global rankings of universities. What helps the IISc retain its excellence?

The institute was endowed in the late 1890s and early 1900s by a far-seeing group of elites of the time—Jamsetji Tata was the prime mover, but the maharaja of Mysore also donated land and money, the nizam of Hyderabad donated money, and the British were persuaded to be enthusiastic enablers. Eminent scientists were early directors, including Nobel laureate C.V. Raman.

A fascinating piece of history is that Tata travelled on the ship that Swami Vivekananda took to the 1893 World's Parliament of Religions in Chicago, and they seemed to have discussed the parallels between a modern research university and the action-oriented asceticism Swami Vivekananda advocated. In a letter, Tata tried to enlist Vivekananda to the common cause:

Esplanade House,
Bombay.
23rd Nov. 1898

Dear Swami Vivekananda,

I trust, you remember me as a fellow-traveller on your voyage from Japan to Chicago. I very much recall at this moment your views on the growth of the ascetic spirit in India, and the duty, not of destroying, but of diverting it into useful channels.

I recall these ideas in connection with my scheme of Research Institute of Science for India, of which you have doubtless heard or read. It seems to me that no better use can be made of the ascetic spirit than the establishment of monasteries or residential halls for men dominated by this spirit, where they should live with ordinary decency and devote their lives to the cultivation of sciences – natural and humanistic. I am of opinion that, if such a crusade in favour of an asceticism of this kind were undertaken by a competent leader, it would greatly help asceticism, science, and the good name of our common country; and I know not who would make a more fitting general of such a campaign than Vivekananda. Do you think you would care to apply yourself to the mission of galvanizing into life our ancient traditions in this respect? Perhaps, you had better begin with a fiery pamphlet rousing our people in this matter. I would cheerfully defray all the expenses of publication.

With kind regards, I am, dear Swami

Yours faithfully,
Jamshedji Tata[21]

The IISc is different from other institutions of higher education in India, including the IITs and IIMs, in that it was mandated to keep research as its core focus. It admits, for example, more postgraduate and PhD students than undergraduate students, which is rare for a higher educational institution of its size.

The IISc's excellence ensures that its funding is not solely dependent on the University Grants Commission. Many other government agencies, such as the Defence Research and Development Organisation, Indian Space Research Organisation, and the Department of Science and Technology, contribute to the pool. The IISc allows its faculty the time and resources to conduct research and follows an international standard peer-review system to grant tenure to its faculty.

To the credit of successive governments, the IISc has maintained relative institutional autonomy in how to govern itself and deploy funds for research, infrastructure and teaching. Beyond academic research, the United Nations Educational, Scientific and Cultural Organization, in fact, did a case study on the IISc two decades ago, emphasizing how the interactions with industry were vibrant and how the institute was meaningfully engaging with practical problems faced by society. If you take a walk around the IISc campus, as we have, you can feel the sense of intellectual energy and enthusiasm that infuses both faculty and students.

The New Temples: Public Research Universities

Elitism is sometimes a bad word. Yet in research, elitism is essential, since being on the frontier is really hard. If India chooses the path we suggest, it will need more high-quality research universities like the IISc. They will do the path-breaking research that will feed our businesses and elevate them from being incremental innovators to becoming break-out innovators.

Increase the Number of High-Quality Research Universities and Their Funding

The Indian government's move to declare twenty universities as Institutes of Eminence (IOE), which presumably would give them more autonomy and more access to funding, demonstrates the right intent. However, because the original recommendations, which included a then yet-to-be-started Jio Institute, sponsored by the Reliance Foundation, ran into controversy, newer recommendations seem to be based on public rankings. If so, only institutions that are already doing well qualify (for instance, the IISc and five of the six original IITs are on the list). These, presumably, already have a substantial degree of autonomy and funding. We need instead to focus the awards on younger institutions that can benefit more. Furthermore, even within venerable existing institutions, the emphasis on research and on training PhDs must increase.

Research

One approach is to substantially increase the funds available for research, for instance, by creating an independent, government-funded National Research Foundation (NRF) that so many past committees have recommended. The foundation should fund original research by awarding grants to deserving competing proposals, with significant amounts reserved for a few thrust areas.

The current proposals for the National Research Foundation are unambitious—$5 billion to be allocated over five years, with 70 per cent coming from industry.[22] This is tiny for the task we have in mind, even in the unlikely event that industry will step up. Within the decade, a government embarked on the path we propose will have to devote significantly larger amounts of money than it does today to support basic research in universities, including buying scientific equipment and training PhD students. We propose tens of thousands of crores initially, turning into lakhs of crores in the next decade. This will be a huge jump from today, but it will be the minimum needed for India to be a player. For context, suggesting this is the right level of aspiration, the United States spends around Rs 5 lakh crore today on just the National Science Foundation and the National Institutes of Health, let alone all the defence and private money that goes to fund and endow university research. The total endowment of just Princeton University, where Rohit did his PhD, is $36 billion, or, approximately, Rs 3 lakh crore.

We must find room for greater spending on research in higher education, and we can if we prioritize better. Last year, the Central government's budget for higher education was Rs 44,000 crore.[23] At the same time, as we pointed out in the introduction to this book, Rs 16,500 crore, more than a third of the Central government's higher education budget, was recently offered as a capital subsidy to a Micron factory that will assemble and test chips. In addition, Rs 2.25 lakh crore was devoted to fertilizer subsidies. These numbers are staggering in their mismatch on what the nation prioritizes for its future.

Some of the enhanced allocation to research will support the usual range of projects that researchers come up with—and there could be surprising breakthroughs among these. But most scientific areas will need a minimum quantum of money and enough researchers in India to make a difference. While we typically do not advocate that the government should direct business or research, the government may have little choice but to pick a few areas—such as sustainable energy storage, development of new medicines or vaccines, or artificial intelligence—hopefully after wide consultations with experts on where India may have advantages. The chosen areas should be critical to future economic growth, strategic from a national security perspective, and where private industry alone will not make investments commensurate with our needs and ambitions. Limiting the number of thrust areas will ensure projects have the funding to take India, with reasonable probability, to the frontiers of research. In contrast, funding spread thinly, widely and for short periods of time will likely end up wasted.

The NRF will have to dole out enormous quantities of money, so it is critical that the system be transparent and independent. Once the thrust areas are decided at the political and academic policy levels, in each area, committees of independent qualified academics and professionals, not bureaucrats, should decide what to fund, based on detailed applications and evaluations of those applications by experts. Once funded, there should be regular evaluations of the projects for funding to be continued.

The intellectual property that is produced should partly belong to the researchers and the university, so that they get some monetary rewards from its commercialization and can plough back the money into further research. Universities will then also have the incentive to facilitate a research culture.

Since research has many positive benefits for the country, a second function of the NRF should be to fund research infrastructure, extending grants even to some well-run private institutions. Many science, technology and engineering institutions do not have basic equipment needed for research, such as, say, a spectrometer, or even a well-equipped laboratory. While they may not be institutions of eminence, their faculty and students can participate in research—and, who knows, a C.V. Raman may emerge—but only if they have the necessary resources and encouragement.

Faculty

Research universities must train first-rate PhD students, who can then fill the many faculty positions at other such universities, but also at the many other universities and colleges of high quality, that are focused on teaching and producing employable graduates. Smart students will give up careers as bankers or consultants if they see they are paid reasonably well when they do their PhDs. So, a third function of the NRF will be to fund PhD programmes at universities.

Given that research has taken a back seat at some of our pre-eminent institutions, it will take time to revive the research culture. New, often privately funded, institutions, like Ashoka University or O.P. Jindal Global University or Ahmedabad University or Azim Premji University, may also take the lead in research. It would be good if public universities can compete for talent—so the NRF should fund a number of professorships at public universities, intended to attract eminent professors at competitive pay scales.

Some candidates for such professorships may be in India, but that pool will be quickly exhausted, so we should also search globally. We may find professors of Indian origin working abroad, but we should also be open to citizens of other countries, including our neighbours. We need to be willing to attract the best and brightest from anywhere, some of whom will bring the know-how and expertise that India could spend decades acquiring on its own.

To be competitive, we should liberalize academic researcher salaries. The state cannot simply regard them as civil servants and peg their employment to that pay scale. Top academic researchers have a global market competing for their talents, and India cannot afford to be uncompetitive.

Academic Freedom

Academic culture requires the freedom to debate, to subvert hierarchies and challenge the existing received wisdom with radical ideas. Authoritarian governments resent that and try and intervene by rewarding favoured personnel and ideologies within universities and punishing disfavoured ones, often with the help of pliant administrators or boards. This will be the path to mediocrity, as will allowing bureaucrats and politicians to dominate the National Research Foundation. If we are to preserve free thinking, if we are to attract the best and brightest in the world, the governance issues we discussed earlier in the context of the state will be important in academia as well.

Upgrade the Quality of Teaching Institutions

Turning to teaching, there are simply too many small colleges in India. For example, as of 2019, 36 million students were enrolled in a total of 51,649 institutions of higher education in India—an average of 697 students per institution; for China the number is 42 million in 2699 institutions—an average of 15,561. A small college cannot offer the subject choices that a larger institution can, nor can it incur the fixed costs of a strong placement office or an office to develop links with industry through projects or internships. Colleges will need to merge, or form looser affiliations with nearby colleges, so that students have more choice.

One way to improve quality throughout the system is to insist that every institution must be accredited—that is, evaluated for teaching quality and quality of student support—within five years of being set up, and then every five years. To do this effectively, the NAAC, the organization in charge of accreditation, will have to enhance capacity significantly, without compromising the quality of accreditation. If a college is found to be performing well, it should be given more autonomy from UGC norms.

If a college is found below par, it should be given a couple of years to fix its problems while it is placed under enhanced oversight. At that point, if a fresh evaluation finds insufficient improvement, it should be placed under a UGC-appointed administrator who will either close the college gracefully after current students graduate or merge the college with stronger colleges in the neighbourhood. This, of course, will require the UGC (or any alternative body that will be the regulator) to have the power to close underperforming institutions.

Students should also be able to identify underperforming colleges and avoid them. The government should cull from its databanks and make public the employment status and the average incomes of college graduates, say three years after graduation.[24] Banking supervisors should put additional risk weights on student loans to those in underperforming colleges, while the government should refuse to guarantee them. These will place economic pressure on underperforming institutions to shape up or shut down, over and above the regulatory pressures.

Benefiting from the World

While India's tertiary education system is being revamped, it should recognize the extent to which India is dependent on institutions around the world and reshape that engagement to India's benefit. India has always sent students abroad for master's and PhD degrees—both of us are examples. We should continue to do so, but also try and attract our trained students back, despite their global market value. Improved opportunities for research in India and better remuneration for top academics will contribute enormously in this regard.

In the last few decades, as our undergraduate system has failed to keep pace, Indian students are increasingly going abroad for undergraduate degrees—according to a Ministry of Education report, over 7,70,000 of them in 2022 alone.[25] These statistics are fuzzy because people leaving India do not have to report why they are doing so, but in the fiscal year 2022, $5.2 billion in foreign exchange was taken out by Indians for studies abroad—the number is likely a lower bound.[26]

India's diaspora is a resource India will draw on when it has the need, but these numbers also suggest an opportunity. If we upgrade and expand the number of our high-quality universities, many of the students we now send abroad in such large numbers for their undergraduate degrees will stay. They can pay and will be an enormous source of university funding, while saving on the outflow of billions of dollars. Many foreign students from neighbouring countries, from the Middle East and from Africa will come for our education. Not only will this be another source of funding, it will also be an implicit export since it will earn foreign exchange. We must encourage the best among them to stay. They must not feel they will be treated poorly because they are of different ethnicity, race or religion. India needs to re-emphasize its historic openness to all, else it will lose the global competition for talent.

At the same time, we must encourage scientific and research collaborations with research institutions abroad, sometimes with our National Research Foundation lubricating the way with research grants. Collaborations will be a way of reinvigorating existing faculty at our top universities, of making connections with the diaspora, but also making use of our trusted status (say, relative to China) among rich democracies. It will be a fast way to get to the frontiers.

In Lament

We must also remember that it takes much effort to build an institution but little to fritter away its excellence. Rohit attended Delhi School of Economics for his master's. It is an institution of great pedigree, with the likes of Jagdish Bhagwati and Amartya Sen having walked its corridors. It has trained many of the current crop of Indian economists. Slowly but surely, however, the institution's glamour is fading, with good faculty leaving. It could have been different.

A direct comparison with the London School of Economics (LSE) is telling. Just as Delhi School of Economics is directly under the control of the University of Delhi, the LSE is directly under the control of the University of London. But, over time, the LSE was given greater autonomy in terms of whom to hire, what courses to offer, even how much fees to charge, within some broad guidelines. As the modern finance industry in London thrived, the LSE trained some of its most prominent bankers. It also continued to invest heavily in its PhD programme.

Delhi School of Economics did not diversify its master's programmes to teach finance, insurance and market-related courses;

its PhD programme, too, has not kept up with global standards or its own glorious past. From Rohit's experience, this has been not due to a lack of vision or effort on the part of the faculty. The tight control by the larger university bureaucracy simply would not let it innovate. We need many more institutions like Delhi School of Economics in its full glory; it is disappointing that we have not given it the autonomy to ensure continued excellence.

9

Capabilities: Health Care

The Covid pandemic scarred India deeply. While no nation's efforts were without blemish, given such a large-scale and unimagined contagion, India's unpreparedness for the ghastly second wave, despite forewarnings from around the world, reflected weaknesses in our governance as well as gaps in our health system. While we can vaccinate effectively on a national scale, primary care is inadequate in many areas of the country. An investigation of the pandemic experience would tell us what needs fixing, but we don't seem to want to find out.

There are other signs that all is not well. The outbreak of war in Ukraine highlighted the vast number of Indian students receiving a medical education there. Why are we not able to provide medical education to our students when we have a scarcity of doctors in India, and when many personnel diagnosing patients and prescribing medicines in India's hinterland do not have any formal degrees?

In the midst of all this, committed individuals and institutions are doing spectacular work, both in the public and private space, trying to make health care accessible. How can we learn from these success stories to give 1.4 billion people a network of primary, secondary and tertiary medical units that delivers good-quality health care?

Health Care: A Lay of the Land

Every citizen should have easily accessible health care of decent quality. This is the goal we must continuously strive towards. As a collateral benefit, health care could become a service we export to the world. Let's see where we are today and what we must do to get to the goal.

In 1943, a committee chaired by Joseph William Bhore was tasked with envisioning modern public health services for India. It outlined a Western European-style architecture, with three tiers offering primary, secondary and tertiary levels of care. Ordinary health issues, such as a septic cut, would be tackled by the primary health centre (PHC), while serious operations would be done at a hospital at the tertiary level, and intermediate care and minor operations would be done at the secondary level. Each level would support the other through a referral system.[1]

A recent report by the World Health Organization notes that India is yet to achieve even the short-term goals for the first ten years laid out in the Bhore Committee report: At the end of the first ten years, each district in India was supposed to 'have 25 primary health centers (PHC) each serving a population not more than 40,000 and one 30-bedded hospital to serve two PHCs. Each PHC should have a staff of 15 comprising two medical officers, four public health nurses (PHNs), one nurse, four midwifes, four public health inspectors, two pharmacists, one clerk and other support staff.'[2] This was no mean task the Bhore Committee had set out for our health system, ninety years ago; but did we mention timely implementation before?

Today, while the Bhore architecture still drives the design of the public-sector health system, the inability of the public sector to deliver both the necessary quantity and quality of service has led to a massive exodus of even the poor to the private sector. While this has helped fill gaps, and even displaced the public sector in some areas, the health-care system as a whole does not work efficiently.

One measure of the quality of health care is the infant mortality rate, which is the number of children that die under one year of age in a given year per 1000 live births. It is still high in India at 26 (as of 2021), while Vietnam is at 16, China 5 and rich OECD countries average 6.[3] There is wide disparity within India, with the infant mortality rate of 6 in Kerala at the OECD level, and a disappointing 41 in Uttar Pradesh, 40 in Chhattisgarh and 46 in Madhya Pradesh, which are closer to the levels in Sub-Saharan Africa.[4]

Today, the rapid rise in new diseases like asthma—due to pollution—and diabetes—due to unhealthy lifestyles—is burdening urban India, even while old ailments like tuberculosis and malaria are still largely with us. Rural India is still struggling with access to basic health care. What accounts for this state?

Poor-Quality Providers

India, as many of us have experienced, has excellent hospitals and world-renowned physicians. But much of India has a very different experience of health care.

At the outset, there are too few qualified doctors. One estimate suggests that India graduates approximately 80,000 MBBS doctors each year from around 560 degree-granting colleges, which is about three times what the United States graduates.[5] However, in 2019, India had only 0.9 doctors per 1000 people, while the United States around the same time had 2.7 and China had 2.5. Part of the problem is that the capacity of medical colleges in the past was smaller. Moreover, not everyone who graduates stays in India. Consequently, the overall number of doctors with formal education and training even now is small, given our population. There is also a huge variety in the quality of doctors, ranging from internationally reputed heart surgeons to doctors who cannot diagnose better than informal providers without degrees.

Despite a largely free public health-care system, a study finds the market share of fee-charging primary-care private providers exceeds 83 per cent in rural Madhya Pradesh, even in markets where a qualified public-sector doctor is available. Around 60 per cent of primary-care visits are made to private providers with no formal qualifications (though they may have medical knowledge from a variety of sources, including having worked in a doctor's office).[6]

Part of the reason for the shift towards private medical providers is that those in the public facilities are absent 40 per cent of the time, and when they are present they spend much less time per patient (only 2.4 minutes on average) than the private provider in diagnosing them. As a result, both the public-sector provider and the underqualified private-sector provider diagnose equally correctly (an abysmal 4 per cent of the cases in the study) and are equally correct on the suggested treatment (about 27 per cent of cases). Both also prescribe unnecessary treatments about 70 per cent of the time, leading, for example, to antibiotic overuse. Interestingly, the same doctors who work in the public hospital spend more time with the patient and diagnose far more diligently in their parallel private practice, much as with teachers in government schools and private tutorials. Incentives matter!

Other studies show that in public hospitals and health centres, medicines are unavailable, medical equipment is broken, there are long waiting lines and the service is of poor quality. According to the National Sample Survey 2017–18, less than one-third of the population now gets treated in public hospitals or health centres. Obviously, the poor depend more on the public health system than the rich. Even so, of those in the bottom 20 per cent in terms of per capita monthly consumption expenditure, only 36 per cent seek treatment in public hospitals.[7]

The rural–urban divide is also pronounced. Again, according to the last round of the National Sample Survey 2017–18, around one-fourth of doctors with MBBS degrees were working in areas classified as rural, whereas around two-thirds of the population still resides there.

What about the alarming preponderance of informal providers without formal degrees (either an MBBS degree or a qualification in traditional medicine, also termed AYUSH)? It turns out that a rise in incomes in the population does not diminish the public's use of informal providers, though they may seek more qualified practitioners if they have more serious ailments. One reason may be that in richer areas, greater competition with qualified providers forces informal providers to improve their knowledge. Indeed, informal providers in Tamil Nadu and Karnataka demonstrated better medical knowledge than MBBS doctors in Bihar and Uttar Pradesh![8] Clearly, as with education, there is the public-sector/private-sector problem, the problem of too few qualified providers and the low average quality of service provided.

Few Resources, Ad Hoc Spending

India spends too little on health care. According to a 2019 NITI Aayog report, the government spends 1.13 per cent of the GDP on health, 'which is grossly inadequate [compared to] similar spending by other countries'.[9] Even adding household and corporate spending, India spends about 3.5–4 per cent of the GDP on health care, far lower than the 10 per cent of the GDP the world spends.

Furthermore, too much of medical spending, about 60 per cent, is ad hoc or out-of-pocket expenditure (OOPE). It is neither based on prepaid private insurance (as in the United States) or tax-financed government health spending (as in the UK's National Health Service). This means that households are hit with a huge expense when some member needs serious medical care. According to a recent study by researchers at the National Institute of Public Finance and Policy, which uses data from 2014, around 8 per cent of all households over the period of one year were pushed below the poverty line due to out-of-pocket health-care payments. Assuming there are 25 crore households in India, this means 2 crore households or 8–10 crore people every year![10]

In many other countries, households pool together in private insurance schemes, where in exchange for a steady premium, the insurance company pays the large bills. Essentially, since everyone does not get sick at the same time, the steady annual premium paid by all households is enough to cover the payments for all the households that have emergencies that year. A large sudden unexpected shock to income is converted into a steady manageable set of predictable insurance premium payments. This is the fundamental principle underlying private insurance.

Public health insurance also pools risks similarly, with the taxes we pay substituting for premiums. Two central advantages of risk pooling are, first, that households bear less risk—think of a poor agricultural worker not having to worry about a medical emergency that could cost lakhs of rupees. Second, the demand for medical services is more predictable—the worker will take his daughter to hospital once he knows she is covered, rather than praying the ailment goes away.

Other countries are not so badly off. The WHO estimates OOPE to be only around 40 per cent for low- and middle-income countries. OOPE came down in China from 60 per cent in 2000 to 35 per cent in 2019. In the US and Thailand, OOPE is around 10 per cent.

Even when an insurer aggregates the premium payments of the insured, it does not necessarily arrange for good service. According to its annual report, the Employees' State Insurance Corporation (ESIC), which covers a whopping 10 per cent of the total population, has accumulated a staggering $10 billion (Rs 80,000 crore) in unspent premiums. So health insurance premiums are deducted from middle-class and lower-middle-class employees' wages, but due to the public insurer's low capacity to provide service, the claims ratio (the ratio of claims to premiums) has remained below 50 per cent. A rule of thumb in the United States is that the claims ratio should be about 80 per cent, suggesting the ESIC is simply not supporting the health of its insured adequately.[11]

Fragmented System with Poorly Utilized Resources

Because the formal system proposed by the Bhore Committee does not work as desired, a patchwork of overlapping private and public providers has emerged. From the public-sector side, we have primary health centres, community health centres, district hospitals, medical college hospitals and super-speciality tertiary centers. The private sector has informal providers, doctors, clinics, nursing homes, standalone hospitals and corporate hospitals, as well as a variety of pharmacies and chemists.

Also, more than 98 per cent of all health service providers in the country have less than ten employees, and over 90 per cent of all facilities have less than fifty beds. So, there are very few integrated facilities that can take a patient from preliminary diagnosis to final treatment. With the patient navigating the resulting maze on their own, and with limited information about the quality or integrity of referrals, patients zigzag among multiple types of providers, leading to what Nachiket Mor, former chairman of Gates Foundation India, calls excessive 'doctor shopping'.

This deeply fragmented health-care system could still perhaps deliver good value if there was a rich enough network that shared information on patients, the success rate of operations and procedures, and patient reviews. What in data science geek land is called interoperability—the ability of computer systems or software to exchange and make use of information—could lead to more informed customer decisions. At the moment, no such system exists.

Of course, even if they acquired the information, the few large buyers of health-care services are not in a position to put pressure on subpar providers because they typically engage in what's called 'passive purchasing'. The World Health Organization defines passive purchasing as a combination of budgetary allocations through bureaucratic assessments, and the simple process of paying bills when presented with orders for health-care equipment, medicines, care personnel and other expenses. The purchaser does not engage much in monitoring the quantity or the quality of health services its customers receive or exercise effort in influencing them.[12]

Strategic purchasing, on the other hand, means the purchaser searches continuously for the best means to optimize health systems performance by deciding which services should be purchased, how they should be purchased and from which providers. An attempt is made to link the allocation of funds to providers based on information on their performance or the health needs of the population they serve. Of course, there is a continuum of purchasing behaviour between these poles, but it is uncontroversial to conclude that India lies firmly on the passive side.

Finally, skilful regulation could improve the public's experience. Given the enormous dependence on informal providers, the regulator cannot simply ban those without formal qualifications. However, leaving the entire sector unregulated, or worse, subjecting it to extortionate bribes, cannot be the answer, especially when the qualified do not do much better. Thoughtful regulation is required at three levels: medical qualifications or capabilities; quality of care and service delivery by providers; and price and coverage of health insurance.

Health Care: Key Ingredients of the Vision

What we want from our system is decent health care for all at moderate costs. However, the country should also have cutting-edge facilities that will drive research and new medical practices, which can attract patients from around the world as well as train the teachers that our medical colleges need. How do we achieve both at the same time? In the following pages we look at four case studies that offer institutional solutions that seem to have worked and try to draw some lessons for the design of the health-care architecture.

Mohalla Clinics

As the Bhore Committee indicated long ago, health care starts with easy access to a capable primary-care provider, who can treat simple ailments, and refer more complicated ailments to polyclinics and hospitals. The Delhi government's Mohalla Clinics offer one example. These were launched in 2015 'to provide quality primary healthcare services accessible within the communities at their doorstep' and 'to reduce the over-crowding of people seeking treatment for common illnesses at hospitals'.[13]

Each Mohalla Clinic serves around 30,000 people from a two- or three-room clinic; and each clinic is equipped with a doctor's office, a pharmacy and laboratory testing kits.[14] There is an air-conditioned waiting area with chairs, an attractive place for some people to just walk in and cool off! Several clinics are specially designed porta cabins or repurposed shipping containers that can just be placed anywhere on government land.

Patients take a number when they walk in, their details are filled in on a tablet, and their prescriptions and records are maintained using specialized software. The clinic is open 4–6 hours a day, six days a week; and when demand is significant, the clinic may work multiple shifts. Each clinic has at least a doctor, a nurse/midwife and a pharmacist, and offers basic first aid, diagnosis, prenatal and postnatal care, a large number of medicinal drugs, a variety of diagnostic tests, and referrals to polyclinics (the second tier of care), specialists and Delhi hospitals for advanced care.

Some doctors have a private practice and work in the clinic to supplement their income at times when they are unlikely to have private patients. For the mohalla patients, the clinic offers a welcoming environment, easy access to a physician and consistent quality service, with a massive saving on the time that would be spent waiting in a public hospital to see a doctor or to get medicines.

Importantly, Mohalla Clinics are free, both for doctor consultation and medications available at the clinic. So how does the system perform on quality for the patients and cost dimension for the government? While more rigorous impact evaluations are needed, early studies report broadly positive experiences for both medical staff and patients, and the clinics are cost-effective in comparison with other public as well as private options in Delhi.[15] There are still few patients from the middle class, but the idea is to make the experience good enough to eventually attract them. As we argued earlier, the middle class will be vocal protestors if quality deteriorates, so they incentivize providers to maintain the positive experience.

Jan Swasthya Sahyog

Jan Swasthya Sahyog (JSS) was founded by professionals from India's premier medical institute, the All India Institute of Medical Sciences (AIIMS), in a cluster of forested tribal villages near Bilaspur town in Chhattisgarh. This is a remote area where the usual means of transport is a bicycle. JSS has a well-functioning system of outreach workers who are the primary contact with patients. These workers are typically recruited locally and do not have formal medical qualifications. However, they are trained to recognize and deal with basic ailments and illnesses (animal bites are a frequent problem in the area), and carry a package of medical drugs for quick treatment. Over time, they get on-the-job experience as they consult with more qualified staff, as well as more training, which allows them to move up the ranks.

Patients with more serious problems go to the health and wellness centres (HWCs), staffed by at least one experienced and better-trained provider. Each HWC is visited weekly by a team consisting of a doctor, a pharmacist and a lab technician. The HWC can consult the team through mobile phone or Skype on days when the team does not visit. The HWCs are also linked to an eighty-bed hospital and medical team in the town of Ganiyari for more complicated cases.

JSS does not focus only on health care in isolation. It runs crèches for children younger than three years, addressing an important gap in early-childhood care, looking for, and treating, malnutrition.[16] JSS's motivated workers, embedded in the community, have also created community support structures—for instance, patient groups for each major disease (including alcoholism), so that patients can urge each other to comply with the treatment. Finally, JSS runs in parallel to the government-run system, but most of the services offered by JSS are simply not offered by the government system.

JSS offers an example of how moderately qualified workers with well-qualified support can create effective health care in rural India using only limited resources. Central to their effectiveness is their pledge: 'Respect for the poor, the village folk, an understanding of their problems, and an unfailing commitment to them shall inform and permeate all our work . . .'

Aravind Eye Hospital

Another values-based organization that is doing good work at scale, and in the process still making enough money to fund itself, is the widely studied Aravind Eye Hospital. Started by Dr G. Venkataswamy in 1976, when he retired at the age of fifty-eight from Madurai Medical College, the hospital operates eyecare networks around India. Like JSS, it supplements the little that government does, without trying to displace it. Given the enormous demand for health services in India, Aravind Eye Hospital focuses on high service volumes without compromising quality, all at affordable cost. The low-cost objective, implemented through its unique assembly-line approach, is not so much to make profits but to serve more customers. The hospital charges 50 per cent of its customers a full price, offers a discounted rate to another quarter and serves the rest free.[17]

Aravind Eye Hospital started off with outreach through eye camps, where it identified those (primarily) in need of cataract surgery and brought them to the camp hospital or the regular hospital. Over time, it did a better job at predicting camp attendance based on past data and assigned doctors to each camp so that they would be fully occupied. Within each camp operating theatre, it typically placed two beds, so that as the surgeon was completing work on one patient, the next patient would be prepared for surgery. Not only did this reduce the need for surgical space, it also optimized the use of the scarce resource:

the surgeon's time. Of course, the large number of operations each surgeon did made them experts at such operations, and the time per cataract surgery came down.

As demand for Aravind Eye Hospital's services grew, it started vision centres and community clinics, which were a more permanent presence in community outreach. In the early 2000s, these vision centres were linked to headquarters, so that a doctor could communicate with patients and offer diagnoses, an early version of telemedicine. Aravind Eye Hospital also innovated, designing and manufacturing its own cheap intra-ocular lens for about one-hundredth the cost of what was available in the market. In 2012, the UK's NHS did about 5,00,000 surgeries, while Aravind Eye Hospital did 3,00,000. These surgeries cost the NHS £1.68 billion, whereas Aravind Eye Hospital spent £13.8 million, about one-hundredth!

Aravind Eye Hospital also has an interesting wage model. About 40 per cent of its doctors are permanent, earning a market wage. Approximately 35 per cent are fellows, qualified ophthalmologists from elsewhere on a two-year training programme to develop skills, and the remaining are residents. The latter two categories earn a fraction of the market wage for ophthalmologists but are compensated through the enormous learning and cachet they get. Finally, many of the nurses and other para-professionals are high-school graduates from the villages near the hospital, are trained at the hospital and then employed in Aravind Eye Hospital's various programs.

Christian Medical College, Vellore

Dr Ida Sophia Scudder founded the Christian Medical College (CMC) at the turn of the twentieth century with the objective of providing health-care service to women and children. Her father was a missionary doctor on the outskirts of Vellore. According to legend, while initially Ida was reluctant to be a missionary or a doctor, during her time in India she saw three women die in childbirth because their orthodox families wanted assistance only from a female. Ida realized her mission in life, and after studying medicine in the United States, she came back to India to fulfil it by setting up CMC in Vellore. Privately managed and mostly privately funded, the hospital has now grown into one of modern India's best teaching and research hospitals.

Back in 1971, management guru C.K. Prahlad wrote a case study on the hospital that was taught widely in the IIMs.[18] Prahlad observed that initially the hospital was funded by donations from abroad and churches in India, and then eventually by grateful patients. Many doctors were sent abroad for specialized training, and several others, including researchers, came to Vellore from the US for long periods in a spirit of service. As we saw in the case of Aravind Eye Hospital, the hospital divided pricing for patients into four categories—private patients who contribute above cost, patients who pay a standard price, some who get a discount and the rest free. It was left to the doctors to give fee concessions to the patients based on their evaluation of the patients' needs and their ability to pay. Cost reduction, while maintaining excellence, Prahlad further observed, helped lower fees and was an important objective for the hospital—the ethos was never to run the institution as a business.

Importantly, and this cannot be emphasized enough, throughout its history, CMC has set medical research and teaching as part of its mission, along with treatment. It is credited with the first open-heart surgery in India, the first detection of HIV in a blood sample, the first reconstructive surgery for leprosy in the world, the first bone-marrow transplant in India and so on. In a press interview, T. Jacob John, a leading virologist and retired CMC professor, extolled the egalitarianism and mutual respect between faculty and students, which helped create a strong research culture.[19]

Among its activities, CMC runs a community hospital and training centre, which works with the rural and tribal population in the surrounding areas. More generally, CMC emphasizes knowledge creation, sharing and a spirit of community. In that sense it works like a large US research university, but with more public empathy.

What Do We Take Away from These Case Studies?

There are many health-care initiatives in India and much innovation. We do not have the space to do justice to them all. Nor do we presume to have all the answers. Yet a few principles seem clear from even the cases we have examined.

Numbers

First, given India's massive needs, we need a triage system resembling the Bhore Committee template, using competent but not necessarily formally qualified personnel at the primary-care level to diagnose easy cases and treat ailments early, and to move difficult cases up to tiers where personnel are more qualified, and diagnosis and treatment more difficult. The primary-care workers can also play a role in preventive care so that fewer people fall sick. Consequently, they reduce the pressure on scarce highly qualified personnel, allowing them to focus on difficult cases. Most important, many of today's uncertified medical providers have the experience to offer primary health care—we do not need all of them to be certified doctors.[20]

Perhaps, though, to ensure public health safety, all providers should be required to pass a test certifying basic competence at diagnosing and treating common ailments. Organizations like JSS and CMC, which have sound training programmes, could be empowered to issue their own equivalence certificates of basic competence. Provider certificates could be maintained in a searchable electronic registry, so that with a simple online search any potential patient can check if their provider has the basic qualifications—this suggestion of an electronic registry extends beyond medicine to all degrees, given the possibility of degree fraud in India. And for those informal providers that cannot pass the test, easy-to-access training programmes should bring them up to par. Chhattisgarh once proposed such a programme to train informal providers, but it was opposed by doctor organizations and never took off. India cannot be overly cautious here, since the status quo would leave patients exposed to untrained and potentially inept medical providers.

India also needs many more doctors. As with education more generally, the shortage is not with the numbers willing to learn but with teachers; on average, between 2018 and 2021, 7.8 lakh students passed the National Eligibility cum Entrance Test (NEET) for admission to a medical college, suggesting they were deemed capable of starting medical education. But unfortunately, there were seats for only one-tenth or so of these.[21] Many of those who did not make it to Indian medical schools went to study in China, Ukraine, Russia and the Philippines—ironically, about as many as managed to study in India. India needs to expand quality medical education, along with quality tertiary education, as discussed earlier. One obvious idea, modelled on CMC, is to aim for each district in India to have a large medical college and hospital which is connected to the local community and backed by local government and private funds to achieve excellence, not just in care but also in research and teaching.

Type of Provider

These cases also suggest there are many ways to provide services. Any form of ownership brings its own set of problems, as we have seen. For instance, how does one prevent an opportunistic private provider from ripping off an unsuspecting poor patient by either delivering poor quality or by overcharging? Conversely, how does one prevent an under-incentivized public system from settling into apathy, with providers not showing up or being effective only when moonlighting in their private practice?

JSS, Aravind Eye Hospital and CMC are private operations that do employ many at market wages, but they are suffused with a spirit of voluntarism. Delhi's Mohalla Clinics are part of a public-sector effort run by the state government, but they employ doctors from the private sector. There are checks and balances on the doctors. For instance, in Delhi, if a Mohalla Clinic gets overcrowded, a new shift is opened to share the load, so that the medical team can spend adequate time with each patient. Furthermore, detailed information is available with the administration about the performance of each doctor in each clinic, so that underperformance can be addressed. At both JSS and Aravind Eye Hospital, detailed information collection helps the management monitor individual performances; but also, the spirit of service embedded in the culture of each organization helps straighten out those who might be motivated by other interests.

Put differently, it is not whether an organization is public, private or voluntary; what matters is how the combination of contracts, information availability and culture combine to create quality output. The never-ending ideological debates of public versus private hurt rather help. People should simply be given greater choice, and what works best will emerge.

Patient Choice and Strategic Purchasing

How does one give patients more choice and redress? Recipients of government-provided services often have no choice where they receive service from, so they get poor service. As soon as there is some competition, with the patient free to choose alternative providers, the incentive to provide better service increases, especially if patients have accurate information on the quality of service at each provider. After all, if no one patronizes a government facility, it will eventually be closed and the providers transferred. We must give patients, especially poor ones, more informed choice.

JSS, Aravind Eye Hospital and CMC operate in parallel with the government system, offering services at affordable prices—some positive price is often useful to ensure that patients feel they have a right to be treated well and also to ensure they do not overuse the medical services. While both JSS and Aravind Eye Hospital are eligible for government reimbursement for some of the services they provide, in practice government reimbursement requires considerable additional bureaucracy, and reimbursement is often delayed. Ideally, the government would reimburse quickly and keep monitoring whether it needs to reduce staff in its own system, so that there is not too much wasteful duplication. Alternative possibilities include the government allowing patients to formally choose a primary-care centre, whether public or private, for basic health care, and then allowing them to change their choice every year based on their experience. The government would then pay primary-care centres a flat annual fee based on the number of patients that sign up.

The recently introduced Pradhan Mantri Jan Arogya Yojana (PMJAY), which provides a health cover for hospitalization of Rs 5 lakh per family per year to over 12 crore poor and vulnerable families, aims to reduce their out-of-pocket expenses. It meets a clear need because a health emergency can devastate a poor family and push a lower-middle-class one into poverty. It also offers the poor a choice among participating hospitals. If information on service quality of the various hospitals is made available to the poor as they make their choice, PMJAY can improve health-care quality. In addition, the single-payer government can make strategic purchasing decisions, including dropping some hospitals, based on the information it gets.

The ESIC, which we encountered earlier in the chapter, can also move to strategic purchasing of medical services, even as it spends more on its insured customers. Of course, it is also possible that the government–private-sector interface in PMJAY or ESIC is poorly managed, too many operations and procedures are questioned, payments are delayed, and the best providers exit the system leaving the field to the worst. Only time will tell.

Information and Technology

It is estimated that around 6 billion health transactions take place in the country every year. This information can and should be used to make health-care services more effective. For instance, when a primary health centre refers a patient to a hospital, that hospital should be able to pull down the relevant history of medical transactions and test results for the patient. This is especially important if the health-care system is likely to remain fragmented for the foreseeable future, with no single organization providing the range of services an individual needs.

What India needs in this domain is a 'health stack' analogous to the India Stack.[22] But today, this requires a gargantuan task of coordination, for health is a state subject, and within each state a myriad of data systems coexist, including many informal ones. Nevertheless, we believe the rewards from data sharing will be well worth it. Of course, any health stack must be backed by robust data protection and privacy laws.

Finally, we have seen some of these providers supplement outreach with telemedicine—the doctor far away uses the moderately knowledgeable provider in the primary health centre to examine the patient carefully and then offers a diagnosis. This may increasingly be the way India brings good health care to its most remote areas, while optimizing on the scarce resource, good doctors.

Decentralization

Health care is primarily a state subject in India. But, as we've been arguing, states in India are also large entities. Managing a health-care system from state capitals, let alone through budgets decided at the national capital, will deliver suboptimal results. Even as we increase budgetary allocations, decentralizing health-care design and delivery must be a top priority. The case studies we presented here suggest that mission-driven health-care facilities that are rooted in local communities, and engage in training and even research, have a far greater chance of putting the increased budgetary allocations to better use.

There is plenty of evidence to show that when Covid struck, local health workers were at the forefront—this was the arm of the state that showed up even as many others higher up went missing. Even after the deadly second wave, these workers contributed greatly in the massive task of vaccinating the country. We must recognize that all health is ultimately local. Even as we rethink health care, we must also constantly push the actual implementation of these plans further down from state capitals.

10

Addressing Inequality

Large sections of society will tolerate inequality in the hope of eventually becoming well off themselves, an idea the economist Albert Hirschman called the tunnel effect. Suppose you are stuck on the road in a tunnel, waiting for traffic to move. The lane next to you, which is headed the same way, starts moving—you are happy, for you hope that you will also move. Of course, if the adjacent lane keeps moving for a long period of time while you stay stuck, hope will give way to anger and perhaps a feeling that you have not been treated fairly.

It is difficult for all lanes to move at the same pace in a developing country, to have both growth and equality simultaneously, as another famous economist, Simon Kuznets, documented. So as one lane starts moving, disparities will increase. Society must start thinking of how to set the other lanes in motion too. A thoughtful bureaucrat once told Raghu that India moves in cycles of growth followed by redistribution, then growth again, and that is what keeps it stable. The frequent protests by various communities in India today, demanding to be included in reservations for education and jobs, and the recent farmers' resistance to changes in farm laws is a reminder to those already moving that those left behind are losing patience.

The path we propose aims to create jobs for all. This will be the best way to spread prosperity. In the short run, though, we have to be alert to the possibility that it may not eliminate existing inequality and may even exacerbate some aspects of it. In the vast landscape of inequality and interventions to address them, we examine four issues in more detail: affirmative action, women's labour force participation, improving agriculture and a catch-all category of safety nets. We will offer a broad picture of how, beyond the improvements in capabilities we have discussed already, other support systems need to be better designed to keep all the lanes in Hirschman's tunnel moving. Let's start with affirmative action.

Affirmative Action

Equal opportunity is at the core of a just society. Beyond its economic and political merits, which we will come to, it is a moral imperative for society to provide a level playing field to each individual. The word 'society' is important. It is natural for parents to desire the best for their children, so left to themselves, most parents will not give up privileges accruing to their children willingly; hence society delegates to the state the task of creating opportunities for the underprivileged, sometimes by limiting the privileges of others.

Turning to the economic argument, unequal treatment leads to an inefficient use of resources and talent. How many Ambedkars have we missed out on because they somehow weren't able to escape the clutches of social hierarchies? Discrimination can be self-fulfilling—people who are repeatedly told they have no way ahead can start believing it and not put enough effort to hone their talents. As Nobel laureate V.S. Naipaul famously remarked, 'After all, we make ourselves according to the ideas we have of our possibilities.'[1]

Having successful role models that look like them gives the disadvantaged a sense of their own possibilities. Networks of their own community in places of power may also lend a helping hand—we all benefit from the lucky break that someone sympathetic to us, our own 'Matthew Sir', gives us. Indeed, the privileged never realize how much of a helping hand they get when their competence is taken for granted, for instance in a job interview. Equally, they do not realize how much the underprivileged have to excel to escape the shackles of low expectations. On the political side, the denial of opportunities to any identifiable section of people eventually creates strife when they become conscious of the sustained discrimination.

Despite the clear advantages of a level playing field, modern societies have discovered it is not easy to create one. Badly designed polices can reinforce identities and divisiveness, pulling society apart. With this in mind, Articles 14 and 15 of the Constitution addressed the issue of equality: it emphasized that all are equal before the law, rejecting any discrimination on the basis of identity. However, it also permitted the state to intervene to ensure equality of opportunity: 'Nothing in this article . . . shall prevent the State from making any special provision for . . .' Note the careful balancing act required by the state. It can and should help the disadvantaged in order to equalize conditions, but excessive support, or in the wrong way, would make conditions unequal again.

Reservations

The Indian state intervened primarily through reservations in higher education and public-sector jobs. Initially, these were for the extremely disadvantaged, formerly 'untouchable' castes (scheduled castes or SCs) from the Hindu, Buddhist and Sikh religions, and for tribal communities of all religions (scheduled tribes or STs). After seventy years of this policy, since expanded to cover other backward classes (OBC is a collective term used largely for other socially and economically backward castes), enduring questions remain: Are reservations an effective way of eliminating disadvantage? Do caste-based reservations only benefit the already elite among the backward castes? Since the private sector in the economy is expanding, while the public sector is shrinking in relative terms, shouldn't we extend reservations to the private sector too? But if we keep doing this, wouldn't we forever be prisoners of caste in society and, hence, of identity politics? By extension, would policy never be able to press for a more general emphasis on the delivery of public goods and services?

Leaving these questions aside for the moment, it is clear that reservations alone are not a sufficient tool for advancement. For starters, they kick in too late as a support in an individual's life. We argued in the previous few chapters how health and education in early life are most beneficial in determining an individual's capabilities in adult life. Indeed, research suggests that no amount of intervention in later years will make up for deprivation in the early years.[2]

Aside from these concerns, reservations in colleges are an overly narrow instrument, focused on admitting underprivileged students but not on better outcomes for those who get admission. For instance, according to data made available by the Ministry of Education, 60 per cent of all recent dropouts in the top seven IITs are from the reserved categories and 40 per cent belong only to the SC/ST communities.[3] Almost surely, admitting some with a reduced standard into demanding institutions, without making significant efforts to bring them up to speed, puts enormous pressure on the students. It is to their credit that so many in the reserved categories manage to shine, but we must do more for those who don't.

Public-sector jobs are too few for reservations there to substantially offset the exclusion and discrimination faced by disadvantaged castes. Nevertheless, given the prestige such jobs are held in, those who get them become role models for their community. Unfortunately, the slow growth of jobs elsewhere has made government jobs the only ticket for many, not just for the youth from historically disadvantaged communities, to improve their social and economic status.

Also, by their very nature, reservations tend to favour the better-off in any community for which seats are reserved. Over time, this creates privileged elite within the community and demands from

excluded subgroups for separate quotas. Take the prominent example
of the conflict between the Malas and Madigas in Andhra Pradesh,
where the former, for historical reasons, have been more able to avail of
the opportunities afforded by reservations than the latter. The Madiga
Reservation Porata Samithi has demanded further bifurcation of the
reservation.[4] And, in the words of prominent Dalit writer and social
activist Anand Teltumbde, the Malas have 'argued that the Madigas
should not grudge their progress because they had worked hard for it
while the Madigas just ate, drank and loafed'.[5] A similar allegation is
often made by some upper castes begrudging reservations for the Dalits
and OBCs.

As we consider reservations, we should also not forget that
handicaps come in many forms: women, the economically poor, the
Dalits among non-Hindu religious minorities and so on. How should
we accommodate their claims? Can we keep reducing the unreserved
pie further?

Reservations Plus

India urgently must consider a 'reservations-plus' paradigm. The
previous chapters argued for providing better basic public services—
early childhood nutrition, decent health care, a focus on basic literacy
and numeracy, and more and better-quality opportunities for higher
education. This should be done with more energy directed towards
backward regions that have an overrepresentation of disadvantaged
groups. This will allow for the possibility of promoting equal
opportunity even within these groups.

Of course, everything has been tried before! The earmarking of
funds for the regions with high proportions of SC and ST populations
has been tried since the 1970s, when concerns were first raised
that reservations were not benefitting the truly backward in these
communities. That scheme met with limited success. However, we
believe that with the broader re-energized focus on early childhood

we have suggested in previous chapters, additional funds should make a difference.

In public institutions of higher education, we must measure the progress of reserved-category students better and help them come up to speed. While institutions will hopefully have an easier job if the system does a better job at preparing children from disadvantaged communities in the early years, institutions should not escape accountability. The reservation-plus paradigm demands catch-up classes, regular check-ins on students to ensure they are feeling welcome and not falling behind, and even counselling support where needed. Customized tutoring, as AI becomes more effective, could also help.

How else should we proceed going forward? Indian society itself, partly as a result of economic liberalization, has moved towards reducing some of the most reprehensible forms of social discrimination. For instance, a detailed survey comparing areas in Uttar Pradesh over time finds that there have been significant changes in upper-caste attitudes towards Dalits between 1990 and 2007, with Dalits much less likely to be seated separately at weddings and more likely to be served by non-Dalits, for example, by midwives at childbirth. Dalit occupational choices have also moved away from those traditionally attributed to their caste.[6]

What India needs, of course, is more growth, opportunities and jobs outside the public sector, something we have focused on in earlier chapters. The heart-warming stories of Dalit entrepreneurs who have made it out of poverty to riches in the new liberalized India suggest that much is possible. The competitive market helps equalize opportunities.[7] As prominent Dalit scholar Chandra Bhan Prasad often remarks provocatively, 'Adam Smith and Thomas Macaulay are my two heroes.' The former extolled the liberating effects of the competitive market, while the latter lauded the virtues of English-language education in India.[8] Both have aided Dalit upward mobility. However, as we noted earlier, individuals really encounter the competitive market only as adults. Before that, much has to be done to prepare them.

Economic advancement is not enough for social discrimination to disappear. A recent study of hiring for their India operations by elite US and European multinational corporations in India finds that students from disadvantaged castes suffer at the interview stage. This may be active discrimination against those castes, or it may be that the (typically upper caste) interviewers subconsciously favoured those from their background. Regardless, students from disadvantaged castes were hurt. Interestingly, those from the disadvantaged castes who do get through the interview perform better on the job and have higher promotion rates than others, suggesting they had to jump over a higher hurdle to be selected.[9]

Redesigning Reservations

Should we end reservations? No, but every policy needs a periodic update, and so does the design of reservations. A five-judge bench of the Supreme Court recently remarked that social 'backwardness is not something which is temporary. Rather, it goes down to centuries and generations. But economic backwardness can be temporary.'[10] The court essentially took the view that while the social and economic reasons for reservations intersect, they are not the same. Social backwardness is a more entrenched form of inequality than economic backwardness.

When a caste faces continued social discrimination, caste identity is an easy way of identifying disadvantage, and thus an effective means for the government to offer economic support, such as reservations. Visible economic progress made by some members of such castes enhances community confidence and their social status. Government benefits give members of these groups a sense of equal citizenship and should continue till economic progress and societal awakening largely eliminate social disadvantage.

When a caste faces economic but not social disadvantage, a variety of proposals to improve the targeting of government benefits are worth considering. For instance, some scholars, such as Anand Teltumbde, have proposed that a reserved category could be dynamically divided into two categories of nuclear families: those that have availed of reservations and those that haven't. The latter could have priority when filling up the reserved seats for the category.

Relatedly, in 2007, the government-appointed National Knowledge Commission laid out how affirmative action should gradually seek to address a multidimensional notion of deprivation in which caste forms one, but not the only, variable. As the economy grows, a small but increasing proportion of the reserved seats could be assigned using such a deprivation index. It will have its own teething problems, with the wrong people excluded or included, but it will at least try to move us in a more holistic direction of affirmative action. It can also address the exclusion of women or of those who are poor but not from a disadvantaged caste.

What about private universities and firms? They should focus on diversity as a desirable goal, not just to correct disadvantages but also to strengthen the quality of their intake and output. For instance, the hardships a student has overcome to reach the entrance to the college often signals their determination and resilience. Such a student should be given some additional preference by a university over someone else who is otherwise approximately equal on every other dimension. The student's score on the multidimensional index of deprivation discussed above could be one guide to the hardship distance a student has travelled. Similarly, social pressures, as well as government nudges and norms, should push private firms to work harder to hire from truly disadvantaged groups.

The bottom line is that we need to eliminate economic sources of disadvantage, both through better public services and targeted government support. Hopefully, over time, the economic success of the disadvantaged will reduce social discrimination. Until that happens, though, those who are socially discriminated against deserve support. We also need a broader awakening throughout society. We should be especially wary of creating new sources of social and economic discrimination, such as those based on religion.

Women and Labour Force Participation

One of the most disheartening aspects of the Indian economy today is the low participation rate of women in work aside from homemaking. The women's labour force participation rate (WLFP) is defined as the percentage of the population of women that is either working or actively looking for work. According to the latest data released by the Centre for Monitoring Indian Economy (CMIE), WLFP was 8.8 per cent for the financial year 2022–23.[11] Allow that to sink in. That means out of hundred women of working age, barely nine are working or looking for work outside domestic work. In virtually every category of the disadvantaged—SC, ST, OBC, religious minority, etc.—women have far fewer jobs than men. In India, women are truly disadvantaged.

There are some differences between the CMIE data and other surveys like the Periodic Labour Force Survey (PLFS). This turns on the definition of what it means to be looking for a job and how a category, such as unpaid work at home (for a family business), is counted. Recent data released by the PLFS, for January–March 2023, puts the WLFP number for urban India at a higher 22 per cent.[12] Even so, twenty-two women out of every 100 (with over 30 per cent reporting doing unpaid work) is the lowest women's labour force participation in the G20, below even Saudi Arabia. What is going wrong, and what can we do about it?

The U-Shaped Curve

If you plot the GDP per capita for a country on the x-axis and women's labour force participation rate on the y-axis, and draw a curve of best fit, you will observe a U shape. Writing in 1995, Harvard economist Claudia Goldin, who won the 2023 Nobel Prize in economics, noted,

'Its U-shape is revealed both across the process of economic development and through the histories of currently advanced economies.'[13]

When countries are poor, mostly agrarian, and have low levels of automation, women work in the fields, do other manual labour and work in low-quality services. Some of their labour is paid, but often they are unpaid workers on family farms and in production at home. WLFP is high. But, as countries get a little richer and households are pulled out of extreme poverty, women's participation in the labour forces declines.

One reason is that as a household's income rises, its members need to do less work to maintain their consumption level, so, typically, social norms dictate that women stop doing paid outside work. Prominent intellectual Chandra Bhan Prasad has pointed out that it may be a matter of pride for some Indian households with rising incomes that females in the family are not required to go outside the home into unsafe environments or to undertake unsafe jobs.[14]

Also, as households get richer, their consumption shifts from cheap goods made in neighbouring households to goods and services produced in factories or offices. Women are, relatively speaking, less likely to work outside the home, in part because they usually are prime caregivers for children, and in part because of safety issues outside the home. In India, a particularly important factor is marriage, with married women participating less in the workforce than unmarried women, regardless of whether they have children.[15]

Eventually, though, as incomes rise further, women become more educated and they have fewer children, they have more choices when it comes to jobs as well as greater flexibility with their time. Society becomes more open to women working and better-funded police improve safety. WLFP starts to increase again.

India Is Stuck at the Lower End of the U-Curve

India has broadly followed the first part of this trend, the decline, but it is yet to see the rise.[16] Importantly, the decline has been concomitant with a huge increase in the enrolment of female students at almost every level of the education system. Enrolment in primary school is, as noted earlier, almost universal now. Even in higher education, the number of females enrolled in colleges and universities for 100 males was fourteen in 1950–51, sixty-seven in 2002–03 and 107 in 2020–21.[17] So, more and more women are getting educated. They do differ in what they study; for example, females are overrepresented in the study of education (perhaps they intend to become teachers) and underrepresented in engineering. While educated women may be more open to working, they are also more likely to be unemployed. The latest data, for example, shows that the labour force participation rate is higher among illiterate women than among women who have an undergraduate degree.[18]

From an economic perspective, productive capacity and incomes decrease if so many women are not doing the best work they are capable of. The country is much poorer than it should be. Many women, frustrated in their ambitions, will lead less fulfilling lives than they could have had. Paid employment increases a woman's bargaining power at home, leading to greater gender equality, including a greater role in household decision-making and greater ownership of household assets.[19]

Women also make the workplace more productive. A recent IMF study argues that you shouldn't think of men and women as simply substitutable labour. Men and women increase each other's productivity by bringing different sets of skills and perspectives to the workplace. Having a gender-diverse team of consultants has an added benefit, above and beyond simply having more consultants.[20]

Given the enormous social and economic benefits to women's participation, why is it so low in India? Alice Evans, an economist at King's College London, points out that women's labour force participation rate among British Indians is around 70 per cent (about as much as for native-born British) and 40 per cent among British Bangladeshis, even though women's participation rate in Bangladesh is higher than in India.[21] While there may be some peculiarities in who chooses to emigrate from each country, if this emigrant population is not dissimilar in attitudes to the population that stays in the country, these facts would suggest that the system in India is more unfriendly towards participation by women.

What Can We Do?

There are no easy fixes. A change in family and societal attitudes on the proper role of women can help, as can changes in attitudes among women themselves. For instance, it should not be that marriage, by itself, should bind women to the home. We should celebrate women who work outside the home, ranging from successful professionals to social reformers.

We also must work on creating more jobs that are both appealing and easier for women. The Economic Survey of India 2017–18 noted how textile, apparel and footwear industries employ more women. But India is unable to occupy the space that China is vacating in low-skilled textiles and apparel, ceding the ground to, among other countries, Bangladesh. The sector is one of the largest employers of women in Bangladesh. We do not need to repeat the reasons why such manufacturing is weak in India, only noting it also hurts women's participation. Indeed, everything we have suggested on job growth for India would also help women's participation.

Nevertheless, there are specific attributes of jobs that would make them more attractive to women. Job search is harder for women, both in terms of accessing job postings and applying and interviewing for them—sometimes because of children or other domestic constraints. Posting jobs where women will see them, including on the Internet, is a 'no-brainer', as is easing the application process and the interviewing process, conducting them virtually wherever appropriate and possible.

Women are also attracted to part-time regular jobs (which allow them to balance work and home) as well as flexible work-from-home jobs.[22] Employers should be encouraged to offer alternative job structures with sliding salary scales, flexible work hours and shared responsibilities, for example, through more half-day jobs. The government should re-examine labour and tax regulations that stand in the way of creating part-time jobs and create some itself.

Reliable and affordable childcare can also help, both in directly creating jobs for women and in giving highly educated or skilled mothers time for work. Historically, women in the joint family who stay at home have provided this service in India. For nuclear families in cities today, professional childcare has become an increasing necessity. Referral services, web-based employment exchanges and databases of user experience can reduce the information gap between parent and potential care providers that keeps this market small.

The home can also be physically connected to the world. India has a large number of female artisans, including women's self-help groups (or SHGs). They are, however, not as economically active as they should be, in part because of the lack of market access. Indian handicrafts account for only 2 per cent of the global handicrafts market, in comparison to 30 per cent occupied by China. The potential for growth, though, is huge, through the right mix of training, design, quality control, branding and connecting to the global marketplace. For example, Tilfi, the firm selling Banarasi saris we read about earlier, has started training female apprentices in a hitherto male-dominated craft.

Safety is a big concern for women in India, both in getting to work and at the workplace itself. A safer commute, enforced by social norms and policing, would help. Women-only compartments on metros and local trains, and free bus travel for women are some measures taken in various cities to encourage women to step out. Another option is to eliminate the commute itself, especially for young women living in big cities, away from their families. China has done so by building safe dormitories near the workplaces. India could learn from China's experience. Night shifts, which seem important in some industries to fully utilize machinery, could also become more feasible in such cases.

Safety at the workplace is also important. One example where this is a particular concern is tourism, a large employer of women all over the world but not in India. The Indian tourism and hospitality industry is staggeringly male-dominated. The next time you go out to a restaurant or on a holiday and stay in a hotel, especially in northern India, try to observe the male–female split of the workforce. It is educative. Interestingly, the split is more equal among flight attendants in Indian airlines—in fact, the majority of the workforce is female—and at 15 per cent, the fraction of female pilots in India is the highest in the world. All this suggests that the situation can be improved through better workplace safety.[23]

The education sector is a large employer of women in India because, among other reasons, women feel safe in schools and college campuses. Given that India needs a revolution in education, as we have discussed earlier, it offers an enormous opportunity to create women-friendly jobs, whether it is by drawing mothers part-time into the school to help with basic learning or drawing PhDs into new universities to teach. Similarly, the greater emphasis on health care we propose will also create women-friendly jobs, ranging from a helper in the Anganwadi to more doctors and nurses in world-class hospitals.

Quotas, too, seem to have worked well in some public-sector jobs. For example, a 33 per cent quota was introduced for women as heads of panchayats (village councils), and today more than 40 per cent of all heads are women. The quota has now been raised to 50 per cent in twenty states. There are many stories of husbands 'remote-controlling' their wives, but there is evidence of women taking on, or at least growing into, the role and bringing about meaningful change. Studies suggest when women panchayat leaders have a free hand, they work harder towards the provision of basic public services such as water and sanitation.[24] As this book is going to print, legislation that would reserve one-third of seats in the lower houses at the Centre and states for women candidates is gaining momentum.

In summary, there is much India can do to employ women outside the home. We owe it to our largest minority to do better.

Improving Agricultural Incomes and Resilience

We have focused on manufacturing and services as the drivers of future growth, with workers leaving low-productivity agriculture. But to address inequality we must focus on agriculture too. In 2022, agriculture's share of the GDP was 16 per cent, but its share of employment was still a high 44 per cent.[25] Of course, the agricultural household is not entirely dependent on cultivation (an increasing proportion of which is horticulture, not grain) or on livestock. Indeed, about half of household income comes from wages and salaries and other sources, some of which are outside agriculture.[26]

In 2016, recognizing the problem of low agricultural incomes, the government set an ambitious target of doubling farming incomes by 2023. We say 'ambitious' because the last doubling of farmer incomes, taking out the effect of inflation, took twenty-two years, from 1993 to 2015.[27] While the target has, of course, not been met, the slow growth of agricultural incomes is just one reason the sector needs reforms.

Another reason for urgent reforms is that government interventions are proving increasingly costly and increasingly distortionary. The costs associated with subsidies are rising. One is simply the direct cost. The total fertilizer subsidy bill for the financial year 2022–23 for the Central government was Rs 2.25 lakh crore. To put this in context, the entire budgetary allocation for primary and higher education by the Central government in the same financial year was Rs 1.05 lakh crore.[28] But the indirect costs may be more problematic. The overuse of heavily subsidized urea is poisoning the soil.[29] Similarly, as we saw in Punjab, free power is leading to excessive pumping of ground water, reducing the water table below natural replenishment rates, which threatens future food production. Free power also hurts poorer farmers who cannot afford the powerful pumps needed to reach the water table.

Even minimum support prices, especially for rice and wheat, which are the main crops procured, are problematic because they are set at a level above any reasonable market price. This, then, makes the minimum support price the effective market price, leading to overproduction of rice and wheat, even though our granaries are already overflowing with them, and even though rice guzzles water. Pulses and even vegetables, which are nutritionally more essential, are underproduced.

Perhaps the most important reason for reform is growing climate volatility resulting from climate change. Farmers will need to adapt, which may mean changing technologies of production to, say, more dry farming or drip irrigation, sowing hardier and less water-hungry crops, and diversifying across crops and agricultural activities. New technologies like vertical farming may also become common to make better use of scarce land.

The government's reforms to farm laws, which were passed hastily by Parliament with little debate in September 2020, were arguably about letting farmers have the choice to sell outside the mandi, giving private traders greater ability to buy and store produce, and allowing farmers to contract with agri-businesses with greater ease. Far from welcoming these laws, farmers, especially in Punjab and Haryana, protested.

Much has been written about the reasons for the protests, including whether they were egged on by the middlemen in the mandi (called *arhatiyas*), whose earnings would have been impaired. Farmers seemed to be genuinely worried that by diminishing the role of the mandi, the reforms might leave them with less choice of where to sell and with less information about market prices (if information about transactions that take place outside the mandi is not recorded). At any rate, the laws were withdrawn by the government in November 2021. The episode highlights the need to consult widely, and to understand and address the fears of those affected, before undertaking reforms of this kind.

This does not mean other reforms are not possible. Crop insurance, where crops are carefully monitored using satellite imagery and compensation paid out quickly in case of loss, needs to become more available and effective, especially as climate volatility increases.

We need far more research on the new crop varieties and techniques that will be needed as the climate changes, and more dissemination of that research to farmers through agricultural extension workers. Systems to do all this have become moribund in many states and will have to be revived. This may indeed be a thrust area for government-financed research discussed earlier.

Land leasing must be made easier, with adequate protections for the lessor, so that farmers whose landholdings are too small can lease the land without selling it. The rent they get, including any transfers the government makes to landowners, will be a supplement to their income, even as they labour elsewhere. A farmer who leases in land could enhance farm size, and achieve the scale that would make agriculture more viable.

Finally, we have to expand agri-processing industry so that more value can be added to farm output. Given their scale, farmer producer organizations or farmer co-operatives may be especially suited to opening processing plants. As farmers break from the tyranny of rice and wheat to make other crop choices, industry should be encouraged to partner with farmers to identify crops that industry can process profitably and farmers find remunerative. The measures we will discuss shortly to enhance entrepreneurship should apply here. Eventually, of course, jobs elsewhere will pull farmers out of agriculture, making farming more viable for those left behind. In the meantime, these measures will enhance farmer incomes, increase their sustainability and reduce their volatility.

Safety Nets

Safety nets are meant to help the very poor, as well as those who suffer a sudden misfortune, such as a loss of a job or illness, and have no savings. Start with subsidized or free food grain for the poor, add subsidized cooking gas, subsidized houses for the poor, free health insurance for the poor for hospitalization and so on, and India has created a safety net of sorts. Can we do better?

The Problem with Subsidies Again

As we have seen with farmers, subsidies often lead to wrong decisions. For instance, the market price for rice and wheat averaged Rs 42 and Rs 30 per kg, respectively, in the summer of 2023, but the subsidized price to the beneficiary through the public distribution system is Rs 3 per kg for rice and Rs 2 for wheat, of course, subject to some limits on quantities per person.[30] One immediate consequence is that beneficiaries consume the cheaper wheat and rice, while ignoring other healthier foods. As a result, while they may get the quantity of calories they need in rural areas, and perhaps too much in urban areas where work is not as back-breaking, they certainly do not get enough of the diverse nutrients they need. The subsidized public distribution system induces poor nutritional habits among our people, which weighs on their health over time.

A second problem with subsidization is that the subsidized good may not reach the intended beneficiary. If rice costs Rs 42 in the marketplace and only Rs 3 to the buyer, there is a huge incentive for middlemen to divert rice stocks. The unscrupulous distributor can profit enormously from unclaimed allocations or the creation of fake ration cards for non-existent persons. While no large-scale recent data exists, various estimates from 2005 to 2012 suggest that between 40 to 50 per cent of the subsidized food grain was being diverted.[31]

Another problem is that not all the needy are covered; according to the National Family Health Survey-3, released in 2009, two-thirds of the Below Poverty Line Cards that are used to gain access to the public distribution system were found with non-poor households, and similar trends continued in the National Family Health Survey-4 from 2015 to 2016.[32] At the same time, despite recent improvements in data availability and information technology, too many of the better-off receive subsidies. A recent study found that 60 per cent of those in the top 60 per cent of households by income and assets in the state of Uttarakhand were enrolled in the newly launched PMJAY, the government's flagship health-insurance scheme, even though the stated goal of the scheme is to target the bottom 40 per cent of the population![33]

Direct Transfers and the Promise of Technology

While subsidies distort the decisions consumers and producers make, direct transfers of cash that are not tied to production or consumption decisions do not. Both state and Central governments have shown that they can deposit cash directly in the bank accounts of citizens. Most of the poor have bank accounts, thanks to the government's Jan Dhan scheme, intended to open bank accounts for all. The Aadhaar unique identification number for every adult citizen of the country prevents duplicate transfers or transfers to non-existent persons. The combination makes it easy to make transfers to almost every citizen. We say 'almost' because a small fraction of people, unfortunately the neediest, are still not covered by either bank accounts or Aadhaar.

Be that as it may, once we want to separate rich from poor, and make transfers only to the latter, we run into the problem of inadequate information. The government does not know precisely who is rich. It could base transfers on tax records, but not only would that further dis-incentivize reporting incomes to tax authorities, it would also reward those who are good at hiding their income. The government could exclude those who own a car, property or land, but ownership title may be distributed across children or held in a corporation. It could exclude those who use a lot of electric power, but that would encourage power theft.

Nevertheless, cash transfers to the poor beat distortionary subsidies. Also, money in the hands of the poor is empowering—if they use it to pay a private school's fees, they feel they have a right to get good value for money, as one founder of private schools told us. Consequently, the paying poor will protest if they get rotten service, which helps improve the quality of education (or health care).

It may also encourage investment. As Raghu's student Nishant Vats has pointed out, farmers who get the guaranteed annual transfer of Rs 6000 from the Pradhan Mantri Kisan Samman Nidhi tend to borrow to invest, perhaps conscious that they now have a guaranteed inflow that will prevent destitution. As a result, they increase their incomes by significantly more than the guaranteed Rs 6000 per year.

The logical conclusion from all this would be to replace subsidies with cash transfers, but this is usually politically very difficult. What we can certainly do is to stop any more subsidies, move any incremental supports, especially to the poor, to cash transfers, and try and sweep all forms of cash transfers, at least from the Central government to start with, into one family transfer where appropriate.

For example, assuming India wants to give Rs 8000 to every household every year (the Rs 6000 to farmer households augmented by inflation), and assuming the average household has two adults and two children, it could transfer Rs 2000 into every person's bank account. Economists Maitreesh Ghatak and Karthik Muralidharan suggest keeping the overall transfer at 1 per cent of the GDP, which is what this transfer would amount to.[34] For very poor households, this would be a substantial direct benefit, but it could also be the basis of borrowing and asset creation. The transfers are small but could help put more varieties of food on the table than grain, or put a child in school, or offer the equity against which to borrow to invest. Eventually, as the economy grows, the number could be scaled up.

To make the scheme more targeted, we could follow exclusion criteria, recognizing the difficulties pointed out earlier and hoping that the malfeasance engendered by the small size of the transfer is small: the government could taper transfer payments off to income tax payers as their incomes exceed, say, Rs 2.5 lakh a year; exclude government servants and employees of large firms; taper transfers to those whose land ownership, past vehicle or house purchases, or power consumption exceeds a certain amount, and so on. Some countries have experimented with making lists of beneficiaries public, so that those who clearly meet the exclusion criteria have an added incentive to declare themselves ineligible. The money saved by not sending benefits to the excluded could be added to the pool going to beneficiaries. Further, since some states are already making such transfers, the Centre could coordinate with states to ensure the cumulative transfer serves the purpose.

There is a fear that people may spend the transfers irresponsibly, say, men drinking them away. Yet there is little evidence across countries that cash transfers are spent on 'temptation goods' such as alcohol and tobacco. Instead, studies suggest that cash transfers are typically spent on increasing expenditures on food, including for increasing the diversity of the food purchased, on health care, on livestock and agricultural inputs, and on savings. These expenditures are certainly consistent with what we think India needs.[35]

Conditional Support

Much of what we have discussed so far is unconditional support for the distressed and the poor, a helping hand to let them build assets or their human capital. India also has a National Rural Employment Guarantee Scheme, which offers distressed farmers and agricultural workers hundred days of remunerated work every year. Given the work is physical and hard, and the remuneration modest, it is unlikely that anyone but the needy will take it up. So it is a useful conditional safety net, used extensively during Covid, when urban migrants returned home to their villages.

Given the plight of urban migrants, marooned in cities without work during the Covid shutdowns, or forced to trudge hundreds of miles home to their villages, it is important that we think of an urban safety net along the lines of the rural scheme. A National Urban

Employment Guarantee, structured so that it does not encourage or discourage rural–urban migration, with work assignments ranging from cleaning up public spaces to public road construction, and with more work made available in difficult economic times, is long overdue.

In closing, any kind of reservation, subsidy or transfer creates an implicit property right that becomes very hard to change. So we should weigh any change carefully, experimenting, if possible, before a full and permanent roll-out. Nevertheless, there are many ways the government can be more effective in its support, while reducing distortions in decision-making.

Evoking the tunnel effect again: Some lanes will move fast and others slowly, but overall, we should constantly endeavour to increase the pace of those who are further behind. This is the marker of a just society.

11

India's Engagement with the World

Today, India is approaching middle income as a country. Because of its large population, its overall income is higher than that of many advanced economies. As it is still relatively poor, its 'catch-up' growth rate is higher than that of advanced economies, so it is overtaking one advanced economy after another—recently, the UK, and if all goes well, Germany and then Japan soon after. So hyper-jingoists are already pressing India to flex its muscles openly, to tell other countries, rich and poor, what we want—after all, we will eventually be a superpower, so why not act like one today? This desire to coerce and even insult other countries, to try and cow them, resembles the 'Wolf Warrior' approach taken by parts of the Chinese establishment. Indeed, some have taken to call this India's 'Tiger Warrior' approach.[1] It plays well with a domestic audience but is extremely short-sighted, for it creates an unnecessary outside reaction.

There is an alternative, though—to build economic strength quietly, to emphasize our values and to spread the message that we will be an equal partner in other countries' growth. We must champion openness in trade and investment, for that has served India and other developing countries well, and we should re-examine our own record in this regard. We must also take the lead in making the world more open to service exports. While India should concomitantly build its military strength as it grows, it must signal it does not intend unprovoked aggression, but will put up a tough, determined defence if ever attacked.

India should play its part in addressing the enormous challenges the world faces, especially de-globalization, climate change, migration and ageing. Not only will this hasten our own economic progress, it will also make it more likely that if and when India becomes a superpower, it will be one in its own mould—a superpower that self-confidently emphasizes cooperation, peace, goodwill and creativity rather than coercion and dominance. We believe the choice is clear.

With the successful hosting of the G20 summit in Delhi, as well as many meetings across the country during the course of India's presidency in 2023, India's foreign engagement has gained significant momentum. It is important that this be sustained, and this chapter focuses on some key issues around which we will have to make choices—soft versus hard power, our approaches to cross-border trade and investment in general, setting the standards for trade in services, how to deal with climate, migration and ageing. Geographically, our main choices have to do with how we work with our smaller neighbours, how we create a nearby region we can trade with, how we interact with our large northern neighbour, China, and our relationship with industrial democracies as well as the developing countries that are termed the 'global south'.

Soft Power vs Hard Power

The former dean of Harvard University's Kennedy School of Government, Joseph S. Nye Jr, defines 'soft power' as the 'ability to get what you want through attraction rather than coercion or payments'. Soft power is spread through art and culture, through ideas and political ideals, and through debate and exchange. When what diffuses to other countries is seen as legitimate and persuasive, as having a moral force, soft power is successful in achieving its purpose.

Think of how the economic success of the United States became an important factor in persuading countries to liberalize their economies after the end of World War II, and even more so after the demise of the Soviet Union. This also benefited US firms because it opened up markets to them. Similarly, artistic developments, such as rap music in the suburbs of New York City, now permeate Punjabi pop and Bollywood music. Hard power, on the other hand, is 'the ability to coerce', through carrots (rewards) and sticks (punishments), and it 'grows out of a country's military and economic might'.[2]

Of course, power cannot be an end in itself. What matters is the ultimate objective of the use of the power—whether it helps the country to develop, to spread its ideas and values, and, relatedly, to improve its own security. This is something we need to keep reminding ourselves of, for the exercise of power can draw counterproductive reactions that move us further from the goals of development, influence and security.

China's experience over the last few years suggests the limits to hard power. Chinese leader Deng Xiaoping's dictum in the early years of his country's growth was that China should 'hide [its] capabilities and bide [its] time'. He was clearly concerned that Chinese strength would provoke a reaction. But China under Xi Jinping seems to believe that the time for that dictum is over. As President Xi stated in October 2017, '. . . the Chinese nation has gone from standing up, to becoming rich, to becoming strong.'[3]

For Washington, such statements triggered its latent paranoias— first, that it would be overtaken as the world's supreme power; and second, that China, ruled by an increasingly authoritarian leader of a one-party state, would not be bound by democratic checks and balances. The US economic reaction has been quick and has bipartisan support. From tariffs on Chinese goods followed by limits on US exports of hi-tech equipment to China, and on outward investment to, and inward investment from, China—a whole range of actions aimed at containment have been unleashed. Europe and Japan have also followed in some measure.

Not just the United States, but many of China's neighbours and near-neighbours fear an authoritarian, coercive China. Several of them have territorial disputes with China. Many, including India, have banned equipment purchases from Huawei, the Chinese telecom equipment manufacturer, fearing that the Chinese state will require Huawei to build spyholes into the equipment.

Worried about eventual conflict, many US firms with supply chains that criss-cross into China are trying to de-risk operations by finding alternative suppliers in friendlier countries. Chinese firms are doing the same, de-risking exposure to the United States. While such decoupling is still limited in scale, few US firms would start a large manufacturing project in China today. All of this is hurting Chinese growth. In retrospect, maybe Deng's advice has been disregarded prematurely—China may have flexed its muscles too soon.

As Shivshankar Menon, India's former national security adviser, writes, 'All rising powers in history have chosen to keep their heads down while building their own strength, rather than inviting resistance to their rise to great power status by proclaiming their power and its uses.'[4] He cautions that Wilhelmine Germany and Japan in the 1930s were frustrated in their rise and paid a heavy price for flaunting their ambition and their growing power too early, and concludes 'whether China has made the same mistake recently remains to be seen'.

Turning to India, its cultural heritage, including the great ancient religions that sprang from within its shores, has always been an important source of influence in the world. India's non-violent fight for independence, and the ideas of the man who led that fight, Mohandas Gandhi, helped distil that heritage into something concrete and worth emulating by the world at large. The fact that Mahatma Gandhi's statue is in Parliament Square in London, outside the European headquarters of the United Nations in Geneva and at Union Square in New York, among other places, is a testament to the wide acceptability of his ideas of non-violence and, by association, a credit to India's soft power. You do not see statues of Gandhi's contemporary Muhammad Ali Jinnah in these places because his cause of a theocratic state is not one that stirs the collective human psyche.

India's choice of democracy at the time of Independence and its ability to stick with it, as historian Ramachandra Guha emphasizes in his classic book *India after Gandhi*, contributed further to its moral aura and widening respect, even as its global economic footprint continued to be minuscule. India's welcoming diverse culture, its openness and spirituality, attracted intellectuals like John Kenneth Galbraith and Octavio Paz to India. Many, especially in the developing world, looked up to us.

India's potential to project soft power is especially pronounced because, like the United States, it is a great mixing of people of different languages, races, ethnicities and religions. When India, despite its poverty, proudly went to the world as a united country, it also told the world that its different peoples could live together peaceably and profitably—it offered itself as a successful realization of human coexistence. The richness of spirit, of mutual respect and tolerance, of common identity reinforced during the freedom struggle, more than compensated for the paucity of our people's incomes.

In this vein, a recent report by eminent scholars of modern India conceptualizes the source of India's soft power aptly: 'The foundational source of India's power,' they remark, 'is the power of its example.' They premise this on four pillars: economic growth, social inclusion, political democracy and a liberal constitutional order.[5] They emphasize that India's founding fathers did not try to achieve a false homogeneity but sought 'to find an enduring national strength through the creative articulation of myriad local identities'.

All this said, soft power will not protect a country if others want to use hard power—otherwise, pacifist spiritual Tibet would still be independent. India still sees US support to the Yahya Khan military regime in Pakistan in the 1971 Bangladesh liberation war as a betrayal, sacrificing the shared values of the two democracies for short-term American self-interest. The Mumbai attacks of November 2008, clearly orchestrated by Pakistan, did not lead to global isolation or punishment for the regime in Islamabad. In short, India cannot, in Nye's framework, get what it wants simply by being attractive.

So hard power is essential for India to defend itself, and even to convince other countries that India is a worthwhile friend (and an undesirable enemy). The question is whether India can rely on its own hard power only. And here the answer is clearly no.

India's is a much smaller economy than that of China, United States and the European Union, and will remain so for decades. India will need alliances if it ever goes up against any superpower. However, even though it is not yet of a size that would pose a threat to today's big powers, it is large enough to raise concerns among its neighbours.

Our Smaller Neighbours

India's relationship with its neighbours, never on a strong footing, has had its ups and downs. Leaving aside the relationships with China and Pakistan, which remain in the doldrums, our relationship with Bangladesh, which Indian troops liberated in 1971, has soured as some of our majoritarian politicians have targeted Bangladeshi migrants with abuse. China has increasing influence in Nepal, Sri Lanka and even Bhutan, and a more muscularly nationalist India makes it attractive for these small neighbours to keep India guessing about their alignment. Myanmar's generals have always had a soft corner for China, which turns a blind eye to their lack of democratic legitimacy.

Our Tiger Warriors do not help. For instance, a mural of Ashokan India in our new Parliament, incorporating Pakistan, Bangladesh and Nepal, has irritated our neighbours, as it appears India is claiming their territory. What makes them even more worried is ruling party ministers and politicians talk about Akhand Bharat (undivided India) as if that is not the past but a future goal.[6] When India justifiably bristles if it sees China showing Arunachal Pradesh as a part of China, it cannot be insensitive to its smaller neighbours' concerns.

Deteriorating relations with neighbours can aggravate conflicts in India's own border states. A friendly neighbour will refuse to offer shelter or safe passage to armed separatists, thus forcing them to the negotiating table with our government. An unfriendly neighbour can turn a blind eye to their activities and even actively support them with weapons, thus prolonging conflict, as has been the case with Kashmir. Unfortunately, majoritarian authoritarianism can exacerbate internal tensions even while it antagonizes neighbours, thus weakening national security.

India would become less concerning to its neighbours and draw their energies into engaging more in economic trade and investment if it committed to peaceable inclusive growth, in part by strengthening the democratic checks and balances on our own leaders. Democracies can, no doubt, start wars of aggression—the 2003 US invasion of Iraq, aided by collective US domestic hysteria and misinformation about Saddam Hussein's supposed weapons of mass destruction, is a recent example. But liberal democracies are typically not driven by the whims of one leader—a leader who may live in their own cocoon, surrounded by yes-men who are constantly trying to gauge what the leader wants to hear. Unfortunately, autocracies are, as Putin's Russia has demonstrated!

On the economic front, too, we are losing opportunities. The South Asian region trades and invests far less within itself than might be suggested by the physical proximity between countries. With strengthened infrastructure in each of the countries and improving scope for cross-border connectivity through roads, rail, waterways and air, South Asia is ready for greater intra-regional trade and investment. Standing in the way is politics. We have discussed earlier the detrimental impact on Punjab's economy of having land-route trade to Pakistan and Afghanistan essentially blocked.

The primary regional organization is the South Asian Association for Regional Cooperation (SAARC). Anyone who has been to SAARC meetings (Raghu has) can sense the obvious undercurrents. First, there is the on/off antagonism between India and Pakistan, which typically determines whether or not the meeting is productive. Second, there is the natural fear small neighbours have of being swamped by India, which Indian officials are not always sensitive to. Consequently, SAARC meetings usually end with small steps that preserve the illusion of movement while achieving little.

As the leading power in the region, India must prepare the political ground for much greater cooperation and then propose a bold agenda of shared growth that enthuses its neighbours. It might start with a series of positive steps, unilaterally where necessary: make visas much easier; reduce unnecessary border frictions, including detailed vehicle inspections and paperwork, or frictions in currency exchange; open universities to regional applicants and its hospitals to regional patients; offer to share know-how in areas like reserves and debt management or digital public infrastructure; invite regional firms to list on Indian exchanges; offer seats in its government training institutions for regional officials; increase official lending and backstop regional currency swaps; increase security cooperation against terrorism, including sharing data where it does not compromise our security . . . All of this requires a certain modicum of mutual trust, which may differ across neighbours. This trust must, nonetheless, be constantly nurtured, which entails some risk, but excessive caution will ensure we never make progress.

India has an important seat at global forums like the IMF and the World Bank (where the Indian executive directors represent much of South Asia), the G7 (as a frequent observer), the G20 and climate dialogues. It should start convoking SAARC before important global meetings to see if there are regional concerns that need to be represented. Climate, where we all face similar concerns (more on this later), seems a natural place to build a common position. More regional dialogue, even if much of it is just talk, will result in greater bonds between officials at all levels, which will prepare the ground for bigger moves.

The next step would be to begin negotiating a regional trade and investment treaty, with a concrete plan for increased openness over time. Indian firms will be at the vanguard of cross-border trade and investment, so India should be sensitive to our neighbours' concerns about Indian goods flooding their markets and Indian firms dominating their economies. Where necessary, India should build in some voluntary restraints if the data suggests that the neighbours' fears are coming true. For instance, India could agree to limits on the growth rate of its exports to each country, especially in sensitive sectors like agriculture. More generally, India should be willing to make concessions in order to kick-start the entire project of making South Asia economically strong and vibrant. This will not be a sign of weakness, it will show confidence and common sense.

What about Pakistan? India has always found powerful interests in Pakistan, including the armed forces and intelligence services, opposed to any bilateral rapprochement. Their budgetary allocations, indeed, their very power, is predicated on keeping India as a bogeyman intent on destroying Pakistan. Yet Pakistan is now an economic basket case, and its usefulness to its former backer, the United States, is limited. China has stepped up, but the Chinese demand their pound of flesh and more for any support they provide. Many Pakistanis are increasingly concerned about Pakistan becoming a vassal state to China. While it may still take time for Pakistan to be willing to deal honestly and bilaterally with India, it may also be less obstructionist in regional moves, especially if it believes that they will be helpful in its own economic growth. When eventually the conditions for dialogue emerge, both countries will find their common languages and culture a basis to build on.

Our Northern Neighbour

In the spring of 2020, while India was battling Covid, the Chinese Army occupied territory on the Indian side of the Line of Actual Control. They fought skirmishes leading to casualties on both sides as the Chinese prevented Indian soldiers from patrolling where they have patrolled for years.[7] Despite many previous meetings between President Xi and Prime Minister Modi, India was surprised by Chinese aggression. But this was not the first time India had been surprised—Prime Minister Nehru, too, did not anticipate Chinese aggression in 1962, thinking the relationship between the two countries was governed by the Panchsheel agreement he had signed with Chinese Premier Zhou Enlai in 1954.

India has to understand that the relationship with China will remain volatile so long as China sees India to be weak. In the short run, India has to be firm on border issues while building alliances with others who have disputes with China. At some point, if pressures from the north mount, India may have to rethink its official stance of remaining non-aligned and examine whether it should push for stronger commitments for mutual assistance in case of attack, through arrangements like the Quad Plus (a group comprising Australia, India, Japan and the United States, augmented by New Zealand, South Korea and Vietnam, that engages in strategic dialogue and joint military operations). Over the medium term, our greatest security will come from building up the economy and devoting a reasonable share of spending to defence.

Without becoming paranoid, India has to be alert to a variety of actions short of war, including cyberattacks, election interference and the funding of groups bent on undermining India. This last, especially when it comes to funding from foreign sources more generally, requires a careful balance between identifying true threats to national security without stamping out legitimate inquiry, research, protest or opposition. The distinction—the first undermines the nation itself, while the second challenges the policies of the government of the day—is seldom acknowledged by government agencies. We must remember that idealistic students who protest government actions, say, on the grounds that they harm the environment, are not the enemy, meant to be jailed. They are our children and are trying to help mould a better future.

While thwarting Chinese aggression, India should not shun the opportunity to cooperate with China where possible, so long as India does not become excessively dependent on China. India will develop faster if Chinese firms are allowed to invest in India, outside of strategic areas like telecommunication equipment or defence contracts. That will also give China something to lose if the relationship deteriorates.

In international debates, India can make common cause on some issues with China, for China, too, is a power that has had little say in the structuring of international arrangements. At the same time, there are many areas where China's size and stage of development would make it an unreliable ally. For instance, all too often, India is clubbed with China as a large country with rising emissions. Yet India emits far less than the world average, is less developed and thus needs to avoid being put in the same basket as China. Furthermore, it does not have the presence in solar cells, batteries or EVs that China has, and therefore has some way to go before fully benefiting from growing global investment in emission mitigation.

Industrial Democracies

While India's interests may diverge from those of industrial democracies on occasion, our values are often more aligned with theirs than with the values of authoritarian countries, and our longer-term growth will depend on strong engagement with them. For instance, as detailed earlier, our attempt to take Indian university education to a higher plane will require increasing collaboration between our research establishments and theirs (and the growing conflict between China and the industrial democracies creates a hole India can fill). We will need them to train many of the PhD students we will need for our research and teaching establishments. Their markets will also be where we will export our goods and services, so the goodwill of their public is essential.

There is a tendency for our foreign policy establishment, now that India has a greater voice on the international stage, to constantly harp about India being powerful enough to withstand outside pressures and emphasize its own interests. Typically, that means criticizing industrial democracies and berating them for their hypocrisy. That may play well at home, and there is a lot of hypocrisy in international behaviour, but such carping needlessly erodes our goodwill among the industrial countries' citizens. Interestingly, we often are less vocal about the bad behaviour of authoritarian countries. Foreign policy can and must be about interests, but if underpinned by shared values, it allows us to commit longer term to predictable and reliable behaviour, which will keep open for us the doors that would be shut to more authoritarian countries. Discretion sometimes is the better part of valour.

As we write this book, India–Canada relations have hit a nadir. India has accused Canada of allowing anti-India extremist activities in support of a separate Khalistan. To Indians, it seems galling that a friendly government will not prevent processions celebrating the tragic assassination of Prime Minister Indira Gandhi.[8] To Canada, this is just free speech, upsetting as it may seem. In turn, Canada has accused Indian agents of murdering Hardeep Singh Nijjar, a former Indian and naturalized Canadian citizen, a pro-Khalistan organizer, on Canadian land.[9]

Worryingly, instead of calming matters, the Indian government issued a statement to its citizens to 'exercise extreme caution and remain vigilant', further remarking that there was a 'deteriorating security environment' in Canada that could put the tens of thousands of Indian students at risk.[10] Rohit happened to be at the University of Toronto, giving a seminar when this happened. As Rohit walked through the city campus, seeing hundreds of desi students going about their day peacefully and hearing from faculty about the rising number of permanent residency applications to Canada from India, the dissonance of it all was not lost on him. If India is to engage effectively with the world, it has to rein in its Tiger Warriors.

Trade and Investment More Generally

The world has always traded more within regional blocs than at long distances, despite China's rise as the world's manufacturing workshop.

So there is significant concentration of trade and investment within the North American region (including Mexico), the European region and the East Asian region (including China and Japan). Of these, India is closest to the East Asian region, but not quite in it—in part because it is at loggerheads with China, and in part because it is not a signatory to regional trade agreements, such as the Regional Comprehensive Economic Partnership (RCEP) and the Comprehensive and Progressive Agreement for Trans-Pacific Partnership (CPTPP).

Particularly concerning was our refusal, after seven years of negotiations, to join the RCEP, the world's largest trading bloc, which includes Asian countries such as China, Korea, Japan and those in the ASEAN, as well as Australia and New Zealand. Undoubtedly, the RCEP may lead to more Chinese imports into India, but it will also allow for the possibility of Indian manufacturers becoming part of regional supply chains and exporting across the region. Our refusal to sign the RCEP entrenches the status quo, where inefficient Indian manufacturers try and keep the Indian market to themselves, while slipping further and further behind globally optimized supply chains.

Trade has benefited India tremendously, and it cannot afford to turn its back on it. India must ask to be admitted into regional trade agreements if it is to be a part of the regional supply chains. Not being part of the founding group in most of the current arrangements, India will have to negotiate from a position of disadvantage. But it could benefit from others' desire to have a counter to China.

Of course, negotiations in any trade agreements involve domestic winners and losers, and hence some give and take. Every country develops a negotiating stance, gauging the political heft of losers versus that of winners, without losing sight of the overall economic gains from the agreement. Prior to negotiating entry, it is extremely important that India does its homework on the concessions it needs others to make from a medium-term growth perspective, and decide what it is willing to give up. Some of the mistakes from the past result from our officials going underinformed and underprepared into negotiations, without a good sense of where our economic interests lie. Where significant political constituencies like agriculture are adversely affected, India could ask trading partners to open up their markets to Indian products. For instance, dairy farming, animal husbandry and horticulture account for increasing proportions of farm output. Instead of backing out of talks whenever India is asked to make agricultural concessions, especially on food grains, why not also negotiate the agricultural concessions India wants others to make?

The Middle East and Africa are fast-growing, emerging centres of economic activity. India has the advantage of proximity with these regions relative to competing countries in other regional blocs. It also has a large diaspora in these regions. Not only should India sign more agreements with countries in these regions, especially those in Africa, but it should also offer the same kind of favourable treatment we suggest it offers the SAARC countries. India's championing of a seat at the G20 for the African Union, as well as a proposed India-Middle East-Europe Economic Corridor are steps in the right direction.

Finally, India must battle at the G20 and the WTO against creeping protectionism in industrial countries, not just through import tariffs but also through non-tariff barriers. For instance, in the future, imports into industrial countries may be required to be produced by firms adhering to industrial country pay, labour, safety and emission standards. Many firms in the global south may become uncompetitive, and their workers lose jobs if the firms are forced to meet first-world standards. India should argue that countries should be allowed to improve standards at their own pace. After all, the best guarantor that a country improves worker pay and production standards is if its workers have jobs and the country grows, following which the domestic demand for better standards increases. Of course, India will have more influence if it reduces its own import tariffs.

Moglix and Private-Sector-Facilitating Trade

Rahul Garg grew up in a household where many family members were engaged in manufacturing. A graduate of IIT Kanpur, he spent nine years designing semiconductors, in the process building one of the finest semiconductor design teams in the world and filing sixteen US patents. At thirty, he felt he had met and surpassed every benchmark on R&D and was looking for new challenges. So, he went to the Indian Business School for an MBA and then to Google Asia. After five years there, he decided he had seen the best in the world and felt there was no reason why he could not match them. In 2015, he started Moglix, with the ambition of making it the go-to business-to-business (B2B) supply platform, first for businesses in India, then for the world.

Essentially, Moglix is an intermediary, facilitating transactions and ensuring orders are fulfilled. For buying businesses, it offers to supply over a million inputs, including electrical, tools, packaging, etc. For selling businesses, it offers to display their products on its digital catalog. When a buyer orders, Moglix takes care of the paperwork, the tax reporting (India has a Goods and Services Tax, which requires careful accounting for inputs and outputs) and much of the logistics. If it has the product in stock, it supplies from one of its forty warehouse centres in India (or two in the Middle East) using its fleet of vehicles, including more than hundred delivery vehicles for the last mile. If it does not have it in stock, it orders from the supplier, and facilitates delivery.

Like many of the other entrepreneurs we have profiled, Garg wants to solve big problems, not small ones. Having grown from twenty-five employees to 1600, Garg still feels he has a tiny fraction of the B2B market, though he is India's largest such digital player. He works with a few hundred large firms, he wants to work with 10,000 of the largest enterprises and 1 million of the smaller ones.

Garg believes there is positive momentum for his business in India because the national Goods and Services Tax has replaced myriad state taxes, making the national market seamless. This has created an opportunity for firms like his to tie manufacturers together, which has been further aided by India's improving transportation infrastructure.

Garg wants to go global. Moglix will be a key service provider if India is to develop its own efficient supply chains, and become part of global supply chains. Moglix is already one of the largest B2B players in the UAE and has ambitions to be a presence elsewhere in the Middle East. Garg spoke to us from the United States, where he was busy getting US firms to see the potential of Indian suppliers as part of their strategy to diversify away from China. This is a job that commercial counsellors at Indian embassies used to do, with limited success. Now companies like Moglix are taking it up, with likely greater urgency, effort and success. Garg is less clear about how border tariffs will impact his cross-border business, since it is early days in Moglix's international foray, but knows he will figure it out and make it work.

Trade in Services and the Setting of Standards

In addition to negotiating trade and investment agreements in goods with countries and regions of the world, India should push the agenda for free trade agreements in services if it is to expand service exports. The World Trade Organization has been slow in coming up with detailed proposals for trade in services under its flagship General Agreement on Trade in Services (GATS). The primary reason is a general lack of urgency among industrial countries, as well as a lack of knowledge on how to set rules in areas like the movement of people as opposed to goods across countries, data sharing across borders and mutual recognition of qualifications of service professionals. India should take a leading role here, perhaps coming up with a draft set of rules for others to debate.

For instance, how would we make it possible for an Indian lawyer to advise an American client or argue a case in a New York court, without leaving Indian shores? Clearly, the state of New York will have a bar exam, but is it possible for the exam to be administered virtually and globally? Can we ensure that any qualification requirement to provide a service be proportional to the needs of that service? For instance, do you really need a PhD in psychology to provide most forms of psychiatric counselling? Once a country sets a qualification, could equivalent qualifications obtained by professionals elsewhere be recognized? Where a country is unwilling to recognize equivalent qualifications elsewhere, could it have an easily accessible exam which tests the capability of otherwise qualified applicants? In sum, qualification requirements should not be a means by which work in services is restricted only to domestically qualified workers, and India should press for agreements that restrain such protectionism.

Similarly, the National Health Service (NHS) in the UK is struggling for doctors. Ageing Britain cannot produce enough of them. In fact, on recent visits to Dubai, Rohit learnt that many talented English doctors are also migrating to other countries, such as the UAE, where work hours are lower and salaries higher.[11] It would then seem that the UK should be open to telemedicine delivered from India. This would not just require the UK to recognize Indian medical qualifications but also the NHS to pay for medical services delivered from India.

We believe India should bring together a group of like-minded countries to draft the agenda and pen the first draft for discussions on the global delivery of services. There is enormous power in holding the pen and forcing the discussions to be based on a draft that you've had a first say in. India showed that in the recent Delhi G20 communiqué by getting all parties to sign off on mutually agreed statements on the Russia–Ukraine war, something that had eluded past communiqués. But, achieving consensus with consistency, and over issues of technical and political complexity will require much expertise and homework.

India must also engage fully as new global standards and rules are being set in many other industries of the future. For instance, the guidelines over the issuance of central bank digital currencies are being discussed in Basel. We will soon likely start global discussions on rules for artificial intelligence. These standards and rules are invariably skewed towards the interests of the countries that engage themselves in rule-making. Critical details are thrashed out in long, mind-numbing meetings attended by mid-level bureaucrats. By the time the rules reach the ministerial or governor level, they are largely cast in stone.

India often skips such meetings or sends underprepared officials who have little sense of what has already happened or where India's interests lie—since they have not had the necessary preparatory meetings with India's experts, including the private sector and academics.[12]

Unfortunately, some of our voluble bureaucrats with limited domain knowledge have to wing it when they attend these meetings episodically. As Eisuke Sakakibara, a powerful Japanese official who was known as Mr Yen in his time, laughingly told Raghu, 'The greatest problem in international meetings is to get Japanese officials to speak up and Indian officials to shut up.' We must speak up but prepare more so that others want to hear us!

Climate, Migration and Ageing

Where all this comes to a head is in the talks on climate action. When serious conversations on climate change first began in the 1990s, India saw it as a diplomatic problem.[13] One-third of the people of the world were expected to reside in China and India, so industrial countries felt that these two countries should go green as they developed if the world were to meet the emission targets. Green development is obviously costlier, since it imposes additional constraints on investment. So India protested, backed by impeccable logic: We didn't create the mess. So why are we being expected to step up when it's clean-up time?

China leads in annual carbon emissions in the world today, followed by the United States and then India. According to a World Bank report, if we divide emissions by population, Qatar was at the top in 2019, emitting 32.7 metric tonnes of carbon dioxide per capita, the US emitted 14.6, China emitted 7.6 and India was at 1.8. If carbon emission budgets are allocated on a per capita basis going forward, India uses much less than its fair share, while the US uses too much. If we take into account the carbon stock that is in the atmosphere, which has been put there largely by rich countries since the Industrial Revolution, the rationale for them to do more to bring down their carbon emissions is stronger still.

Nevertheless, the lack of any agreement implies that global warming is proceeding apace. India is seeing up close the problems created by a changing climate. Unseasonably hot temperatures are ruining harvests. Extremely high wet-bulb temperatures in our concrete-filled cities are making them unlivable except for those with air-conditioning. This makes life worse for the rest as air conditioners heat up the air outside. We are seeing repeated city flooding during the monsoon because we have built over floodplains. Paradoxically, we are also experiencing a dramatic fall in groundwater levels across the country as we fail to capture the run-off from heavy downpours.

Scientific research forecasts such growing climate volatility. For example, various studies from twenty years ago predicted a rise in extreme temperatures and rainfall events that we are witnessing today.[14] The melting of the Himalayan glaciers, the rise of the sea level in coastal lands and the slow turn of lush agricultural areas towards aridity are all happening. The environment is being further stressed by factors such as urbanization, migration patterns and pursuit of growth policies without green accounting. Given all this, we have to recognize three realities that should govern our policies.

First, regardless of what happens at the international level, climate change will affect South Asia more than almost any other part of the world—the devastating floods in Pakistan in 2022 are just a preview of what is likely to happen in the region. That means we have to push forcefully for international efforts at mitigation, that is, reducing the greenhouse gases that are going into the atmosphere. It is not their problem any more; it is ours too. Indeed, a recent study predicts that India (and China) will be very vulnerable to climate-induced downgrades to its country debt rating.[15]

Second, the scientific community believes that the world can tolerate up to 1.5 degrees Celsius warming since pre-industrial days without huge and unpredictable damage. Almost surely, though, the world will blow through it before mitigation efforts halt and then reduce the carbon in the atmosphere. So India has to prepare for unprecedented climate volatility in this century. This means that it has to begin efforts at adapting to climate change right now, regardless of what it does on mitigation. This entails, for instance, changing the pattern of farm cropping so that crops are less water-hungry and less susceptible to climate volatility, improving the management of water and keeping climate change as an ever-present concern in city planning. A first step would be to bring some order to the haphazard growth of our cities.

Third, to have credibility, India will have to lead in its own mitigation efforts. As a matter of fairness, though, it can ask for compensatory payments. For instance, Raghu proposed a scheme whereby countries emitting above the global average and thus eating into others' carbon budget should pay into a fund, and those below the global average should receive.[16] This would give all countries an incentive to reduce carbon emissions (because they have to pay more or receive less as they emit more), while compensating low emitters like India, and giving them the funds to engage in mitigation and adaptation efforts. This is an area where India can make common cause with the developing countries in Africa, South Asia and Latin America, and present their consensus viewpoint at global meetings.

Finally, consider some steps we can take domestically to put India on the right side of climate history. First and foremost, 69 per cent of our greenhouse gas emissions are related to the generation of power, and power is intricately linked to our development choices and trajectory.[17] Our energy consumption is going to rise quite rapidly as we electrify more and pursue more growth-inducing policies. The big catch, though, is that 70 per cent of our power currently is generated by coal, which is terrible for the environment.

The International Energy Agency predicts that by 2040, India will need to add to its grid as much power as the European Union's entire consumption today.[18] This simply cannot be done only through coal. At the same time, expecting India to transition to renewables rapidly is unrealistic, so we have to fire on both cylinders, of cleaner and progressively diminished coal-induced power, perhaps supported by carbon-capture technologies, and rapidly rising renewables. Carbon taxation of coal-fired industry (which is already in place in some measure) and other incentives to switch to renewables will also play a crucial role. As important will be to facilitate the domestic manufacture of equipment that will help mitigation, such as solar cells, windmills, batteries and EVs, without relying on extensive subsidies.

The transition won't be easy, though—beyond the power grid, coal companies directly employ half a million people and another half million jobs directly depend on the industry. A further 10–15 million people are affected by the economy built around coal mines. One estimate suggests that in some states, like Jharkhand and Chhattisgarh, coal constitutes around 10 per cent of the state's total economic output. In addition, coal freight is currently used by Indian Railways to cross-subsidize passenger travel by about 13 per cent. All green reforms will require careful thinking and planning, with the focus on new jobs that we have advocated throughout the book.[19]

Navroz K. Dubash, a prominent scientific voice on climate change, has repeatedly emphasized that steps to decarbonize industries, decarbonize transport, and manage urbanization and afforestation require policy coordination at the Centre and setting a framework within which states can take their own initiatives in tackling the emerging effects of climate change. Unfortunately, the Prime Minister's Council on Climate Change does not meet frequently, and most of the technical discussion and policy inputs have been left to consultants commissioned by the NITI Aayog episodically.[20] Moreover, energy choices and responses to climate impacts are formulated at the state level, but the financial resources and bureaucratic capacities sit at the Centre. We need far better management of our green initiatives today, which requires sustained attention from the political establishment.

India needs to lay out in some detail how it plans to achieve net zero, summoning Indian researchers and policy analysts together to draw a road map. It then needs to populate that road map with five-year milestones it can be held accountable for. It should fill in details on milestones and actions over the next decade. This will be helpful to India in giving it a sense of what it needs to work on, and should include both mitigation and adaptation efforts, as well as the required financing. Finally, it should present that effort to the world and demand similar details from all leading countries (while helping other developing countries prepare their plans). Ostrich-like myopia or righteous benign neglect in the belief that it is up to others cannot be a strategy any longer.

Because the world is likely to control carbon emissions too slowly to prevent climatic catastrophes from happening more frequently, we should prepare for the worst in our neighbourhood. Some low-lying countries, such as the Maldives, may need many of their people to emigrate permanently. At the same time, ageing countries across the world need young qualified migrants. Could India architect a more sensible global approach to legal migration, from climate-affected nations to willing ageing recipient countries, matching the qualifications of would-be migrants with the needs of recipient countries?

Hard Power

Even as India grows economically, it has to develop its defensive capabilities. The wars of the future will be based much more on getting the right battlefield information quickly and acting on it with precision weapons capable of firing at long distances, even while preventing the enemy from doing the same. A new defence vision will require less emphasis on massed tanks, manned aircraft and aircraft carrier battle groups, and more on smart artillery, drones and hypersonic missiles. Much of this requires dual-use technology, such as artificial intelligence, and cyber capabilities, as well as R&D in making weapons smarter, more accurate and resilient to interference. The path we have suggested for India should help it build stronger defences, but only if the military becomes more nimble in its vision and cooperates better with India's private sector. The armed forces will require a whole new set of skills to complement existing ones, and they should not hesitate in taking the decisions that will perhaps make them a smaller but more capable and effective force.

India's Place in a New World Order

The existing world order, devised in the immediate aftermath of World War II by the United States, is skewed against late arrivals like China and India. It is structured for a unipolar world, where the US plays impartial policeman (at least that is the ideal) and Europe its loyal aide. This structure is breaking down. The US is itself involved in many disputes, and its administrations display increasing volatility and unpredictability in their engagement with the world. At times it is reluctant to play policeman, at others overly eager. We need to rethink global arrangements, respecting the fact that the US is still the most powerful economy in the world but also creating space for others who want a say.

In this regard, India's constant harping for a permanent seat on the UN Security Council reflects a lack of imagination in our foreign policy establishment. The UN is a weak organization, emasculated precisely by the vetoes of the permanent members. Instead, India should offer a new view from the global south of what fair global arrangements—a globalization 2.0—would look like. That means spending much more time with South Asia, Africa and Latin America in proposing and architecting a consensus, rather than pleading with the industrial West to give us crumbs off the table. Almost surely, it would mean a revamp of existing organizations but also the creation of new ones— for instance, a World Climate Authority and a Global Migration Organization. An India that has the backing of the developing world will have a much greater voice than an India that speaks only for itself and only incidentally for the rest.

Returning to the theme that started this chapter, our influence on the world should be a consequence of everything else we do. A superpower in creativity and innovation while having the hard power that allows us to defend ourselves effectively—that will truly make India a *vishwaguru*. Self-belief should make us secure and more confident in our foreign policy, which includes resisting the temptation to play-act for the domestic political gallery. Rather than demanding recognition for what we may have done in the past, let us get recognition for what we are doing today and for what we aim to do in the future. Beyond focusing on our developmental agenda, this starts with leading initiatives to peaceably address the challenges the world faces.

12

A Creative Country

Government jobs will not employ more than a small fraction of our people. Existing firms, too, will make a small dent in the desired numbers. The bulk of the jobs in the future will be created by enterprises that are not yet born and will be started by our people. How do we foster that spirit of questioning, creativity and enterprise that is so necessary for India to succeed? How do we get more people to ask 'Why?' when they see a problem, rather than simply walk quickly past it? How do we get more of them to come up with possible solutions no one has thought of? And what will get them to go beyond theorizing to trying out the ideas and not giving up if they fail? There are times in a country's history when its energy and ferment take it to impossible heights of imagination and genius—think of Florence during the Renaissance or England during the Industrial Revolution. How can we make the next hundred years our 'century of flourishing', as Deirdre McCloskey would put it?

Innovation and Creativity as a National Endeavour

India needs to become an entrepreneurial nation. Malti, a villager who makes more idli batter than she needs and sells it to her neighbours, is displaying enterprise; as is P.C. Musthafa, whom we encountered in the introduction. Yet both are asking the same question: Why does everyone have to make batter every day, and how do we change that? They come up with different answers, and both answers will result in entrepreneurship, but everything starts with questioning . . . And critical questioning is what democracies do better.

This is perhaps why authoritarian countries can build strong armies and even innovate in top-down-directed national projects, like building ballistic missiles or sending satellites into space, but fail when it comes to bottom-up, consumer-led innovation and commercialization—think of North Korea or the Soviet Union. China, with its decentralized approach in the decades since the late 1970s, was more vibrant and bottom-up than its socialist peers, but in the last decade it has turned more to the top-down, state-led direction. We believe that unless China turns away from this path, it may become stronger militarily but will slow economically.

We have already discussed what must be done to improve people's capabilities. Malti gains confidence from the basic mathematics she learnt in school as she buys in bulk rice, urad dal and heeng—all ingredients for idli batter. A conducive business environment also matters—she should only have to satisfy the panchayat committee that her process is clean and hygienic, instead of fearing a visit from the rapacious food inspector. Let us now turn to other key aspects of facilitating creativity and enterprise.

Entrepreneurship and Status

The caste system places intellectuals at the top, perhaps because they conceptualized the system. So the academic researcher enjoys respect. Modern India also places successful large entrepreneurs—like Bhavish Aggarwal, who co-founded the ride-hailing service Ola Cabs—on a pedestal. That is good, for we need many more Olas. But we also have to move many of our youth from working on the farm or taking civil services exams to looking around them, finding problems to solve and starting small enterprises to solve them. Often, self-employment requires an ability to experiment, to 'tinker' as one tries to find a creative solution to a real-world problem and to work with others as one sells the solution more widely.

This was how famed entrepreneurs like Thomas Edison succeeded, and it requires two important changes in our mindset. First, we should elevate the status of tinkering—whether working with one's hands or with software or with the mind to solve practical problems. This requires more than just the vocational training we advocated earlier, it needs a change in mindset inculcated in the early years of schooling. It is about getting students to think about practical problems and getting them to work, if possible in groups, to find creative products or services to address them. It also means rewarding that creativity. Our best schools obviously do this with labs, class projects and science fairs, but the practical emphasis should spread more widely, both across the curriculum and across all schools. The Central government has taken an initial step in this direction, setting up 10,000 Atal Tinkering Labs in schools, as has the Delhi government in moving from the Happiness Curriculum towards the Entrepreneurship Curriculum in the last years of school.[1]

Second, we should address the instinctive suspicion that every businessperson is a rogue, intent on misusing the system, getting an unfair advantage and ripping off the customer. Relatedly, we should dispel the stigma of failure. Some of this can be embedded in the school curriculum, celebrating entrepreneurs like Jamsetji Tata even as we cherish our freedom fighters. But respect will also come from how we transform business practice. Transparency and a level playing field for all, which we discussed earlier, should help—if the best entrepreneurs are seen to succeed, not because they are proximate to the government but because they build products or services that consumers desire, then respect for the businessperson increases.

Technology can help by allowing small businesses to build reputations for good and reliable service (think of public customer reviews) as can effective regulation, such as a requirement for regular audits. Quick investigation and enforcement in case of fraud can distinguish the unscrupulous businessperson from the well-intentioned risk-taker. Simultaneously, however, our investigating agencies should have a better understanding of business, so that a failure doesn't lead them immediately to a presumption of fraud. Furthermore, investigating agencies themselves should have internal monitoring systems, as well as be subject to oversight by Parliament and by boards of eminent citizens so that businesses are not subject to politically motivated investigations or harassment by corrupt officials.

Respect for businesspeople has certainly grown substantially since the early days of liberalization, because of the celebrated achievements of businesspeople like Sachin Bansal, Uday Kotak and Nandan Nilekani. A fascinating compendium of case studies of Dalit entrepreneurs suggests that entrepreneurship is increasingly being seen by Dalits as an alternative route to equal status, preferable even to a government job.[2] This will be an important collateral benefit of increasing entrepreneurship opportunities even as India works on enhancing the capabilities of all, including disadvantaged communities, for it will help achieve both our social and economic aims.

Finally, while the public's respect for businesspeople has increased, the government is still ambivalent. An interesting event in 2015 brought home to Raghu the lowly official status of private businesspeople in India.[3] President Obama was visiting Delhi. The entire Indian elite flocked to meet him at a reception at the Indian President's house. True to form, the bureaucrats running the reception had identified everyone's precise place in the social hierarchy and lined them up to shake President Obama's hand. It was a long line, starting with the Indian prime minister, the former prime minister, cabinet ministers, the leader of the Opposition, military chiefs . . . retired dignitaries from the ruling party, ministers from various states . . . the Indian President's grandson, serving bureaucrats . . . and at number eighty-three, the aged chairman of India's largest private-sector group, accounting for over $100 billion in market value, followed by other tycoons and bankers. Certainly, public service should be rewarded with higher status to compensate for its lack of monetary rewards, but isn't number eighty-three in the hierarchy for India's top businessman alarmingly low?

Printing Rockets

IIT Madras's Research Park is an unusual oasis of large open spaces and tall buildings in the midst of the crowded Taramani area of Chennai. The buildings are chock-full of start-ups. On the first floor in one of the buildings is AgniKul's rocket factory.

Srinath Ravichandran, AgniKul's co-founder, always wanted to be an astronaut. But after finishing an engineering degree, he drifted into finance and eventually ended up working for an insurance firm in Los Angeles. There, he reconnected with his first love, space, attending conference after conference. As he saw the rise of Elon Musk's SpaceX, he realized that he too wanted to build rockets, but smaller ones, and in India.

So he spammed dozens of professors back home, asking if any would be interested in working with him on building rockets. Only one, Professor Satya Chakravarty of IIT Madras, expressed interest. IIT Madras made a 'plug-and-play' area available on rent, complete with utilities and zoning permissions, and the venture started attracting space engineers from all over India. Soon the shape of the rockets that AgniKul intended to send into space started emerging.

They would be small, intended for payloads of up to 100 kg and would go to a distance of about 400 miles from earth. And they would be 3D-printed, which meant each part could not exceed 40 centimetres on any side, since that was the maximum size the 3D printer could accommodate. The rockets would be modular, in that smaller payloads could be lifted by the same rocket with fewer engines. And they would be propelled by liquid fuels, which means they could be transported across the world, unlike solid-fuel rockets, which are essentially missiles, liable to explode.

The virtue of a small rocket is that it can send small satellites into orbit quickly without commingling many payloads. A large rocket has to carry many small satellites, possibly from many different firms. Not only does it take time for its payload to be made up, but the satellites too may affect each other adversely, and there is a substantial loss in case the rocket misfires. AgniKul can send up even single-satellite payloads, with the rocket tailored to the weight that is being sent up. Hence it has no need to ask a customer to wait. Since only a few satellites are being sent up at a time, the potential loss from any rocket malfunctioning is small.

There is also virtue in 3D-printing the rocket, especially in the design phase. Complicated engines can be designed and printed without welding, which minimizes what can go wrong. Moreover, since the rocket was designed from the bottom up without pre-existing blueprints, the designers could 3D-print different versions of the same part easily and iterate to find what worked best.

Agnibaan, the firm's first rocket, will soon be launched from India's space centre in Sriharikota.

Srinath employs about 200 engineers from a variety of engineering schools across India. They are everywhere in his

Chennai factory, huddled around computers, designing rocket parts and programming the software it needs. Srinath benefited from the advice of around thirty-five retired engineers from the fabled ISRO, one of India's best-run public-sector enterprises. However, AgniKul has not relied on ISRO, except for the launch facility and the flight termination system that ISRO put in to blow up the rocket if it strays in flight. Srinath says that getting his own flight safety system approved and certified would take too long.

Srinath works closely with professors from IIT Madras and also has a twenty-year lease on the space he has in the park. The park has been very useful in reducing start-up costs—it would be hard to find such ready-to-use space in a big city and so close to premier technological institutions. Importantly, government inspectors don't often make their way into the park. There is a buzz in the park as employees of so many start-ups meet and talk and exchange ideas. They are likely planting the seeds of many more start-ups.

AgniKul's small rockets not only have commercial applications, they will also give India's defence forces an independent ability to send up small monitoring or communications satellites quickly, in case they need to place more eyes on certain spots or replace destroyed satellites. Today, most such technology is dual-use.

AgniKul, is a moonshot, almost literally. The path ahead is not without risk—it has missed target dates in the past, and it does have global competitors. It certainly takes some chutzpah for a finance executive to think he can build rockets. But this is the kind of entrepreneurship India needs, willing to take risks and going all out to create intellectual property embedded in sophisticated products at the frontiers of technology.

Government as Enabler

Industrial policy consists of a government picking sectors or firms to support, a form of corporate freebie we have argued against earlier in this book. It is coming back across the world. Of course, India never abandoned it fully, despite its decidedly poor past experience picking sectors to support. This is not to say that the government should remain passive. It can enable, without directing too much.

For instance, the transaction costs of setting up business—such as renting premises, contracting for utilities like power, water, broadband and cloud, finding accountants and so on—can be prohibitive. IIT Madras's Research Park offered AgniKul a 'plug-and-play' facility, which minimized these costs. Commercial players might also open such facilities. If the start-ups attracted to a facility have similar customers, are part of the same supply chain or use similar inputs, they can generate ideas, partnerships or lower costs by clustering together. The facility provider can set up a common workshop or tool room with expensive but useful tools for common use. The facility provider may just set up the plug-and-play facility or, like IIT Madras, play a role in selecting and investing in the firms it invites into the facility, in which case it becomes more of an incubator.

The data revolution we described earlier should enhance the availability of debt financing for small enterprises. One of the great remaining difficulties for small firms is the dearth of patient risk capital, that is, equity financing that does not require immediate dividends and can absorb initial losses. A consequence is that many high-growth risky young firms are not financed, while others are financed with foreign venture capital, ensuring that the bulk of the returns are made by foreigners. Of course, they take risks that Indian investors are unwilling to take, but there are now growing amounts of patient capital in Indian pension funds and insurance companies, a portion of which can be deployed as part of a diversified portfolio in risky new ventures.

In the United States, a change in regulations in 1979 made pension funds more willing to fund start-ups. Before the change, pension fund managers followed a 'prudent-man' rule, which required them to make investments that only a prudent man would make. Their cautious interpretation of what was 'prudent' led them to believe that investments could only be made in large, profitable 'blue-chip' firms. The labour department then clarified in 1979 that 'although securities issued by a small or new company may be a riskier investment than securities issued by a blue-chip company, such an investment may be entirely proper'.[4] The clarifications acted as a 'safe harbour' for fund managers, implying that those who complied with the clarifications would be seen as having satisfied the prudent-man rule. Soon after, the volume of investment by pension funds in venture capital funds, which was then further invested in small and risky innovative companies, took off. In 2015, India's Pension Fund Regulatory and Development Authority indicated a desire to move steadily to a liberal prudent-man rule. Progress thus far has been slow. It should move faster so that Indian venture capitalists and innovative Indian businesses get the funding they need.

Finally, some governments want to fund small innovative firms directly and consequently set up government venture funds. The history of government funding has been a chequered one at best, partly because government officials have neither the expertise nor the right incentives to manage such funds well.[5] For instance, the successful venture capitalist will have to pull the plug on 90 per cent or more of the firms she finances, while riding on the stupendous success of 10 per cent. If a fund is unwilling to terminate bad investments and continues financing them, as a government fund is wont to do, the many losses will swamp the few gains. So rather than engage in direct government financing, government pension funds and insurance companies should invest small parts of their portfolio in well-managed private venture capital funds.

Tejas Networks

Consider an Indian technological success story, Tejas Networks, which was just awarded *Dataquest*'s Pathbreaker of the Year Award 2022. Tejas is India's largest telecom products company, with sales to more than seventy-five countries. It is ranked among the top ten suppliers in the global optical transmission and fibre broadband equipment segments. Tejas supplies 70 per cent of the requirements of the BharatNet project, the world's largest rural high-speed broadband roll-out.

Tejas invests a substantial amount in R&D, an amount that is all the larger because of the relatively lower cost of highly skilled engineers in India. As Tejas's just-retired CEO, Sanjay Nayak, puts it, 'If Indian engineers can make products for Google from India, why can't they make products for Indian companies that we can sell to the world?' Over the years, the company has filed for 349 patents, of which 127 have been granted (this is impressive but still a long way from world-leading Huawei, which has 3325 patents in 5G alone).[6] While the company makes its hardware other than chips, its emphasis on software that links hardware helps keep down costs, because it can reuse an existing hardware design by reprogramming with upgrades.

Things were not easy for Nayak.[7] After the company was started in 2000, it suffered two near-death experiences—the first in 2009, when its largest customer, Nortel, filed for bankruptcy; and the second after a telecom scandal in India over the allocation of 2G licences led to many telecom companies slowing purchases. Nayak gradually rebuilt sales and profitability. 'It took us much more time than we had thought,' he says. 'But building a good company is a marathon, not a sprint!' He attributes the recovery to the engineers, who have stuck with the company through thick and thin. But Nayak himself did not lose faith in R&D,

investing over a quarter of the company's revenues in R&D even in its worst year. However, on all other aspects, Nayak ran a frugal ship, leading to a successful IPO in 2017.

Tejas has also advised India's participation in the 5G standard-setting body, 3GPP, as its seventh voting member. It recently won a deal with Bharat Sanchar Nigam Limited (BSNL), India's state-owned telecom company, to upgrade BSNL's networks without increasing dependence on imported equipment. Tejas is now supplying products for India's transition to 5G and is positioning itself as a supplier of 5G networks to other developing countries. One of Nayak's selling points is that Tejas offers reliable, trustworthy products without the backdoor-spying capabilities that might be built into products from existing superpower-linked suppliers. If India had strong privacy legislation, protecting data from even the Indian government's intrusion (at least without strong judicial oversight), this would be a formidable selling point. Unfortunately, it does not.

Having taken Tejas this far, Nayak recently sold a majority position in the company to the Tatas and gave way to a new CEO, who has had eighteen years of experience in Juniper Networks, an example of how India's diaspora can be a valuable source of talent in India's technological leap.

Government Purchases

Government purchases, as in the case of BSNL awarding Tejas the deal to upgrade its networks, can be a boost for Indian business. Defence, space agency or government medical purchases can play an enormous role in catalysing innovation. Through its choice of provider, the government may also determine technological choices for an industry and coordinate movement towards some specific standards. It is therefore important that government purchasing is done with the most transparent structures and the best independent experts advising the government, so that its choices are the best available. It is also important that wherever quality is not compromised, the government slant contracts towards smaller young firms, for these are the ones that would benefit the most from visible government support.

Government contracts can also play a role in more day-to-day entrepreneurial activity. For instance, in Chhattisgarh, the government contracts out the midday-meal scheme to local women's cooperatives, who in turn buy local produce for the meals they cook. Such contracting can be an enormous boost to the cooperatives as well as local vegetable farms, for it creates steady demand. Many functions that come under the government purview, such as street cleaning, where there is a measurable output, could also be contracted out to small local businesses.

Of course, there are dangers in government purchases, the foremost being corruption and, relatedly, tardy and uncertain payments. Once there is a whiff of corruption, the benefits of government purchases—the vote of confidence signalled by a guaranteed, steady stream of payments from a buyer with unimpeachable credit—disappear. Renewal of the government contract becomes uncertain; officials do not want to pay on time for fear that they would be hauled up later for aiding corruption; and the private provider spends more time in court appearances than in producing the product. This is why transparent procedures for allocating contracts, and independent and transparent monitoring of delivery, are so essential.

Finally, the government can coordinate, even subsidize, investment that is necessary for an industry to take off. For instance, widespread availability of charging stations is necessary for consumers to be interested in buying EVs. On the other hand, firms putting up charging stations want reassurance on customer demand before deciding to invest. The government could bridge the gap. For instance, in some remote areas, the government could work with manufacturers to ensure that charging stations are put up, sometimes even agreeing to bear losses if the demand falls short.

Commercial Development of Sunrise Sectors

Basic research, whether in artificial intelligence, resilient crops or molecular biology, starts at the university. We have already discussed the need to create and fund elite universities.

For everything except basic research, commercialization must be kept in mind as research develops. One problem, though, is that many of the most innovative companies working in India are incorporated outside, since Indian regulations on early-stage ownership and financing are too onerous and limiting, and foreign investors prefer a tried-and-tested legal system and regulators in countries like Singapore. India needs to make its regulations for entrepreneurial start-ups more firm-friendly as well as competitive with other countries' systems.

Rather than looking to firms that are active in industry for advice, angel investor Sharad Sharma advocates using voluntary expert *sutradhars* (facilitators) who can advise the government on policies, standards, regulations and international agreements needed for effective development of thrust areas. Such sutradhars could be modelled on the Indian Software Product Industry Roundtable (iSPIRT), which advised the roll-out of the India Stack. ISPIRT consists of a mix of retired and active industry players, academics and investors who commit to offer impartial advice in the interest of the country and agree to not benefit financially from any of their recommendations. The value of such bodies advising the government is that they bring industry experience without the bias of the self-interested. Indeed, iSPIRT has launched a checklist of changes needed to persuade companies to stay in India.[8]

Talent Search

There is plenty of talent across the world that might help India create innovative technologies—the new CEO of Tejas comes from the US firm Juniper Networks. Foreigners and expatriates have played important roles in other countries. For instance, Morris Chang, who founded TSMC, the leading chip foundry in the world today, was educated at Harvard, MIT and Stanford, and worked for Texas Instruments in Dallas, moving to Taiwan only when he was passed over for the top job at Texas Instruments.

There are plenty of would-be Morris Changs that India can attract. But organizations in India, as everywhere else, have a resistance to outsiders, especially if they are brought in near the top. 'Why is no one internal good enough?' goes the refrain. In truth, comfortable insiders fear outsiders, even if they are good for the organization. Outside talent brings new knowledge, new perspectives, even new behaviours that can be very energizing. Yet it is because outsiders are different and refuse to accept the status quo that they can also be threatening. As few organizations are confident enough to accept outside talent, such talent really flourishes when it comes into, or creates, new organizations—as was the case with Morris Chang. Fortunately, India needs many more new universities and research-based firms, so that we have plenty of room for returning talent.

The government can make it more attractive for the talented to move to India. It can liberalize the regulations and lower the taxes that make such moves difficult; it can make it easier for expatriates to place their children in good schools. China's Thousand Talents programme, to attract expatriate Chinese back, is worth studying, for the successes it had. It will be important for India to emphasize that this programme is a way for it to hire experts. It will have to assuage fears in other countries that this will not be a mechanism to steal intellectual property, something China did not do satisfactorily. It will have to assuage domestic talent that it, too, will benefit from the capabilities and the competitiveness that returnees bring.

Don't Make Old Mistakes, Even Though We Will Make New Ones

It bears reiterating that the most important task of any government intent on making India a start-up nation is to strengthen our democracy, enhance free speech and encourage a culture of debate. Authoritarianism snuffs out free thought. There are, of course, many ways the government can aid entrepreneurship more directly. We have suggested a few, and we should constantly evaluate outcomes and correct course if policies do not work. As far as possible, though, the government must enable many to succeed, rather than choosing a few winners. Even the most well-meaning government has difficulty making good choices, which is why industrial policy pushed too hard has failed so often. India should not repeat its past mistakes.

PART III

WRAPPING UP

Prelude

'A populist is, basically, a gifted storyteller; someone who can tell a false story well. And the way to fight them is by telling a true story better.'

—Suketu Mehta, *This Land Is Our Land*

Part I set our choices up, suggesting that low-skilled, manufacturing-led exports were not the only path open to India for development and that, indeed, such a path was becoming increasingly difficult to follow. Low-skilled manufacturing, and manufacturing more generally, has become far more competitive. Furthermore, for many products, the manufacturing portion of the supply chain does not add substantial value, nor is it necessarily a way to capture other elements of the supply chain. To be like China is also very difficult unless one wants to dispense with our vibrant democracy. Instead, to create higher-value-added jobs, whether it is through the creation of intellectual property or through remunerative employment in manufacturing or services, India must focus on improving the capabilities of its people. And this is likely to be easier to effect in a more democratic India.

In Part II, we outlined the elements of the strategy, starting with an enabling governance structure, the steps needed to improve nutrition, education and health care, and culminating with an enabling business environment, including in India's relations with the world.

In Part III, we wrap up. Since India is at a crossroads, and we have described the choice we want India to make, we should also discuss the road we would advise against, the road India is arguably currently on. Much of our concern is not just with the unwarranted obsession with low-skilled manufacturing, which we discussed in Part I, but with the kind of authoritarian society India is becoming on its current trajectory. This is inimical to its becoming a thinking, innovative and creative nation. So what better way to end than to imagine a dialogue between us and a sceptic, one who is convinced of the current path we are on?

13

The Wrong Way

We write this book to persuade, not to shout down critics. We imagined that a concerned citizen, who is much more sympathetic to the nation's current trajectory, read through the first two parts of the book and reached out to us to have a more detailed dialogue. In homage to Mahatma Gandhi's *Hind Swaraj*, we term the concerned citizen the 'Reader', and if you pardon us the conceit, we take on the role of 'Editor'. So, here goes . . .

Reader: I find your book to be unnecessarily critical. You yourselves point out a lot of good that is happening in India. Moreover, how can India be on the wrong track if we were recently elected by the G20 to be its president, and our leaders are received with pomp and ceremony around the world?

    Editor: You raise important questions. At any time and under any government, there is a lot of good going on in India—some because of the government and some despite it. Some ruling parties publicize the good news better; some leaders have a better sense of political timing and political rhetoric; and some regimes are more determined to suppress criticism and hide bad outcomes. But under any government, along with the significant good, there is also much that is not being done, and some things that are being done are really bad. All of these must be analysed and put in the public domain.

So let us get into the facts. The G20 presidency rotates across all members; so every member becomes the president at some point. India was scheduled to become G20 president in 2021, but the government requested Italy to shift places with it so that India's turn coincided with our seventy-fifth year after Independence. It is indeed wonderful for India to have hosted the event, since world diplomats came here and took back with them a bit of the promise of India. The government has a natural incentive to play down the rotating nature of the presidency, especially in the year before the polls. Your assumption that India was elected is an understandable error.

Having said that, as we mentioned earlier, the G20 finale in September 2023 in Delhi was spectacular, and there is much to praise in how it was organized. It is also wonderful that our leaders are being received with pomp across the world. Such a welcome reflects respect for what India has achieved over the last few decades as a democracy and as an economy. Foreign governments are also self-interested. If our leaders come with defence deals or aircraft deals in hand, the political calculation is that cost of the pomp is minuscule given the scale of the business deals at stake. And there are strategic considerations too in the reception, in that the West sees us as a hedge, a counterbalancing force against a powerful China. We should, however, make better use of these welcomes than we currently do, pushing for more openings for our businesses and farmers.

Reader: Okay, then, let us turn to facts. We are the fastest-growing economy in the G20. We've come a long way since 2014. Aren't you criticizing just for the sake of criticism?

Editor: Poor economies grow fast because they are in catch-up-growth mode, as we indicated earlier. We are the poorest economy in the G20, so we should be the fastest growing. The right comparison is not with the rest but with our own recent past. From that perspective, we just had the worst decade of growth since the economic reforms introduced by Prime Minister P.V. Narasimha Rao and Finance Minister Manmohan Singh in the early 1990s.

The key question is what the numbers say about the medium term: the jobs situation right now is abysmal, the lower middle class is hanging on by its fingernails, growth is becoming more unequal and female labour force participation is stagnant at a low number. Yet quarterly growth numbers are settling down between 5 and 6 per cent.

One explanation is that our current growth is largely jobless, which means we need far more growth to create the necessary employment, or else the demographic divided will evaporate in front of our eyes.

Another possibility is that our growth and GDP have been overestimated since 2013, when we changed the method of estimating the GDP. As Arvind Subramanian, former chief economic adviser, has pointed out, growth in important indicators like imports, exports, credit, tax revenues and profits slowed considerably in the latter period relative to the former period, while GDP growth miraculously stayed strong. A government survey suggests that household consumption growth collapsed, but that survey has not been released publicly. So we should admit the possibility that we haven't even been growing at the official rate. If so, the lack of good data may be making us overly complacent about the accumulating dangers of the current policy path we are on.

Reader: Our stock market is booming, and my investments are paying off. What is the market missing if you are right?

Editor: There are a few reasons for the market's current buoyancy—some good and some not so good. By the time our dialogue is published, matters may be different. So it is a volatile barometer.

First, as we write, hopes that global growth will continue uninterrupted by recession are increasing. Across the world, stock markets are buoyant—indeed, we travel a lot, and every country's paper has long articles on why that country is doing so well. Also, with US–China tensions continuing, emerging-market investors want an investment alternative to China. India is benefiting from inflows, as are other emerging markets—India is right in the middle of the pack as we write, with South Korean and Brazilian stock returns since the beginning of the year significantly higher.

Finally, the not-so-good reason. For a variety of reasons, including demonetization, the pandemic and the implementation of GST, we have seen an increase in the profitability of large firms in this country, while small and informal firms are doing relatively poorly. But only the former are quoted on the stock market, which offers a misleading picture of the broader economy. Indeed, high-employment sectors with many small firms, such as apparel and leather, have shrunk since June 2016, the period just before demonetization.

Reader: Okay, I need to think a little more about this. The government wants to take us on a manufacturing-led growth path. Why are you against manufacturing?

Editor: We are not against manufacturing. Why would anyone be? We are against pouring enormous subsidies into attracting the lowest end of the manufacturing supply chain, assuming that will attract the rest. We have tried to explain in this book that the world is changing rapidly. There is diminishing value added in low-skilled assembly. Moreover, the chance of climbing our way up is not going to be easy—there is no necessary connection today between the low-skilled assembly segment and other parts of the value chain. In the words of an industrialist we spoke with, we are competing for the right to be serfs, not just today but also tomorrow. We must think bigger, aim bigger, to adapt to the world of tomorrow.

Reader: I guess your point is about what the best use of government resources is. I still have more questions about your economic agenda. Why are you for freebies like the cash transfer you propose?

Editor: The term 'freebies' is loosely bandied about as a political insult, but essentially the politician's definition of 'freebie' amounts to this: the subsidies and transfers my political opponent proposes are freebies, while the ones I propose are essential for development. We should examine every subsidy and transfer for whether it delivers on its objective. Essentially, we want a safety net for the poorest and the most unfortunate, while also giving them some money power to invest in their future. After all, we need people at every level of the economic pyramid to build their human capital. That is what the proposed cash transfer aims to do.

Reader: What about national champions? Won't it be great if we had a few large companies matching other companies across the world in scale?

Editor: Absolutely, it would be spectacular to have globally competitive national companies. But if it means that we build them up by favouring them over other domestic companies, or by shutting out global competitors, or by asking global competitors to sign up to joint ventures with the government's favourite industrialists, our consumers will have to pay a price just to fatten the profits of our largest industrialists. And in the longer run, it is not clear that they will be competitive if they have grown with the help of protection and subsidies. So rather than favouring some firms, let us build a more conducive environment within our country for all firms to grow. Champions will come, and some are already emerging, as our case studies suggest. But champions may also need to go if they cannot keep up with competition.

Reader: Okay, maybe we need new ideas on how to grow. But we keep hearing that we are a vishwaguru. Does that not count for something?

Editor: What is a vishwaguru? The literal translation is, of course, a teacher to the world. From that specific viewpoint, we are a net importer of modern ideas or intellectual property from the world, at least today. We will, we're confident, be a net exporter in the near future, but as things stand, we are not.

Don't get us wrong. India has been the spiritual centre of the world for centuries in the past and an intellectual powerhouse too. But we allowed the developments of modern science to bypass us, colonialism drained our resources, and we observed the Industrial Revolution from afar. No doubt, our confidence as a people faltered, and we had to remind ourselves of our past glory to keep our morale up. We are now rebuilding our economy and society, which also means our intellectual and technical capacities. In this endeavour, drawing inspiration from the past is good, but living in the past is not.

Do you recollect that old Hindi adage, *Mehnat itni khamoshi se karo ki safalta shor macha de*? It means, 'Work hard in such silence that your resounding success sounds your arrival.' We will be a vishwaguru when it is our time, and hopefully it will be soon, but first we need to put in all the work to get there. Also, let others proclaim us a vishwaguru.

Reader: Okay, but I really like our leader, who makes bold decisions without being paralysed by endless consultations. Hard decisions, such as demonetization and the strict lockdown during Covid, were taken swiftly. Why should we not centralize decisions under such a leadership?

Editor: Political charisma and likability are a great binding force in a country, provided they are used in the right way. However, debate and consensus building almost always improve decisions. Both the overnight bank nationalizations in 1969 and the declaration of the Emergency in 1975 were done suddenly and without much consultation. Few would assert they benefited the nation.

Under this government, the sudden demonetization of large currency notes in November 2016 broke the back of the informal economy and small enterprises, inflicted hardship on millions of people, with no discernable effect on black money. Economic growth, which was picking up till then, started weakening steadily till it tanked in 2019, just before the Covid pandemic.

The sudden lockdown announced in March 2020, without any planning or preparation, created the worst quarterly economic downturn among large economies and certainly in post-liberalization India, and sent millions of migrant families walking home, carrying their children on their shoulders. We have discussed the lack of preparation after the first Covid wave, which undoubtedly increased the ferocity of the second wave in April–May 2021. This was mismanagement by any metric, papered over by the much better roll-out of vaccinations after the damage had been done.

The political decision of pushing through the farm laws in September 2020 without consultation or attempts at persuasion created a massive wave of protest and closed the door on deep agriculture reforms for the foreseeable future. Unfortunately, our farmers still desperately need sensible agricultural reforms, and they are unlikely to get them soon.

What unites these bad decisions? It is the leadership's desire to project boldness and decisiveness; an unwillingness to take expert opinion into account or to persuade opponents who may have valid suggestions. Because the decision is sudden, it is also accompanied by little preparation. Such actions may have much more damaging and long-lasting effects on our citizenry than incremental decisions taken by a weaker, but consensus-driven, leadership. After all, India's most reform-oriented budgets came from coalition governments in the 1990s.

Reader: Has democracy not given our leader an overwhelming mandate? How can you question decisions such a popular government takes?

Editor: That is a great question. Elections give the government a mandate. It is also natural that any government will make mistakes in its honest pursuit of what it thinks is best for the country. Therefore, any elected government requires constant scrutiny and criticism, which then leads to the government undertaking course correction where appropriate. That is how a democracy is supposed to work.

Where there is no criticism, you have the policies of the Soviet Union, where the official party line was the only public version people heard, until the system collapsed. Of course, it was not that all the common people were fooled. Many knew the deficiencies of the system. However, the people in power, shielded from the common man's experience by the trappings of office, never had the right information to make good decisions.

When you put your finger in the flame, you feel pain, which causes you to withdraw your finger, thus preventing more serious damage. If the pain is suppressed because you have taken a local anaesthetic, you will not feel the pain, but you also will not be able to course-correct by withdrawing your finger, and your body will suffer worse damage. Relatedly, the suppression of criticism hurts the government because it is left in the dark.

Finally, it is interesting that the government has managed to portray both demonetization and Covid management as triumphs. If you believe so, ask yourself this: While other countries have announced independent inquiries into their handling of the pandemic, we have not. Why not? If you lost a relative or friend during the pandemic, don't you deserve an answer as to what we could have done better? If the government did such a great job, it should welcome an inquiry.

Reader: I have one last question on the economy. You say we are doing badly on jobs. Then why are the youth not mobilizing and protesting more if they are so unhappy? Surely you are wrong.

Editor: Do you remember the protests by the youth when the army introduced the Agnipath scheme in the summer of 2022, or when irregularities were reported in hiring in Indian Railways in January 2022. Even the farmers' protest in the winter of 2020–21 was a cry to protect their livelihoods. But no single political entity has been able to channelize the frustrations in a consistent, purposeful voice. That does not mean the frustration does not exist below the surface—it just erupts in different ways, as, for example, in the current troubles in Manipur, where the Meiteis are looking for reservations on a par with the Kukis.

There are other factors also at work. As T.N. Ninan has pointed out, RBI surveys suggest that the current political leadership has managed to make the public feel that 'even if their immediate economic situation is difficult, or has not improved, they have become more hopeful about the future'.[1] This may be a political achievement of sorts but not an economic one, for it is not backed by any fundamental improvement in their standard of living.

There is also widespread hope of a government job. Despite the small odds of succeeding, millions of youth are writing exams, hoping they will get into some government job. Given all the buzz about the new India and the sparse statistics about the true extent of the jobs crisis, when they have exhausted their attempts it is not irrational for them to conclude that there might be something wrong with themselves, not the system.

Most people get just about enough through free food grain and transfers to get by. But to keep them from focusing on their plight, we need distractions. Divisive issues of culture and religion are a major source of distraction, accentuated by social media and cheap data on our mobiles.

Walk to any city or *kasba*, and now even a village, and you will see young people hanging out with their affordable smartphones, whiling away the hours on the Internet. Hear us out, even though we may sound like jaded uncles—Raghu for sure, but Rohit too!

Data on mobile handsets has set off a revolution in India, opening up access to business, education and governance. But it has also come with an inadvertent consequence: dissipating the latent energies of our youth because the outside option of jobs has not been very promising. They are spending hours debating what wrongs Mughal emperors did or did not do in medieval India, and what all this means for our current times. Entire history books are being written on WhatsApp.

After having cracked the problem, in large part, of abject poverty, the transition to a minimally decent standard of life for hundreds of millions of our youth has not materialized. And a youth that voted for a government on the promise of *achche din* is not mobilizing despite the disappointment, because social media is very effective at distracting them. This, however, cannot last. And we as a nation will need to have answers for these youth when they ask us, 'Where were you, when we were entranced?'

Reader: Hmm . . . I'll have to think about your explanation. Let's turn to institutions. Are India's institutions under threat? If so, why?

Editor: As we argued earlier in the book, our founding fathers believed in the good intentions of our government leaders. They did put in place checks and balances on arbitrary behaviour, but these proved wanting during the Emergency. While we have tried to strengthen institutions since then, this is work in progress. For instance, Raghu remembers how Arun Jaitley as finance minister used to reminisce about craven press behaviour during the Emergency. The press is still structurally dependent on the government, and an opportunistic government takes advantage of it. This must change, for without a free press an important check on government misbehaviour is lost.

More generally, we have to strengthen democratic institutions, such as the Supreme Court and the Election Commission, even if only to enhance our growth prospects. We have suggested some ways, including making the appointment processes in these organizations more independent, but if we start the process, institutions will strengthen each other. Our goal is not a liberal–elitist project, it is a mass–democratic one that seeks robust institutions at its foundation to ensure that the fruits of development go to every Indian.

Reader: Okay, let's switch gears away from the economy to our *samaaj* and *sankskriti*, our society and history, our culture. You are wrong there, and I'm more confident of being right there.

Editor: Friend, we are not righting or wronging each other here. We are having a dialogue and trying to find the right path through discussion. Also, please remember, no matter what questions you ask, we should not doubt their intent. We all want India and every Indian to succeed. And yes, let's switch gears to samaaj and sanskriti. Go for it!

Reader: Let me get straight to the point. I want a government that looks out for Hindu interests. After 1200 years of subjugation, is that a bad thing? Most minorities are foreigners, or at least not fully Indian, and they should know their place in this country. Going back to our Hindu roots will make us a strong nation. It is quite simple.

Editor: See, this question is an emotive issue, so please hear us out. It is the duty of the government to look out for Indian citizens. Since approximately 80 per cent of Indians are Hindus, there will invariably be policies that address Hindu interests and their way of life. And that is a good thing. But the government cannot discriminate against anyone from another religion, at least not in our constitutional framework, and we must be proud of this.

At the time of Independence, two countries were formed on very different principles. Pakistan branded itself as an Islamic republic. We in India wanted simply to be a republic that sees all its citizens as equal in front of the law. But we wanted to be careful that minorities, especially the Muslims who were facing the insecurity of having chosen to remain in India, felt at home. This is a key founding principle of modern India and, we would argue, in our own interpretation of Hindu dharma too.

What does going back to our Hindu roots entail? We are the land of Ram and Krishna, of Shiva and Durga. There is a timelessness to Hinduism. But while we retain Hinduism's conceptual core, it also allows us to constantly adapt to change, to the reality of our circumstances. That is what the Ramayana and the Mahabharata teach us, to take our spiritual ethos from the wonders of storytelling to the practicality of our lives.

It is this openness of thought we would argue, as have many before us, that first led to other related but somewhat distinct traditions emerging from within our land—Jainism, Buddhism and Sikhism. It is also this openness that welcomed people of all faiths to our shores; Muslims, Jews, Christians, Zoroastrians and many more. Atheism, too, is an 'ism' within Hindu philosophy—you may have heard of the Charvaka sect that questioned God and premised rationality and experiential learning as the founding principle of constructing all morality and ways of life.

It is this openness that allowed this timeless culture, religion, set of ideas, whatever your preferred name for it, to thrive, despite competing ideas repeatedly coming from abroad. If Hinduism had been closed, rigid and insecure, it would arguably have been broken with the repeated battering by foreign religions. But because it was open and diffuse, almost Hayekian, if you allow us to use an economic analogy, it evaluated all ideas that came to its shore and developed a modus vivendi with the best of them, sometimes even making them its own. So it is not a coincidence that the Sufism sect of Islam achieved its greatest heights in the subcontinent concomitantly with the Bhakti movement.

In this organic cosmopolitanism, influenced in large parts by our Hindu ethos, we all became part of this land and its constantly evolving culture. We firmly reject the thought that only those who follow Hinduism in their personal lives are some sort of 'real' Indians. Aren't A.P.J. Abdul Kalam, A.R. Rahman, Dilip Kumar, Dadabhai Naoroji, Homi Bhabha, Jamsetji Tata, Julio Ribeiro, Manmohan Singh, Mansoor Ali Khan Pataudi, Mary Kom, Maulana Azad, Amrit Kaur, Sam Manekshaw, Shabana Azmi and Shah Rukh Khan important contributors to modern India? Aren't several of our best schools, colleges and hospitals founded by, and in many cases still run by, committed Christian missionaries? Are all of them any less Indian in your eyes?

Do you remember the famous *Mahabharat* TV show of the late 1980s? Do you know its script was written by a Muslim, Rahi Masoom Raza? The iconic voice of Samay, that is, time, was envisioned by Raza. The director B.R. Chopra said that once he heard Raza explain how Samay would narrate the story of the Mahabharata, he knew he had found his writer. So, all the dialogues that Krishna spoke to Arjun on the battlefield of Kurukshetra, which had hundreds of millions glued to their television screens every Sunday morning on Doordarshan, came from Raza's pen. In fact, the character of Arjun was also played by a Muslim actor.

The qawwali, a famous musical form that is associated with the great Amir Khusrau, was honed on the streets of Nizamuddin, Delhi, in the thirteenth century. Seven hundred years later, Indian actor

Ranbir Kapoor was pictured in the film *Rockstar* humming to the song 'Kun Faya Kun', shot at Nizamuddin Dargah; the words 'Kun Faya Kun'—meaning, 'be, and it is'—are central to the Quran.

What we are trying to say is that the cultures have enmeshed and created a beautiful, truly Indian, language. How can we deny this beauty that is a lived experience of so many of us? And how can we now try to disentangle them, as if they were two sides of a river that never meet, as if the bridges were never constructed? You may not like the enmeshed culture, but Hinduism has not been threatened by it, and we do not need to defend it by giving other religions a second-class status. We should not convert India into a version of Pakistan.

Indeed, to attempt to do so will be profoundly harmful to the country. When our majoritarian politicians label Indian Muslims as 'Babur ki aulaad', or talk about 1200 years of *ghulami* (slavery), they question Muslims' belonging, their very identity. Many Muslims will resist peaceably. As author and journalist Ziya Us Salam said in an interview with anchor Karan Thapar, 'I will not fulfill their dream of having a Muslim mukt Bharat . . . This is not my land, this is not your land, it is our land.'[2]

Reader: All that is fine. But haven't we been appeasing minorities, especially Muslims, for too long?

Editor: We hear you. 'Appeasement' is a word that can mean many things. Yes, politicians have occasionally caved in to radicals from various religions, but the notion that Muslims have been made economically better off than others through government policies is simply not supported by any data. For example, an RTI inquiry in 2014 elicited the following response from the Uttar Pradesh state government: Only 2 per cent of sub-inspectors, 3 per cent of head constables and 4 per cent of constables in the state were Muslims.[3] This is astonishing. Government jobs, as we have seen, are much sought after, so the low percentages cannot be for want of applicants in a state where nearly 20 per cent of the population was Muslim according to the 2011 census. Equally worrisome is the decline in percentage of Muslims as one goes up the police hierarchy. Yet such statistics can be seen again and again in almost every measure of well-being. Indian Muslims are not faring well economically. So what does this 'appeasement' mean in practice?

Oh, and one more thing. We have given examples of Muslims who have contributed hugely to nation-building. But there should be absolutely no need for Muslims to 'prove' they belong, in the same way as we don't ask an anti-social Hindu, or, for that matter, a Sikh or a Christian, to verify their citizenship credentials through his or her actions. He is an Indian citizen and enjoys the associated rights even if he violates the Constitution. So, too, must we treat every Muslim citizen, whether saint or sinner, as fully deserving of all constitutional protections. We may not like the sinners of any religion, but we must afford them equal protection. Politicians who attempt to create a second-class citizenry of Muslims, for instance, by bulldozing the houses of Muslim protesters without due process, are creating fissures in our society that will weaken our nation.

Reader: Haven't we been slaves for 1200 years before Independence? How do you dispute that?

Editor: While this claim is bandied about, it totally misreads history. It excludes great Indian emperors like Akbar or Shah Jahan, because it wants to treat all Muslims as foreigners. But it also excludes southern Hindu kingdoms, like the Chola kingdoms of Rajaraja I and Rajendra I, which traded with the Khmer Empire and Song China as well as with Arabia. It excludes the Vijayanagara Empire and the kingdoms of the Marathas. Is free India to be associated only with the periods when Hindus ruled Delhi?

We should not leave the telling of history to politicians. Instead, we need professional, apolitical historians. 'Apolitical' means they do not slant the facts to support their view. Traditionally, Indian historians were left-leaning, but that trend is changing now, and different views are emerging, which is all good for looking at our history through different lenses.

But whatever the historical facts, they don't justify the targeting of minorities today. There is a disturbing trend of old uncles becoming history buffs and continually spewing venom against minorities. A Muslim youth today bears no responsibility for what Aurangzeb did to Guru Tegh Bahadur in 1675. We should understand our history, but we cannot be prisoners of our past.

We need a leadership that preaches communal harmony rather than fans old grievances. Trust us: once you fan the flames of division, there is no end to the fissures that can be exploited in a land as diverse as India. And those who have preached hatred, who have espoused the cause of one community over that of another, are not credible peacemakers in a war of all against all. The greatest threat in a forest full of dry tinder is to start a fire, thinking you can control it.

Reader: You say you want to treat everyone equally. Then why do so many in the so-called intellectual class not want a uniform civil code? Why should only Muslims be allowed to practise polygamy? This is hypocritical, isn't it? And will they not have more children and swamp Hindus?

Editor: We agree with you that some of the arguments against a uniform civil code are hypocritical. In a modern society, everyone must be the same in front of the law. Yet the ultimate rationale for a uniform civil code, as India's Law Commission suggested in 2018, must not be to achieve a bland uniformity—else we should insist every marriage be a civil marriage in front of a government official—but to ensure that the fundamental rights of every citizen are protected.

In many religions, men enjoy stronger rights than women. The reason to object to polygamy is that men have the right to marry many women at the same time, but women do not have a similar right (the Draupadi-vivah is illegal).

But let us examine the facts on polygamy more closely. Which religion do you think has the largest instance of polygamy in India? The only reliable data that get to this question come from the National Family Health Survey (NFHS). It has had five rounds, from 1992–93 to 2019–

21. Aggregating data from the last three rounds of the NFHS, when the question of polygamy was posed, the largest occurrence of polygamy in India (in terms of percentage within that religious community) is among Christians, at 2.1 per cent of marriages. This is driven by the Christians living in the North-east. For Hindus, the rate is 1.4 per cent, while for Muslims it is 2 per cent. Since there are five times as many Hindus as Muslims, this means there are many more polygamous marriages among Hindus than among Muslims. Assuming every additional wife has the same number of children, simple maths says that there is no chance that Muslims will swamp Hindus because of polygamy.

Turning to the rights of the wives: clearly, the first Hindu wife enjoys strong legal rights. Importantly, the second (illegal) wife of a Hindu man enjoys no rights, nor do her children, since the marriage is not recognized by law. So while the first Hindu wife enjoys stronger rights than the first Muslim wife, the positions reverse with the second wife. If we truly want to do something about the position of women in polygamous marriages, it is not sufficient to declare Muslim polygamous marriages illegal; we should also do something about wives' rights in illegal polygamous marriages in all religions.

The data also clearly reveals that the fraction of polygamous marriages has been coming down steadily in all communities in India, including among Muslims. Instances of polygamy fall with increasing family wealth and rising education levels among both men and women. This is true across religious groups. Polygamous rates among Indian Muslims are also significantly lower, at every income level, than among Pakistani Muslims.

All this suggests that polygamy is a relatively small issue and getting ever smaller. But if we are really exercised about the position of women and want to remedy it, let us recognize that the solutions need deeper reflection than simply declaring Muslim polygamy illegal.

More generally, there is a sense that the universal civil code implies applying the Hindu code to everyone else. But Hindus also enjoy privileges that others do not. For instance, the Hindu Undivided Family (HUF) structure is used to transfer ancestral property across generations and to save taxes in family businesses. Allowing all religions to benefit from the tax exemptions accorded to the HUF will entail a significant loss to the exchequer. Conversely, doing away with HUF exemptions will enrage the Hindu families that have been avoiding taxes through this structure.

Similarly, if we want women to have the same freedom as men, Christian and Hindu women should have the freedom to divorce, as enjoyed by Muslim women. Hindu women still don't have the inheritance rights enjoyed by Hindu men or by non-Hindu women, despite legislative amendments in 2006. Put differently, creating a uniform civil code will require a tremendous amount of consensus building. Perhaps this is why in 2018, the Law Commission, tasked with examining a uniform civil code, suggested that the legislature first guarantee equality within communities, between men and women, rather than equality between communities. This means going against the orthodox status quo in every religion, not just Islam. Our preferred solution would be for the state to nudge progressives, especially women, within each community to create a community consensus on reforms and then legislate them.

Reader: Okay, you make an impassioned case. I have one last question since you raised the north–south comparison. I have heard talk about reapportionment of parliamentary seats in 2026. I am for it, because it is democratic. What are your views?

Editor: This is an excellent question, but the issue has to be addressed delicately. First, the facts. In the 1970s, the government was very concerned about population growth. So as to not reward states that did a poor job controlling population with more electoral power, India passed a constitutional amendment freezing parliamentary representation of each state at the level indicated by the 1971 population census. This amendment was meant to hold for twenty-five years. But in 2001, Prime Minister Atal Bihari Vajpayee's government renewed the amendment for another twenty-five years. It will come to an end in 2026. Of course, since then, the poorer states, like Bihar and Uttar Pradesh, have continued growing in population, while richer states have slowed down. Bihar's population grew by 25.4 per cent between 2001 and 2011, while Kerala's population grew only by 4.9 per cent. This means that some Lok Sabha constituencies in the south represent less than 2 million voters, while some in the Hindi belt represent almost 50 per cent more people. If we want to move to equal representation, that is, each Lok Sabha seat representing approximately the same number of people across the country, the Hindi belt will have to get many more new seats. Anticipating such an increase in seats, the new Parliament building has over 800 seats in the Lok Sabha, while the actual number of seats today is only 545.

Of course, matters are not so easy. The southern, western and richer northern states pay more in taxes, which are then transferred to the poorer, more populous states. And the transfers are large. Furthermore, the allocation of seats to the Hindi belt will disproportionately favour parties who have their voter base there. The broader point is that population changes since the amendment freezing seats will now imply massive regional adjustments in political power if seat numbers are readjusted according to current population. The southern and western states can well feel aggrieved that they are being penalized for their economic growth—which results in their paying higher taxes, having fewer children and less political power.

The matter has to be addressed with sensitivity—perhaps counting migrant workers into the population of richer states, while deducting them from the population of poorer states, and spreading the seat adjustments over several decades so that they are not abrupt. Once again, any attempt to make changes in the status quo without sensitivity and consultations could result in bitterness, even conflict. We must hope the government of the day in 2026 will understand this.

Reader: I have a lot to think about. I hope we can continue the dialogue.

Editor: Through dialogue comes mutual understanding. We certainly must.

In Conclusion

India is at a crossroads. We must embark on the Indian way, which builds on our strengths rather than our weaknesses. Our strengths include our spirit of inquiry and debate, which allows us to challenge feeble and misguided thinking; our desire to be creative and inclusive; our willingness to protest indecency and injustice, which makes rule of law, democratic consultation and a readiness to accept and act on criticism essential parts of our government. Taken together, these are key elements of our ethos, which we must strive to strengthen. These not only make life in India more empowering and fulfilling for every citizen, they will also help us build the economy of the future.

And that economy will be based on creativity, innovation and skilled work. It will be based on building the human capital of every citizen rather than augmenting the financial or physical capital of a few of the wealthy. Our Indian way will be different from the way other countries have grown into prosperity, but it will be uniquely suited to us and our times. The way we grow will be a beacon for other developing countries in the global south. It will help us become a leader in finding solutions to global problems like climate change.

Political Leadership

Much of this book has been about harnessing the energy of the people. But the massive reforms we advocate will happen more easily if we have political leadership of the highest order. We need an enlightened leadership that can inspire citizens to action—action not intended to avenge past wrongs or to stamp on some community or to dominate other nations, but to better the nation economically, socially and culturally, and thus build a better future for all its people. This leadership should preach unity and tolerance, not divisiveness and hate. Its agenda will be nationalistic, but it will take its responsibilities towards the world seriously. Its objective will not be power but sustainable development, though national power will surely accompany growth. And when India does attain that power, it will hopefully use it wisely.

All too often, our leaders promise that they will do it all, thus advocating that people be passive and wait till the leadership and their government deliver—typically, a very long wait. Instead, our leadership will have to acknowledge our people are dissatisfied with the status quo but also convince each individual that they have the power to change it. In doing so, they will galvanize people into action. As we have said before, India is too vast and complex a country to be governed from the top. But it can be inspired from the top.

What We Can Do

We can wait for inspired leadership that will break the mould. That is how so many of our discussions over chai end—with a lament about what's out there. Yet the moment produces the person. Winston Churchill, a heavy-drinking, racist and failed politician who switched back and forth between the Liberal and Conservative parties, proved to be a great prime minister for Britain during World War II.

Rather than waiting, let us move forward, taking India's future into our hands. We don't have all the answers, but you collectively have.

Whether you are a politician, a social worker, a bureaucrat, a regulator, a member of the security forces, a businessperson, an agriculturist, a professional, an academic, an artist, a homemaker, a student or one of a myriad other contributors to that multifaceted mosaic we call India, there is something you can do differently, some new idea you can implement that will make us all better off. Eventually, a new leadership will emerge—that sees what you are doing and weaves it together into a new vision. In the meantime, let each one of us be the change we want to see. The choice to act is ours and ours alone. We cannot have any more excuses.

Acknowledgements

We started this book during the Covid pandemic, as we started thinking about the direction India was headed in. Then, as now, there are two polar opposite narratives—one of unmitigated optimism about India's path and one of unmitigated pessimism. Our sense was that neither narrative fully appreciated the facts on the other side. Nor did they account in full measure for changes in competition, technology and geopolitics that could affect India's development path. This book is an attempt to make sense of where India is at present, cutting through the fog of poor or inadequate data and misrepresentation, which then allows us to lay out the kind of future it can aspire to. The book offers hope that India can grow to its immense potential and play a valuable role in helping address global challenges, but we caution that this will happen only if India does the hard work, is willing to embrace innovative paths, and resists premature triumphalism and divisive politics.

Any book is a collective effort, even if it has two authors. Rohit got married while this book was being written. His wife, Swasti, has brought immense intellectual depth to his work, and her ideas, critiques and warmth contributed fundamentally to this book. His parents-in-law, Kshama Sharma and Sudhish Pachauri, stupendous writers themselves, were pillars of support, sharing generously their method of writing. His parents, Seema and Kapil Lamba, and sister, Nishtha, the original inspirers and cheerleaders, were indulgent soundboards and constantly encouraging as the book took shape.

Raghu's wife, Radhika, has always been a full partner with him on every intellectual venture, helping him think through ideas, reading drafts, correcting, criticizing and, always, encouraging. Her insights have helped shape this book right from the early proposal to the final drafts. Raghu's children have been supportive as always, offering useful suggestions on the main themes of the book, and helping us think about alternative titles and covers (often the hardest part of the book). His brother, Mukund, encouraged us to write this book and made a number of important introductions. Raghu's father's integrity and sense of duty, and his mother's kindness and compassion for the underprivileged have been guiding lights in his life. Their influence makes its way into all his writing.

Radhika Marwah, our editor, has been the epitome of professionalism. She has been extremely supportive and offered valuable and insightful suggestions throughout the writing. She especially deserves our gratitude because she was willing to work with an extremely compressed schedule and, given our different time zones, at the oddest times. Vineet Gill, the copy editor, and all the fantastic staff at Penguin, including Ahlawat Gunjan, Manali Das, Peter Modoli, Rinjini Mitra, Aastha Verma and their teams, have also done an incredible job with the book.

We have benefited from discussions with many. The genesis of the book was in a set of discussions during the pandemic with Mekhala Krishnamurthy, Varad Pande, and Srinath Raghavan. A number of others joined us in those discussions, including Gautam Bhatia, Chandra Bhushan, Sajjid Chinoy, Rohit De, Navroz Dubash, Devesh Kapoor, Nachiket Mor, Karthik Muralidharan, Dipa Sinha, Aradhya Sood, T. Sundararaman and Raeesa Vakil.

Rahul Chauhan was a co-author with us on some op-eds for the *Times of India* that became the basis for some of the chapters in the book. We are grateful for his help, especially in the sections on jobs and on the PLI scheme. Raghu thanks Vindi Banga and Syeda Hameed for making introductions to entrepreneurs, and Chikki Sarkar for motivating us to actually put pen to paper.

During the course of writing this book, we benefited from conversations with a number of people. These include Rukmini Banerji, Vindi Banga, Peyush Bansal, Aditi Chand, Jai Decosta, Rahul Garg, Jacob Goldin, Dr Yusuf Hamied, Ajay Jakhar, Udit Khanna, Sunil Munjal, P.C. Musthafa, Sanjay Nayak, Sam Pitroda (he also introduced us to Radhika at Penguin), Prateek Raj, Rodney Ramcharan, Srinath Ravichandran, Sharad Sharma and the others at iSPIRT, and Anirudh Tiwari.

Freddy Pinzon and San Singh provided invaluable research assistance, as did Aaryan Gundeti.

Raghuram Rajan
Rohit Lamba

Notes

Introduction

1. Richard Baldwin and Tadashi Ito, 'The Smile Curve: Evolving Sources of Value Added in Manufacturing', *Canadian Journal of Economics*, 2022.
2. Gaurav Nayyar, Mary Hallward-Driemeier and Elwyn Davies, *At Your Service?: The Promise of Services-Led Development*, World Bank, 2021, p. 180.
3. David Tobenkin, 'India's Higher Education Landscape', NAFSA, 12 April 2022, https://www.nafsa.org/ie-magazine/2022/4/12/indias-higher-education-landscape
4. Pranjul Bhandari, 'India's Big Leap in Services: Will It Cross over into Manufacturing', Hongkong and Shanghai Banking Corporation, 14 September 2023. This growth is, of course, from a smaller base than for software.
5. Nikhil Inamdar, 'Semiconductors: Can India Become a Global Chip Powerhouse?' BBC News, 26 July, https://www.bbc.com/news/world-asia-india-66265412
6. Subhadip Sircar and Ruchi Bhatia, 'Goldman's Biggest Office beyond New York Attests to India's Rise', Bloomberg, 14 June 2023, https://www.bloomberg.com/news/features/2023-06-13/goldman-s-biggest-office-outside-new-york-shows-india-s-business-evolution?sref=cY1UiIYj
7. Nasscom data cited in Neelkanth Mishra's newsletter, 8 July 2024.
8. Gulveen Aulakh, 'Micron India Plant to Make Chips Next Year', *Mint*, 23 June 2023, https://www.livemint.com/news/india/micron-india-plant-to-make-chips-next-year-11687539738271.html

9. https://img.asercentre.org/docs/ASER%202022%20report%20pdfs/ allindiaaser202217_01_2023final.pdf

10. India Skills Report, Wheelbox, 2023, https://wheebox.com/india-skills-report.htm

Chapter 1: How Do Countries Grow Rich?

1. Calculations done by the authors using World Bank data.

2. Patrick Wallis, Justin Colson and David Chilosi, 'Structural Change and Economic Growth in the British Economy before the Industrial Revolution, 1500–1800', *Journal of Economic History*, 2018.

3. Claudia Goldin and Lawrence F. Katz, *The Race between Technology and Education*, Belknap Press, 2009.

4. Joe Studwell, *How Asia Works: Success and Failure in the World's Most Dynamic Region*, Grove Press, 2013.

5. This is modelled in a theoretical paper by Rudiger Dornbusch, Stanley Fischer and Paul Samuelson, 'Comparative Advantage, Trade, and Payments in a Ricardian Model with a Continuum of Goods', *American Economic Review*, 1977. The phenomenon in Asia is referred to as the 'flying geese', with early developers moving into more sophisticated sectors and leaving sectors requiring lower skills to late developers 'flying behind them'.

6. All these data are from the World Bank's database: https://data.worldbank.org/indicator/NY.GDP.PCAP.CD

7. Rohit Lamba and Arvind Subramanian, 'Dynamism with Incommensurate Development: The Distinctive Indian Model', *Journal of Economic Perspectives*, 2020.

8. Dani Rodrik, 'Premature Deindustrialization', *Journal of Economic Growth*, March 2016. In particular, see Figure 5 in the paper.

Chapter 2: Why Has India Not Built a Global Manufacturing Presence?

1. The six blind men felt different parts of an elephant, and each had a different description of what an elephant was. Perhaps we, too, are extrapolating from aspects of the China–India differences we have 'felt'.

2. From the Barro-Lee Tables, see Robert Barro and Jong-Wha Lee, 'A New Data Set of Educational Attainment in the World, 1950–2010', *Journal of Development Economics*, 2013, updated data available at http://www.barrolee.com/data/dataexp.htm

3. Yasheng Huang, 'Human Capital Development: The Reason behind China's Growth', *Economic Times*, December 2009.

4. *Doing Business*, World Bank, various editions.

5. Richard McGregor, *The Party: The Secret World of China's Communist Leaders*, HarperCollins, 2010, pp. 175–76.

6. These data are taken from TheGlobalEconomy.com: https://www.theglobaleconomy.com/rankings/household_consumption/

7. Mehul R. Thakkar, 'Peddar Road Flyover Opposed by Lata Mangeshkar and Locals Remain only on Papers Today', *Hindustan Times*, 6 February 2022, https://www.hindustantimes.com/cities/mumbai-news/peddar-road-flyover-opposed-by-lata-mangeshkar-and-locals-remain-only-on-papers-today-101644161743008.html

8. Harsha Vardhana Singh, 'Trade Policy Reform in India since 1991', Brookings India working paper, 2017. See Table 4.

9. For example, see 'The Chakravyuha Challenge of the Indian Economy', Economic Survey of India 2015–16, https://www.indiabudget.gov.in/budget2016-2017/es2015-16/echapvol1-02.pdf

10. Abhishek Anand and Naveen Joseph Thomas, 'Reigniting the Manmade Clothing Sector in India', OP Jindal Global University working paper, 2022. The paper describes in detail the difficulties for textile manufacturing in India introduced due to the import ban on purified terephthalic acid in 2014.

11. M. Rajshekhar, 'Why Is Industry Fleeing Punjab?', Scroll, December 2015, https://scroll.in/article/772899/why-is-industry-fleeing-punjab

12. This is based on research done by Pramod Kumar, director of Chandigarh's Institute for Development and Communication, as quoted in M. Rajshekhar, 'Why Is Industry Fleeing Punjab?', Scroll.

13. M. Rajshekhar, 'Why Is Industry Fleeing Punjab?', Scroll.

14. Manas Chakravarty, 'Jaw-Dropping Numbers from the Index of Industrial Production', Moneycontrol, 14 August 2023, https://www.moneycontrol.com/news/opinion/jaw-dropping-numbers-from-the-index-of-industrial-production-11173871.html/amp

Chapter 3: The Transformation in Trade and Services-Led Development

1. Gaurav Nayyar, Mary Hallward-Driemeier and Elwyn Davies, 'At Your Service? The Promise of Services-Led Development', World Bank publication, 2021, p. 27.
2. For a detailed discussion of these ideas on the revolutionary change in the services industry, see Chang-Tai Hsieh and Esteban Rossi-Hansberg, 'The Industrial Revolution in Services', *Journal of Political Economy: Macroeconomics,* 2023.
3. Gaurav Nayyar, Mary Hallward-Driemeier and Elwyn Davies, 'At Your Service? The Promise of Services-Led Development', pp. 62–71.
4. Mary Hallward-Driemeier, Gaurav Nayyar and Elwyn Davies, 'For Services Firms, Small Can Be Beautiful', *VoxEU*, Centre for Economic Policy Research, January 2022.
5. Gaurav Nayyar, Mary Hallward-Driemeier, and Elwyn Davies, 'At Your Service? The Promise of Services-Led Development'.
6. Subhadip Sircar and Ruchi Bhatia, 'Goldman's Biggest Office beyond New York Attests to India's Rise', Bloomberg, June 2023.
7. Ibid.
8. Gaurav Nayyar, Mary Hallward-Driemeier and Elwyn Davies, 'At Your Service? The Promise of Services-Led Development', p. 45.
9. Besart Avdiu, Karan Bagavathinathan, Ritam Chaurey and Gaurav Nayyar, 'The Impact of Services Trade on Non-Tradable Services in India', Ideas for India, 2022.
10. Emily Oster and Bryce Millett Steinberg, 'Do IT Service Centers Promote School Enrollment? Evidence from India', *Journal of Development Economics,* 2013.
11. Robert Jensen, 'Do Labor Market Opportunities Affect Young Women's Work and Family Decisions? Experimental Evidence from India', *Quarterly Journal of Economics,* 2012.
12. Benjamin Weiser, 'Here's What Happens When Your Lawyer Uses ChatGPT', *New York Times*, May 2023.
13. Erik Brynjolfsson, Danielle Li and Lindsey R. Raymond, 'Generative AI at Work', NBER working paper, 2023.
14. Carl Benedikt Frey and Michael A. Osborne, 'The Future of Employment: How Susceptible Are Jobs to Computerisation?', *Technological Forecasting and Social Change,* 2017.

Chapter 4: Where Should We Place Our Hopes?

1. Philip Wen, 'China Finally Has a Rival as the World's Factory Floor', *Wall Street Journal*, May 2023, https://www.wsj.com/articles/india-china-factory-manufacturing-24a4e3fe
2. Ibid.
3. Niall Macleod, 'Reshoring the Supply Chain: Where, What and How Much?', UBS Research, January 2021.
4. The numbers are based on calculation using data on global value chains available at World Integrated Trade Solutions, see https://wits.worldbank.org/gvc/gvc-output-table.html
5. This section draws on speeches by Dr Hamied, an interview with him as well as an interview conducted by Tarun Khanna for *Harvard Business Review*.
6. Josh Lerner, '150 Years of Patent Protection', *American Economic Review*, May 2022.
7. Shannon K. O'Neil, *The Globalization Myth: Why Regions Matter*, Yale University Press, October 2022. See figure on p. 7.
8. Sabrina Kessler, 'Why US Firms Are Reshoring Their Business', Deutsche Welle, August 2021.
9. These numbers are taken from the World Tariff Profiles for years 2015 and 2023 put out by the World Trade Organization: https://www.wto.org/english/res_e/publications_e/world_tariff_profiles23_e.htm
10. 'Production Linked Incentive Scheme (PLI) for Large Scale Electronics Manufacturing', Ministry of Electronics and Information Technology Notification, April 2020, https://www.meity.gov.in/writereaddata/files/production_linked_incentive_scheme.pdf
11. Nathan Lane, 'Manufacturing Revolutions: Industrial Policy and Industrialization in South Korea' (forthcoming), QJE.
12. 'Languages Most Frequently Used for Web Content', Statista, https://www.statista.com/statistics/262946/most-common-languages-on-the-internet/
13. Ngozi Okonjo-Iweala, 'Globalization at an Inflection Point', World Trade Organization, https://www.wto.org/english/news_e/spno_e/spno39_e.htm

14. Chris Miller, *Chip War: The Fight for the World's Most Critical Technology*, Simon & Schuster, October 2022.

15. Nicholas Welch and Jordan Schneider, 'China's Censors Are Afraid of What Chatbots Might Say', *Foreign Policy*, March 2023, https://foreignpolicy.com/2023/03/03/china-censors-chatbots-artificial-intelligence/

16. Yu Jie, 'China's Quest for Self-Reliance Risks Choking Innovation', *Financial Times*, August 2023, https://www.ft.com/content/db006725-421a-464d-870e-3e8e48b8814f

17. Alexander Donges, Jean-Marie Meier and Rui C. Silva, 'The Impact of Institutions on Innovation', *Management Science*, April 2022.

18. Michel Serafinelli and Guido Tabellini, 'Creativity over Time and Space: A Historical Analysis of European Cities', *Journal of Economic Growth*, January 2022.

Prelude: Governance and Structures

1. 'English rendering of PM's address at the World Economic Forum's Davos Dialogue', Press Information Bureau, January 2021, https://pib.gov.in/PressReleseDetail.aspx?PRID=1693019

2. 'BJP Hails PM for "Defeating" Covid-19,' *The Hindu BusinessLine*, February 2021, https://www.thehindubusinessline.com/news/national/bjp-hails-pm-for-defeating-covid-19/article33896405.ece

3. Thomas Abraham, 'What Has Gone Wrong with India's Vaccination Programme?', The India Forum, April 2021, https://www.theindiaforum.in/article/what-gone-wrong-india-s-vaccination-programme

4. Gautam Menon, 'Covid-19 and Indian Exceptionalism', The India Forum, May 2021, https://www.theindiaforum.in/article/covid-19-and-indian-exceptionalism

5. Karan Deep Singh, 'As India's Lethal Covid Wave Neared, Politics Overrode Science', *New York Times*, September 2021, https://www.nytimes.com/2021/09/14/world/asia/india-modi-science-icmr.html

6. Parakala Prabhakar, *The Crooked Timber of New India: Essays on a Republic in Crisis,* 2023. See the chapter 'One Billion Jabs: Let's Join the Celebration'.

7. William Msemburi et al., 'The WHO Estimates of Excess Mortality Associated with the COVID-19 Pandemic', *Nature*, 2023, Figure 3, https://www.nature.com/articles/s41586-022-05522-2/figures/3

8. Murad Banaji, 'Making Sense of Covid-19 Mortality Estimates for India', The India Forum, April 2022, https://www.theindiaforum.in/article/covid-mortality-india

9. https://www.indiabudget.gov.in/budget2021-22/economicsurvey/doc/vol1chapter/echap01_vol1.pdf

Chapter 5: Governance for the Twenty-First Century: Structure

1. Constituent Assembly Debates, Volume 7, 4 November 1948, https://www.constitutionofindia.net/debates/04-nov-1948/

2. M. Venkaiah Naidu, 'Lessons from Emergency We Must Not Forget', *Indian Express*, June 2023.

3. 'India Threatened to Shut Down Twitter, Says Ex-CEO Jack Dorsey; Govt Says "Outright Lie"', *Indian Express*, 13 June 2023.

4. This paragraph is based on the essay by Tarunabh Khaitan, 'Restoring Democracy: An 11-Point Common Minimum Programme for the United Opposition', The Wire, July 2023, https://thewire.in/politics/united-opposition-democracy-common-minimum-programme

5. This paragraph draws on the essay by Arvind Datar, 'Eight Fatal Flaws; The Failings of the National Judicial Appointments Commission', *Appointment of Judges to the Supreme Court of India: Transparency, Accountability, and Independence*, 2018, eds Arghya Sengupta and Ritwika Sharma.

6. The following paragraphs draw on the essay by Gautam Bhatia, 'ICLP Turns Four: Some Thoughts on the Office of the Chief Justice and Other Supreme Court Miscellany', *Indian Constitutional Law and Philosophy Blog*, 2017.

7. P. Chidambaram, 'A Time for Supreme Reform', *Indian Express*, August 2020, https://indianexpress.com/article/opinion/columns/supreme-court-legal-reforms-p-chidambaram-6575346/

8. Ravi Chopra, 'Joshimath: An Avoidable Disaster', The India Forum, March 2023, https://www.theindiaforum.in/environment/joshimath-avoidable-disaster

9. Several studies show the benefits of the Mid-Day Meal Scheme towards enrolment, attendance, learning and improving nutrition. For example: Tanika Chakraborty and Rajshri Jayaraman, 'School Feeding and Learning Achievement: Evidence from India's Midday Meal Program', *Journal of Development Economics*, June 2019.

    Abhijeet Singh, Albert Park and Stefan Dercon, 'School Meals as a Safety Net: An Evaluation of the Midday Meal Scheme in India', *Economic Development and Cultural Change*, January 2014.

    F. Afridi, 'Child Welfare Programs and Child Nutrition: Evidence from a Mandated School Meal Program in India', *Journal of Development Economics*, July 2010.

10. These paragraphs draw on an essay by K.C. Sivaramakrishnan, 'Local Government', which is Chapter 31 of *The Oxford Handbook of the Indian Constitution*, 2016, eds Sujit Choudhry, Madhav Khosla and Pratap Bhanu Mehta.

11. Ritva Reinikka and Jakob Svensson, 'Fighting Corruption to Improve Schooling: Evidence from a Newspaper Campaign in Uganda', *Journal of the European Economic Association*, April–May 2005.

12. See, for example, the comprehensive discussion by Himanshu, 'Do We Know What Has Happened to Poverty Since 2011-12?', April 2023, The India Forum.

13. '"Misused, Abused": India's Harsh Terror Law under Rare Scrutiny', Al Jazeera, August 2021, https://www.aljazeera.com/news/2021/8/16/india-uapa-terror-law-scrutiny

14. Timur Kuran, *Private Truths, Public Lies: The Social Consequences of Preference Falsification*, 1995.

15. For instance, Menaka Gurusamy, 'How Not to Reform the Code', *Indian Express*, 16 September 2023.

16. Devesh Kapur, 'Why Does the Indian State Both Fail and Succeed?', *Journal of Economic Perspectives*, Winter 2020.

17. While the data used by Devesh Kapur stops in 2018, the numbers for India haven't changed much. According to the Commonwealth Local Government Forum, local government transfers in India were budgeted to be 3.3 per cent of total government expenditure in 2020–21 and 3.1 per cent in 2019–20. See the full report: http://www.clgf.org.uk/default/assets/File/Country_profiles/India.pdf

18. Pabitra Chowdhury and Rosa Abraham, 'Number Theory: Shrinking Public Sector Employment and Its Costs', *Hindustan Times*, September 2022.

19. There are a variety of sources of data on this, with a range of estimates for the ratio, from above 2 to above 4. We took the mid-point. Duckju Kang, 'Where Are Teachers Paid the Most and the Least Compared to Other Professions in Asia?', Yahoo Finance, June 2019.

    Jean Dreze and Amartya Sen, *An Uncertain Glory*, Princeton University Press, 2013.

    Geeta Gandhi Kingdon, 'The Private Schooling Phenomenon in India: A Review', *Journal of Development Studies*, 2020.

20. Institute for Strategic Studies, 'Personnel vs. Capital: The Indian Defence Budget', *Military Balance Blog*, April 2023.

21. 'Budget Basics: National Defense', Peter G. Peterson Foundation, April 2023, https://www.pgpf.org/budget-basics/budget-explainer-national-defense

22. Union Public Services Commission, 72nd Annual Report, April 2023, https://upsc.gov.in/content/72nd-annual-report

23. Aditya Dasgupta and Devesh Kapur, 'The Political Economy of Bureaucratic Overload: Evidence from Rural Development Officials in India', *American Political Science Review*, 2020.

Chapter 6: Governance for the Twenty-First Century: Process

1. Kaushik Basu, *An Economist in the Real World: The Art of Policymaking in India*, Penguin Viking, 2016.

   Ajay Chhibber and Salman Anees Soz, *Unshackling India: Hard Truths and Clear Choices for Economic Revival*, HarperCollins, 2021.

   Naushad Forbes, *The Struggle and the Promise: Restoring India's Potential*, HarperCollins, 2021.

   Vijay Joshi, *India's Long Road: The Search for Prosperity*, Oxford University Press, 2017.

   Ashoka Mody, *India Is Broken: A People Betrayed, Independence to Today*, Stanford University Press, 2023.

   T.N. Ninan, *The Turn of the Tortoise: The Challenge and Promise of India's Future*, Oxford University Press, 2017.

   Abhijit Banerjee, Gita Gopinath, Raghuram Rajan and Mihir Sharma, eds, *What the Economy Needs Now*, Juggernaut Books, 2019.

2. Devesh Kapur, 'Why Does the Indian State Both Fail and Succeed?' *Journal of Economic Perspectives,* Winter 2020.

3. Philip Keefer and Stuti Khemani, 'Democracy, Public Expenditures, and the Poor: Understanding Political Incentives for Providing Public Services', World Bank Research Observer, Spring 2005.

4. The farm law reforms here refer to the three acts initiated by Parliament in September 2020 on agricultural markets, which were made into law and later rescinded.

5. Aryaman Vir and Rahul Sanghi, 'The Internet Country: How India Created a Digital Blueprint for the Economies of the Future', Tigerfeathers Substack, January 2021, https://tigerfeathers.substack.com/p/the-internet-country

6. Shouvik Das, 'UPI Crosses 10 Billion Monthly Transactions, Confirms NPCI', 31 August 2023, Live Mint, https://www.livemint.com/economy/upi-crosses-10-billion-monthly-transactions-confirms-npci-11693498082161.html

7. Tamanna Singh Dubey and Amiyatosh Purnanandam, 'Can Cashless Payments Spur Economic Growth?', working paper, 2023, https://papers.ssrn.com/sol3/papers.cfm?abstract_id=4373602

8. Cristian Alonso, Tanuj Bhojwani, Emine Hanedar, Dinar Prihardini, Gerardo Una and Kateryna Zhabska, 'Stacking up the Benefits: Lessons from India's Digital Journey', IMF working paper, March 2023.

9. Vrinda Bhandari and Karan Lahiri, 'The Surveillance State, Privacy and Criminal Investigation in India: Possible Futures in a Post-Puttaswamy World', *Univ. of Oxford Human Rights Hub Journal,* 2020.

10. David McCabe, 'Montana Legislature Approves Outright Ban of TikTok', *New York Times*, May 2023, https://www.nytimes.com/2023/04/14/technology/montana-tiktok-ban-passed.html

11. 'India: Data Protection Bill Fosters State Surveillance', Human Rights Watch, 22 December 2022.

12. Gautam Bhatia, 'From a Culture of Authority to a Culture of Justification: The Meaning of Overruling ADM Jabalpur', Live Law, January 2018.

13. 'Ranbaxy Settles Violation Dispute', Bloomberg News, December 2011, https://www.nytimes.com/2011/12/21/business/ranbaxy-settles-violation-dispute.html

'India's Ranbaxy Hit by FDA Product Ban at 4th Indian Plant', Reuters, January 2014.

14. This section draws on 'Gambian Child Deaths Fuel Alarm over Rules in "World's Biggest Pharmacy" India', *Financial Times*, March 2023, https://www.ft.com/content/72effe2f-988d-4618-bb07-16c96e81b6ee; 'Indian Drugs Are a Global Lifeline. For Dozens of Children, They Were Deadly', *New York Times*, November 2022, https://www.nytimes.com/2022/11/03/world/asia/india-gambia-cough-syrup.html

15. See the World Tariff Profiles 2023 report put out by the World Trade Organization, https://www.wto.org/english/res_e/publications_e/world_tariff_profiles23_e.htm

16. 'Electoral Bonds Likely to Carry Validity of 15 Days', *Economic Times*, 12 December 2017, https://economictimes.indiatimes.com/markets/bonds/electoral-bonds-likely-to-carry-validity-of-15-days/articleshow/62035423.cms?from=mdr

17. 'Former CEC TN Seshan: A No-Nonsense Man, He Cleaned Up India's Electoral System', *India Today*, April 2022.

Chapter 7: Capabilities: The Childhood Challenge

1. The World Bank database reports the stunting rates in Sri Lankan children in 2016 (latest available) and the health ministry's Family Health Bureau reports stunting to be just below 10 per cent for the year 2022. For a study on the discrepancy on the height of South Asian children growing up in the West versus those in South Asia, see: Caterina Alacevich and Alessandro Tarozzi, 'Child Height and Intergenerational Transmission of Health: Evidence from Ethnic Indians in England', and references therein, published in *Economics and Human Biology*, 2017.

2. Reynaldo Martorell, 'The Nature of Child Malnutrition and Its Long-Term Implications', *Food and Nutrition Bulletin*, 1999, https://journals.sagepub.com/doi/abs/10.1177/156482659902000304

3. Bipasha Maity, 'Interstate Differences in the Performance of "Anganwadi" Centres under ICDS Scheme', *Economic and Political Weekly*, 2016.

4. National Education Policy, 2020.

5. Alejandro J. Ganimian, Karthik Muralidharan and Christopher R. Walters, 'Augmenting State Capacity for Child Development:

Experimental Evidence from India', *Journal of Political Economy*, January 2023.

6. 'Success Stories with Reducing Stunting: Lessons for PNG', World Bank policy note, 2019, https://documents1.worldbank.org/curated/en/809771561531103886/pdf/Success-Stories-with-Reducing-Stunting-Lessons-for-PNG.pdf

7. Alessandra Marini, Claudia Rokx and Paul Gallagher, 'Standing Tall Peru's Success in Overcoming Its Stunting Crisis', International Bank for Reconstruction and Development and the World Bank, 2017.

8. Michael Kremer et al., 'Teacher Absence in India: A Snapshot', *Journal of the European Economic Association*, 2005.
   Karthik Muralidharan, Jishnu Das, Alaka Holla and Aakash Mohpal, 'The Fiscal Cost of Weak Governance: Evidence from Teacher Absence in India', *Journal of Public Economics*, 2017. There is some academic debate about the extent of teacher absenteeism. For instance, in a research study published by the Azim Premji Foundation, teacher absenteeism 'without reasons' was found to be 2.5 per cent, which is markedly different than the studies stated above.

9. See Annual Status of Education Report (Rural) 2022, https://asercentre.org/aser-2022/

10. 'Where Are the Kids? The Curious Case of Government Schools in Bihar', Jan Jagran Shakti Sanghatan, July 2023.

11. Seema Bansal and Shoikat Roy, 'School Education Reforms in Delhi 2015–2020', Boston Consulting Group, January 2021, https://www.bcg.com/school-education-reforms-in-delhi-2015-2020

12. 'Explained: Why Delhi's School Reforms Are Not Yet a Runaway Success', February 2021, *Business Standard*.

13. Devi Khanna and Amelia Peterson, 'State-Led Education Reform in Delhi, India: A Case Study of the Happiness Curriculum', Brookings Institution, February 2023.

14. Abhijit Singh, Mauricio Romero and Karthik Muralidharan, 'Covid-19 Learning Loss and Recovery: Panel Data Evidence from India', NBER working paper, 2023.

15. Paran Amitava, 'Gloom in the Classroom: A Silent Crisis in Jharkhand's Schools', The India Forum, April 2023.

16. 'Gloom in the Classroom: The Schooling Crisis in Jharkhand', technical report, Gyan Vigyan Samiti, Jharkhand, December 2022.

17. Ministry of Education, Government of India, https://www.education. gov.in/one-teacher-school

18. Guthrie Gray-Lobe, Anthony Keats, Michael Kremer, Isaac Mbiti and Owen Ozier, 'Can Education be Standardized? Evidence from Kenya', BFI working paper, September 2022, https://bfi.uchicago. edu/working-paper/2022-68/

19. Jean Dreze and Amartya Sen, *An Uncertain Glory*, Princeton University Press, 2013.
 Geeta Gandhi Kingdon, 'The Private Schooling Phenomenon in India: A Review', *Journal of Development Studies*, 2020.

20. For instance, teachers' salaries were doubled in 2005 in Indonesia, but this large increase led to no improvement in learning outcomes for students. See: Joppe de Ree, Karthik Muralidharan, Menno Pradhan and Halsey Rogers, 'Double for Nothing? Experimental Evidence on an Unconditional Teacher Salary Increase in Indonesia', *Quarterly Journal of Economics*, November 2017.

21. Karthik Muralidharan and Michael Kremer, 'Public and Private Schools in Rural India', in P. Peterson and R. Chakrabarti (eds), *School Choice International*, Cambridge, MIT, 2008.

Chapter 8: Capabilities: Higher Education

1. This paragraph and the next draws on: Bibhudatta Pradhan and Vrishti Beniwal, 'Worthless Degrees Are Creating an Unemployable Generation in India', Bloomberg, April 2023, https://www. bloomberg.com/news/articles/2023-04-17/india-s-worthless-college-degrees-undercut-world-s-fastest-growing-major-economy

2. See data made available by the Ministry of Education, Government of India, https://www.education.gov.in/statistics-new?shs_term_node_tid_depth=387

3. See the World Bank database, https://data.worldbank.org/indicator/ SE.XPD.TOTL.GD.ZS

4. 'Demand for Grants, 2023–24 Analysis', PRS Legislative Research, February 2023, https://prsindia.org/files/budget/budget_parliament/2023/DFG_2023-24_Analysis_Education.pdf

5. This and the next few paragraphs on labour market data are based on: Raghuram Rajan, Rohit Lamba and Rahul Singh Chauhan, 'Why

India Needs Better, Not Just More Jobs', *Times of India*, 6 December 2022, https://timesofindia.indiatimes.com/india/the-great-jobs-hunt/articleshow/96035338.cms. Numbers updated using PLFS and CMIE databases.

6. Data available at OECD, https://data.oecd.org/emp/labour-force-participation-rate.htm

7. Numbers taken from the National Education Policy, 2020, see point 16.1.

8. Shamika Ravi, Neelanjana Gupta and Puneeth Nagaraj, 'Reviving Higher Education in India', Brookings India, November 2019, p. 14.

9. See the report uploaded by the Department of Animal Husbandry and Dairy for the Livestock Census 2019, https://dahd.nic.in/sites/default/filess/Key%20Results%2BAnnexure%2018.10.2019.pdf. See the newspaper article on veterinarians here: https://www.deccanherald.com/opinion/the-veterinary-frontline-is-in-crisis-1108766.html. The argument here is taken from Devesh Kapur, 'Liberalization sans Liberalism: The Control Raj and the Perils of Ideology and Rents in Higher Education', published in *India Transformed: Twenty-Five Years of Economic Reforms*, edited by Rakesh Mohan.

10. See the Annual Survey on Higher Education, 2020–21, p. 15, published by the Department of Higher Education, Ministry of Education, Government of India, https://aishe.gov.in/aishe/viewDocument.action?documentId=352

11. Uttar Pradesh, too, has brought in an ordinance to pause the enforcement of existing labour laws, but it has to ensure that new legislation does protect worker rights from arbitrary layoffs.

12. India's GER is taken from the Annual Survey on Higher Education, 2020–21, published by the Department of Higher Education, Ministry of Education, Government of India. The GER and per capita GDP for the other countries are taken from the World Bank database.

13. Rahul Verma, 'Politicians Will Pose the Biggest Challenge to NEP', *Hindustan Times*, August 2020.

14. See the Analysis of Budgeted Expenditure on Education: https://www.education.gov.in/statistics-new?shs_term_node_tid_

depth=387&page=1. The numbers here are taken from the 2019–21 report on page 65.

15. Suresh Sharma and Ankita Singh, 'Importance of Scholarship Scheme in Higher Education for the Students from Deprived Sections', IEG working paper no. 395, 2020.

16. 'High NPAs in Education Loan Segment Turn Banks Cautious', *Economic Times*, September 2022.

17. 'Rs 17,668 Crore Disbursed in Education Loan in 2022–23: Dharmendra Pradhan', *Indian Express*, April 2023, https:// indianexpress.com/article/education/rs-17668-crore-disbursed-in-education-loan-in-2022-23-pradhan-8543574/

18. '695 Universities and over 34,000 Colleges Still Unaccredited', *Times of India*, February 2023, https://timesofindia.indiatimes. com/education/news/695-universities-and-over-34000-colleges-still-unaccredited/articleshow/97898819.cms

19. 'Corruption Cancer Destroying Indian Academia', Education World, https://www.educationworld.in/corruption-cancer-destroying-indian-academia/

20. Anurag Behar, 'Eliminating Corruption from Colleges', *Hindustan Times*, April 2019, https://www.hindustantimes. com/education/eliminating-corruption-from-colleges/story-DPkAMWCRNeupra5G4EoG2J.html

21. See the letter uploaded on the webpage of Tata, the company: https:// www.tata.com/newsroom/jamsetji-tata-letter-to-swami-vivekananda

22. Pratik Pawar, 'India Aims to Invigorate Science with Hefty New Funding Agency', *Science*, July 2023.

23. Deepika Baruah, 'Indian Government's National Education Budget 2022', British Council, February 2022, https://opportunities-insight. britishcouncil.org/insights-blog/indian-government%E2%80%99s-national-education-budget-2022

24. These data can be obtained by matching Aadhaar numbers of graduates, their PAN numbers and their tax filings, and can be disclosed as averages so that individual privacy of graduates is maintained.

25. '7.7 Lakh Indian Students Went Abroad to Study in 2022; Many Face Challenges in Finding Jobs Later', *Tribune*, February 2023.

26. Authors' calculations from the RBI's Liberalized Remittance Scheme statistics.

Chapter 9: Capabilities: Health Care

1. Rama V. Baru, 'The Bhore Committee and Recent Debates', *Seminar*, 2019.
2. 'India Health System Review', World Health Organization, 2022, https://apo.who.int/publications/i/item/india-health-system-review
3. These numbers are based on the World Bank database.
4. The numbers for Indian states are taken from the data released by the Ministry of Health and Family Welfare for 2019, see https://pib.gov.in/PressReleaseIframePage.aspx?PRID=1796436
5. Nikhil Rampal and Kritika Sharma, '80,000 Seats, 7 Lakh Takers — Inside Story of Why Thousands of Aspiring Indian Doctors Fly Abroad', ThePrint, March 2022.
6. Jishnu Das, Alaka Holla, Aakash Mohpal and Karthik Muralidharan, 'Quality and Accountability in Health Care Delivery: Audit-Study Evidence from Primary Care in India', *American Economic Review*, December 2016.
7. 'Less Than a Third of Indians Go to Public Hospitals for Treatment', *Mint*, May 2020, https://www.livemint.com/news/india/less-than-a-third-of-indians-go-to-public-hospitals-for-treatment-11588578426388.html
8. Jishnu Das et al., 'Two Indias: The Structure of Primary Health Care Markets in Rural Indian Villages with Implications for Policy', *Social Science and Medicine*, 2022.
9. 'Health System for a New India: Building Blocks, Potential Pathways to Reform', NITI Aayog, November 2019. The press release of the report is here: https://pib.gov.in/PressReleasePage.aspx?PRID=1591934. As of October 2023, the report was currently missing on the NITI Aayog webpage, but it was available and circulated widely since its release in November 2019.
10. Mita Choudhury, Jay Dev Dubey and Bidisha Mondal, 'Analyzing Household Expenditure on Health from the 71st Round of Survey by the National Sample Survey Organization in India', National Institute of Public Finance and Policy research paper, 2019, https://www.nipfp.org.in/media/medialibrary/2019/12/WHO_NSSO_report_2019.pdf
11. Tarun Khanna, Nachiket Mor and Sandhya Venkateswaran, 'Transition Paths towards Better Health Outcomes in India: Optimizing the Use of Existing Pooled Government Funds', Brookings, 2021.

12. 'The World Health Report : 2000 : Health Systems : Improving Performance', World Health Organization, 2000, https://iris.who.int/handle/10665/42281

13. 'Aam Aadmi Mohalla Clinics: Brief Write-up on Aam Aadmi Mohalla Clinic', Government of Delhi, https://dgehs.delhi.gov.in/dghs/aam-aadmi-mohalla-clinics

14. The next few paragraphs draw on Rakshita Khanijou and T. Sundararaman, 'Aam Aadmi Mohalla Clinics (AAMC): A New and Evolving Urban Healthcare Model', Chapter 16 in the technical report 'The Archetypes of Inclusive Health Care: Where Health Care for the Poor is Not Poor Health Care', 2017.

15. For quality, see Chandrakant Lahariya, 'Access, Utilization, Perceived Quality, and Satisfaction with Health Services at Mohalla (Community) Clinics of Delhi, India', *Journal of Family Medicine and Primary Care*, 2020; and for cost-effectiveness, see Charu C. Garg and Roopali Goyanka, 'A Comparison of the Cost of Outpatient Care Delivered by Aam Aadmi Mohalla Clinics Compared to Other Public and Private Facilities in Delhi, India', *Health Policy and Planning*, 2023.

16. We have drawn extensively from the case study 'The Vision of Comprehensive Primary Healthcare Learning from Jan Swasthya Sahyog for Developing Health and Wellness Centers', written by T. Sundararaman, Chapter in 2 in the technical report 'The Archetypes of Inclusive Health Care: Where Health Care for the Poor is Not Poor Health Care', 2017.

17. This section draws on the case study 'Re-visiting Aravind Eye Hospital in Times of Universal Health Coverage', written by T. Sundararaman, Chapter in 6 in the technical report 'The Archetypes of Inclusive Health Care: Where Health Care for the Poor is Not Poor Health Care', 2017.

    V. Kasturi Rangan, 'Aravind Eye Hospital, Madurai, India: In Service for Sight', Harvard Business School Case 593–098, April 1993, revised May 2009.

18. C.K. Prahlad, 'Christian Medical College and Hospital', Indian Institute of Ahmedabad case materials, 1972, https://www.egyankosh.ac.in/bitstream/123456789/6320/1/case%20study-6.pdf

19. Information in this paragraph in based on: Mohana Basu, 'HIV, Polio, now Covid — How CMC Vellore Has Been Leading Healthcare

& Research for 121 Yrs', ThePrint, June 2021, https://theprint.in/
health/hiv-polio-now-covid-how-cmc-vellore-has-been-leading-
healthcare-research-for-121-yrs/680348/

20. See Abhijit Banerjee's essay in Abhijit Banerjee, Gita Gopinath,
Raghuram Rajan and Mihir Sharma, eds, *What the Economy Needs
Now*, Juggernaut Books, 2019.

21. Nikhil Rampal and Kritika Sharma, '80,000 Seats, 7 Lakh Takers
— Inside Story of Why Thousands of Aspiring Indian Doctors Fly
Abroad', ThePrint, March 2022.

22. 'National Health Stack: Strategy and Approach', NITI Aayog,
July 2018.

Chapter 10: Addressing Inequality

1. V.S. Naipaul, *A Bend in the River*, Alfred A. Knopf, 1979.

2. James Heckman, 'Invest in Early Childhood Development: Reduce
Deficits, Strengthen the Economy', The Heckman Equation,
December 2012.
James Heckman, 'The Economics of Inequality: The Value of Early
Childhood Education', *American Educator*, Spring 2011.

3. '60% of Dropouts at 7 IITs from Reserved Categories', *The Hindu*,
August 2021, https://www.thehindu.com/news/national/parliament-
proceedings-60-of-dropouts-at-7-iits-from-reserved-categories/
article35752730.ece

4. In the case 'E.V. Chinnaiah v. State of Andhra Pradesh', 2004, the
Supreme Court held that the scheduled castes form one 'homogenous'
group and that any inter-se classification within the scheduled
castes would be a violation of Article 14. The issue is again being
considered by a larger bench at the court. See https://indiankanoon.
org/doc/746591/

5. Anand Teltumbde, 'Reservations within Reservations: A Solution',
Economic and Political Weekly, 2009.

6. Devesh Kapur et al., 'Rethinking Inequality: Dalits in Uttar Pradesh
in the Market Reform Era', *Economic and Political Weekly*, 2010.

7. Chandra Bhan Prasad, D. Shyam Babu and Devesh Kapur, *Defying
the Odds: The Rise of Dalit Entrepreneurs*', Penguin Random House,
2014.

8. 'Episode 296: Caste, Capitalism and Chandra Bhan Prasad', *The Seen and the Unseen* podcast with Amit Varma.
9. Soumitra Shukla, 'Making the Elite: Top Jobs, Disparities, and Solutions', working paper, Yale University, 2022.
10. 'EWS Row: Reservation Has Social, Financial Connotations, Meant for Oppressed, Says Supreme Court', *Economic Times*, September 2022.
11. Udit Misra, 'ExplainSpeaking: Why India's Workforce Is Becoming Increasingly Male-Dominated', *Indian Express*, June 2023.
12. See Periodic Labour Force Survey (PLFS), Quarterly Bulletin, January–March 2023, https://pib.gov.in/PressReleaseIframePage.aspx?PRID=1928124
13. Claudia Goldin, 'The U-Shaped Female Labor Force Function in Economic Development and Economic History', *NBER*, 1994.
14. 'Episode 296: Caste, Capitalism and Chandra Bhan Prasad', *The Seen and the Unseen* podcast with Amit Varma.
15. Erin K. Fletcher, Rohini Pande and Charity Troyer Moore, 'Women and Work in India: Descriptive Evidence and a Review of Potential Policies', India Policy Forum, 2018.
16. Ibid.
17. Nandita Singh, 'Higher Education for Women in India—Choices and Challenges', Forum on Public Policy, 2008.
    All India Survey of Higher Education 2020–21, Figure 27.
18. Dhruvika Dhamija and Akshi Chawla, 'Decoding Women's Labour Force Participation in 2021–22: What the Periodic Labour Force Survey Shows', https://ceda.ashoka.edu.in/decoding-womens-labour-force-participation-in-2021-22-what-the-periodic-labour-force-survey-shows/
19. Fernanda Bárcia de Mattos and Sukti Dasgupta, 'MGNREGA, Paid Work and Women's Empowerment', ILO Employment working paper 230, December 2017.
20. Jonathan David Ostry, Jorge A. Alvarez, Raphael A. Espinoza and Chris Papageorgiou, 'Economic Gains from Gender Inclusion: New Mechanisms, New Evidence', IMF Staff Notes, 2018.
21. Alice Evans, 'Why Has Female Labor Force Participation Risen in Bangladesh but Fallen in India?' Brookings, October 2022, https://www.brookings.edu/articles/why-has-female-labor-force-participation-risen-in-bangladesh-but-fallen-in-india/

22. 'Women Are Moving Jobs for the Work-from-Home Perk', *Economic Times*, 8 March 2022.

23. Blassy Boben and Rupam Jain, 'Female Footprint in India's Workforce', Reuters, September 2023.

24. Raghabendra Chattopadhyay and Esther Duflo, 'Women as Policy Makers: Evidence from a Randomized Policy Experiment in India', *Econometrica*, 2004.

25. Numbers made available by the World Bank database.

26. Ashok Gulati, Devesh Kapur and Marshall Bouton, 'Reforming Indian Agriculture', *Economic and Political Weekly*, March 2020.

27. Shoumitro Chatterjee, Mekhala Krishnamurthy, Devesh Kapur and Marshall M. Bouton 'A Study of the Agricultural Markets of Bihar, Odisha and Punjab', University of Pennsylvania Center for the Advanced Study of India, 2020.

28. Union Budget 2022–23, https://www.indiabudget.gov.in/budget 2022-23/

29. Ashok Gulati, Devesh Kapur and Marshall Bouton, 'Reforming Indian Agriculture', *Economic and Political Weekly*, March 2020.

30. 'Central Issue Price under NFSA', Department of Food and Public Distribution, Government of India, https://dfpd.gov.in/pds-cipunfsa.htm

31. Ashok Gulati and Shweta Saini, 'Leakages from Public Distribution System and the Way Forward', Indian Council for Research on International Economic Relations, 2015.

32. F. Ram, S.K. Mohanty and Usha Ram, 'Understanding the Distribution of BPL Cards: All-India and Selected States', *Economic and Political Weekly*, February 2009.
Basant Kumar Panda et al., 'Malnutrition and Poverty in India: Does the Use of Public Distribution System Matter?' BMC Nutrition, 2020.

33. 'Analysing the Effectiveness of Targeting under AB PM-JAY in India', WHO, March 2022.

34. Maitreesh Ghatak and Karthik Muralidharan, 'An Inclusive Growth Dividend: Reframing the Role of Income Transfers in India's Anti-Poverty Strategy', India Policy Forum, 2019.

35. 'Results of an Experimental Pilot Cash Transfer Study in Delhi', SEWA, Government of Delhi and UNPD, January 2013.
David K. Evans and Anna Popova, 'Cash Transfers and Temptation Goods', Economic Development and Cultural Change, January 2017.

Chapter 11: India's Engagement with the World

1. Kunal Purohit, 'Modi's "Tiger Warrior" Diplomacy Is Harming India's Interests', *Foreign Policy*, 28 August 2023, https://foreignpolicy.com/2023/08/28/india-modi-diplomacy-bjp-hindu-nationalism-religion-manipur/

2. Joseph S. Nye Jr, 'Soft Power and American Foreign Policy', *Political Science Quarterly*, 2004.

3. 'China's Xi Jinping Lauds "New Era" of Strength as He Opens National Congress', NPR News, 18 October 2017.

4. Shivshankar Menon, 'Modi's India Plans to Be "Vishwaguru" but Forgets Soft Power Is Useless without Hard Muscle', ThePrint, April 2021, https://theprint.in/pageturner/excerpt/modis-india-plans-to-be-vishwaguru-but-forgets-soft-power-is-useless-without-hard-muscle/642359/

5. Yamini Aiyar, Sunil Khilnani, Prakash Menon, Shivshankar Menon, Nitin Pai, Srinath Raghavan, Ajit Ranade and Shyam Saran, 'India's Path to Power: Strategy in a World Adrift', Takshashila Institution, https://takshashila.org.in/research/indias-path-to-power-strategy-in-a-world-adrift

6. Rhea Mogul, 'Why a Map in India's New Parliament Is Making Its Neighbors Nervous', CNN, June 2023, https://www.cnn.com/2023/06/13/india/india-akhand-bharat-map-parliament-intl-hnk/index.html

7. Yamini Aiyar, Sunil Khilnani, Prakash Menon, Shivshankar Menon, Nitin Pai, Srinath Raghavan, Ajit Ranade and Shyam Saran, 'India's Path to Power: Strategy in a World Adrift', Takshashila Institution, https://takshashila.org.in/research/indias-path-to-power-strategy-in-a-world-adrift.

8. '"Celebration" of Indira Gandhi's Killing: What Really Happened at Canada Event?', *Hindustan Times*, 8 June 2023.

9. 'Canada: How Ties with India Soured over Hardeep Singh Nijjar Killing', BBC News, 19 September 2023.

10. 'India Urges Its Citizens to Exercise "Extreme Caution" in Canada', *Guardian*, September 2023.

11. 'UAE, a Destination for British Doctors and Nurses,' Emirates 24/7, June 2023.

12. Yamini Aiyar, Sunil Khilnani, Prakash Menon, Shivshankar Menon, Nitin Pai, Srinath Raghavan, Ajit Ranade and Shyam Saran, 'India's Path to Power: Strategy in a World Adrift', Takshashila Institution, https://takshashila.org.in/research/indias-path-to-power-strategy-in-a-world-adrift

13. Navroz K. Dubash et al., 'India and Climate Change: Evolving Ideas and Increasing Policy Engagement', *Annual Review of Environment and Resources*, 2018.

14. B.N. Goswami et al., 'Increasing Trend of Extreme Rain Events over India in a Warming Environment', *Science*, 2006.

15. Climate Change and Sovereign Credit Ratings, University of East Anglia and the University of Cambridge, https://www.uea.ac.uk/climate/evaluating-sovereign-risk

16. Raghuram Rajan, 'Joined at the Hip: Why Continued Globalization Offers Us the Best Chance of Addressing Climate Change', Per Jacobsson Lecture, 2022, https://faculty.chicagobooth.edu/-/media/faculty/raghuram-rajan/research/papers/joined-at-the-hip3-final.pdf

17. Navroz K. Dubash et al., 'India and Climate Change: Evolving Ideas and Increasing Policy Engagement', *Annual Review of Environment and Resources*, 2018.

18. Sara Schonhardt, 'Why the Climate Fight Will Fail without India', *Scientific American*, February 2023.

19. Navroz K. Dubash et al., 'The Disruptive Politics of Renewable Energy', The Indian Forum, 2019.

20. Navroz K. Dubash et al., 'Building a Climate-Ready Indian State', Centre for Policy Research, 2021.

Chapter 12: A Creative Country

1. 'School Education Reforms in Delhi 2015–2020', Boston Consulting Group, January 2021, https://www.bcg.com/school-education-reforms-in-delhi-2015-2020

2. Chandra Bhan Prasad, D. Shyam Babu and Devesh Kapur, *Defying the Odds: The Rise of Dalit Entrepreneurs*, Random House, 2014.

3. The anecdote draws from Raghuram Rajan, *The Third Pillar: How Markets and the State Leave the Community Behind*, HarperCollins, 2019.

4. 'U.S. Eases Pension Investing', *New York Times,* June 1979, https://www.nytimes.com/1979/06/21/archives/us-eases-pension-investing-pension-investments.html

5. See Josh Lerner, *Boulevard of Broken Dreams*, Princeton University Press, 2009.

6. 'Who Is Leading the 5G Patent Race?', Iplytics.com, 2019, https://www.iplytics.com/wp-content/uploads/2022/06/5G-patent-race-June-2022_website.pdf

7. The next paragraphs draw partly on https://www.moneycontrol.com/news/business/companies/how-sanjay-nayak-brought-tejas-networks-back-from-the-brink-of-failure-2352397.html and partly on an interview with Sanjay Nayak.

8. Stay in India Checklist Index 2021, https://pn.ispirt.in/stay-in-india-checklist-index-aiming-for-5-trillion-economy-by-2025/

Chapter 13: The Wrong Way

1. T.N. Ninan, 'If Consumer Confidence Is a Political Bellwether, Are Current Levels Enough to Help BJP Win 2024?', ThePrint, June 2023, https://theprint.in/opinion/if-consumer-confidence-is-a-political-bellwether-are-current-levels-enough-to-help-bjp-win-2024/1621151/

2. Karan Thapar interview with Zia Us Salam, 'What Does It Feel like to Be a Muslim in Narendra Modi's India?', The Wire, 30 June 2023.

3. 'Negligible Representation of Muslims in UP Police, Reveals RTI', News 18, February 2014, https://www.news18.com/news/india/negligible-representation-of-muslims-in-up-police-reveals-rti-667591.html